Journalism Ethics

A Reference Handbook

CONTEMPORARY ETHICAL ISSUES

Journalism Ethics

A Reference Handbook

Edited by
Elliot D. Cohen and Deni Elliott

ABC-CLIO
Santa Barbara, California
Denver, Colorado
Oxford, England

Library of Congress Cataloging-in-Publication Data

Journalism ethics : a reference handbook / edited by Elliot D. Cohen
and Deni Elliott.
    p.   cm. -- (Contemporary ethical issues series)
    Includes bibliographical references (p.   ) and index.
    ISBN 0-87436-873-1 (alk. paper)
    1. Journalism ethics.   I. Cohen, Elliot D.   II. Elliott, Deni.
    III. Series: Contemporary ethical issues.
    PN4756.J67   1997   97-26874
    174'.9097—dc21   CIP

02 01 00 99   10 9 8 7 6 5 4 3 2

ABC-CLIO, Inc.
130 Cremona Drive, P.O. Box 1911
Santa Barbara, California 93116-1911

This book is printed on acid-free paper ∞.
Manufactured in the United States of America

CONTEMPORARY ETHICAL ISSUES

Contents

5 Court Cases, 123

Robert F. Ladenson

Contents

9 Organizations, 177
Bill Pardue

Glossary, 183

Index, 191

About the Contributors, 197

CONTEMPORARY ETHICAL ISSUES

Chapter 1:
Introduction

Deni Elliott

One unique aspect of journalism is that its ethical lapses most usually occur in the public forum. Overly graphic news photos or tapes, distortions and misinterpretations, false reports, and intrusions into private lives are broadcast on television screens and radio programs and printed in newspapers and newsmagazines. How well journalists have met their responsibilities is a judgment call open to scrutiny with the production of every story. The primary news critics—the subjects and consumers of the resulting news story—do not hesitate to voice judgments about the rights and wrongs of journalistic action. Thus, the practice of journalism ethics begins. No other professional behavior is as open to scrutiny by those working in the profession, those who are used by the profession, and those who consume the final products.

What Journalism Ethics Is

Ethics, the broader discipline to which journalism ethics belongs, is the study of morality. There are two related ways in which morality may be studied:

descriptively and *philosophically*. The descriptive study of morality *(descriptive ethics)* involves an attempt to describe or report the moral outlooks of different cultural groups or subgroups. Such a study does not evaluate or assess these outlooks; it merely records them. For example, a description of the moral outlooks of some Eskimo and American Indian tribes would include reference to the custom of leaving their elderly behind to die when they become unable to travel with the rest of the tribe. A description of the outlook of some Hispanic groups would include the practice of "machismo"; and a description of the outlook of some religious groups, for instance, Jehovah's Witnesses, might include a description of certain perceived obligations, such as the obligation to refuse blood transfusions.

Descriptive ethics resembles "objective journalism," wherein the journalist merely records what the source has stated without attempting to interpret or evaluate those statements. Ethics can, however, also signify the normative evaluation or assessment of the described moral perspectives. Thus, for example, the criticism of machismo as *sexist* goes beyond the mere description of the practice in question. It casts its own moral judgment.

The attempt to rigorously examine, defend, or justify moral judgments, rules, principles, or ideals belongs to the study of morality known as *philosophical ethics*. When philosophical ethics aims at defining and justifying abstract moral standards, principles, or ideals, it is called *ethical theory*. The latter study is associated with the theories of such classical thinkers as Plato, Aristotle, St. Thomas Aquinas, Spinoza, Kant, and Mill, to name just a few. Ethical theories aim at explaining the nature and grounds of morality itself. These theories try to provide answers to such perennial questions as "What makes (morally) right acts right?" "How can we tell the difference between (morally) right and wrong conduct?" "What is moral virtue?" "When, if ever, can people be justly praised or blamed for their actions?" and "What is the meaning of justice?"

When philosophical ethics aims at answering more specific, practical moral questions, it is called *applied ethics*. Applied ethics addresses such problems as abortion, the death penalty, suicide, poverty and affluence, and sexual practice. When applied ethics addresses problems arising in the professions such as law and medicine, it is called *professional ethics*.

Journalism ethics is a branch of professional ethics. In particular, it is that part of professional ethics that addresses problems concerning behavior of reporters, editors, photographers, videographers, producers, and any other professional involved in the production and distribution of news. At the roots of this normative, philosophical study is the understanding that the profession fulfills a necessary function in society. Citizens need to receive and share particular kinds of information to function effectively in their communities, and news organizations have pledged to provide that information. Moral problems in journalism arise in the context of this commitment by journalists. Journalism ethics and its problems must therefore be defined and assessed in relation to the profession.

What Journalism Ethics Is Not

Some common statements about the practice and products of journalism seem inclined to distract the discussion from ethics. Comments such as "All they care about is selling papers," "Local television news exists to make ratings," "Why did we publish it? It was a damn good picture," and "The First Amendment means that no one can tell us what to do" tend to divert journalists' and consumers' attention from careful consideration of important ethical issues. Indeed, morally permitted action is often also legal, esthetically appealing, economically sound, and prudent. Nevertheless, the problems of journalism ethics are not mere matters of law, economics, esthetics, or doing that which is in one's self-interest.

Journalism Ethics Is Different from Law

The confusion between journalism ethics and laws relating to journalism most often arises around the First Amendment of the U.S. Constitution. Along with freedom of speech, religion, and assembly, the First Amendment guarantees freedom of the press. That means, except in very rare instances relating to national security, the government may not intervene in the freedom of a publisher to produce and disseminate whatever message he or she wishes.

Constitutionally acceptable laws relating to the publication of material allow for punishment after the fact, but not for prior restraint. News organizations can be punished for printing material that is false and damaging or for printing true information that unjustifiably violates the privacy of an individual. Judges and juries are increasingly swift and harsh in their punishment of news organizations that fail to exercise good judgment in the use of their tremendous power. Courts, however, are constitutionally restrained from preventing a news organization from publishing information—even if that information is likely to be found libelous or an actionable invasion of privacy after the fact.

Very few of the ethical dilemmas that arise in journalism relate to publication of material that is likely to result in libel or an invasion of privacy lawsuit. Yet, without being a potential legal problem, the published material or process of gathering information for a story can have long-lasting detrimental effects on individuals or on the community. Accordingly, it can still be ethically problematic.

The fact that news organizations can publish virtually whatever they wish to publish does not imply that they should publish all information available to them. The distinction between what is legally restricted and what is ethically appropriate can easily be seen by analogy to one's own life. The law is generally silent on matters of deceit. It is illegal to lie on one's tax returns or to lie when under oath in a court of law. Yet, there are a seemingly endless number of ways that one can act deceptively that are not addressed by law. One can cheat on a test or lie to a friend; one can pretend that a sales check was correct when the clerk had forgotten to include some items in the final bill. How one reacts to these situations is a matter of ethics, not law. In a similar way, how the decision makers in news organizations choose to exercise restraint over what is published and what is not is far more often a matter of ethics than law.

Journalism Ethics Is Different from Economics

In the United States, news organizations are privately owned and operated (partially in reaction to the First Amendment guarantee that government will not interfere in the development or dissemination of news). Aside from National Public Radio (NPR), Public Broadcasting System (PBS), and a handful of alternative news sources, the news organizations are for-profit institutions. The economic reason for their existence is to make money for owners or stockholders, but news organizations have noneconomic reasons that are also necessary to explain their existence.

News organizations fulfill a particular function in the community: they, in a timely manner, collect and distribute information that citizens need to function effectively within that community. This function of news organizations is what differentiates the news organization from other social institutions and businesses in the community. It clarifies how their role is distinct from an advertising or public relations firm. It is not an ethical problem that news organizations work to make a profit. It is, however, an ethical problem if making a profit interferes with the news organization fulfilling its social function. The ultimate goal for any news organization is to serve the community by fulfilling its special role and to do so efficiently enough that a reasonable profit can be realized.

There is no necessary conflict between economic well-being and ethics, but it is morally prohibited—wrong—to make money at the expense of meeting one's social responsibility. By way of example, consider the economic and ethical requirements of physicians and attorneys who are in private practice. They must exist to make a profit, otherwise they could not provide for themselves and their families. Nevertheless, no one would excuse the doctor or lawyer who performed an unnecessary procedure simply because a client could afford to pay for it or because the practitioner needed the money. It is important that news organizations make a profit as an *indirect* effect of performing their duties to the public; however, ethics is not reducible to the bottom line. How industries balance their ethical and economic requirements is, in itself, a matter of ethics.

Personal Preference and Professional Ethics

The distinctions between ethics and matters of taste, opinion, and self-interest are many. Here it is necessary only to notice the aspect of social responsibility to be able to see why it is that taste, opinion, and self-interest fail as guides for appropriate professional conduct.

The First Amendment guarantees that those paying the publication and broadcast bills have complete freedom to produce and display what they like. The major limitation on mass-market news organizations is not the law, but the implicit promise that they have made to their communities to provide a certain kind of service. When the news director broadcasts a compelling tape without regard to the harm it will cause individuals or the community, when an editor decides that the community should not hear arguments opposing a bill that the editor would like to see passed, or when the publisher orders the paper to withhold a story that will cause her harm, the practice is unethical. In these cases, the news organizations are failing to keep their implicit promise to tell citizens the news that they need to know.

As noted earlier, in the United States and other democratic countries, news organizations provide information required for self-governance. The press is the "eyes and ears" and the "watchdog" of the citizens. This role is vital if democracy is to work.

News organizations are free to do much more than produce this bare minimum content of news. They can provide comics, classified ads, editorials, and expertise from column writers on a world of topics. It is, however, the citizens' dependency on them as the source for information about the coming blizzard, the school budget, the results of the campaign, and the outcome of the zoning consideration that makes news organizations unique among other collectors and providers of information. The social responsibility of news organizations is to fulfill this unique role.

News organizations interpret what it means to fulfill that role a little differently among different communities and between different news organizations, but there is a norm of what constitutes adequate news coverage and of what news coverage should be held up as a model. Because of the norm, travelers in different parts of the country know what types of information to expect on the front page of any mass-market daily newspaper that they find; they know that the less important news will appear at the end of the section; they know that the op-ed pages provide space for writers employed by the newspaper as well as citizens at large to express their opinions. Because of the norm, national prizes for high-quality reporting abound, from the coveted Pulitzer Prize to those prizes awarded by regional professional organizations.

The unique social function of news organizations and the implicit promises that they have made to their communities provide the scope for what counts as morally permissible behavior for journalists. That scope is not reducible to law, economics, or personal desire.

Journalism Ethics and the Concept of Harm

Journalism ethics finds its roots in the study of moral philosophy and in the unique responsibility of news organizations. Two thousand years of Western moral philosophy provides the foundation for the practice of ethics in journalism. While there are major differences in the surviving ethical theories that constitute the general curriculum in classes in ethical theory, there are major points of agreement as well. Generally accepted ethical theories require, for minimal morality, that one meet one's responsibilities and that one refrain from causing harm that cannot be justified. Responsibilities include formal job requirements as well as informal role-related responsibilities such as those that arise from being one's mate, parent, or friend. "Do not cause unjustifiable harm" means do not cause other people to suffer pain, death, or disability or deprive them of opportunity or pleasure unless there is good reason for doing so. If someone is caused harm for a good reason, like a child made to suffer the pain of an injection, the harm is justifiable (Gert 1988). A person is acting in a morally permissible way (in a minimal sense) if she is meeting her moral responsibilities and not causing unjustifiable harm. Morally ideal action occurs when people find ways of meeting their responsibilities that cause no harm and promote good.

Justification theories for professionally caused harms rest primarily on how closely the harm is related to the practitioner's job. For example, it is justifiable for a police officer to stop someone who is speeding, thus temporarily depriving that person of the opportunity to keep driving and depriving that person of pleasure (or even causing pain) by levying a fine.

For a parent, being moral or ethical in this minimal sense means taking care of the kids and not causing anyone unjustifiable harm. An example of justifiable parental harm is depriving one's child of opportunity and pleasure by making him sit down to do his homework. Unjustifiable harm would include stealing the neighbor's CD collection so that one's son could have all the music he wanted.

For a teacher, doing one's job means, in part, that the teacher does what needs to be done to help students learn new information and skills. The justifiable harm caused by teachers includes depriving students of opportunity by requiring them to come to class, depriving them of pleasure by giving them exams, and sometimes causing them pain by giving them the grades that they deserve. Unjustifiable harm would include stealing someone else's work (like showing pirated videotapes) so that the students could be exposed to new material. Unjustifiable harm would also include kidnapping a recalcitrant student to force her to get her homework done.

It is important to notice that parenting and teaching role-related obligations are like journalistic obligations in that they are all part of voluntary roles. When one takes on the job, one assumes the obligations of the job. That truism holds for practitioners of the news. Consonant with First Amendment rights, practitioners are free to print or not print anything they want. Nevertheless, once they have taken on the responsibilities associated with journalism, they have an obligation to do what they and their news organizations have promised that they will do (Elliott 1986).

Good parents or good teachers do more than just meet the minimums. They strive for the moral ideal in their actions. This sense of minimal morality provides a starting point for understanding what is meant by ethical behavior. What it means for a journalist (or a news organization) to act morally in a minimal sense is that she (or it) is providing citizens information that they need to have to function effectively in a self-governing society and that she (or it) is not causing unjustifiable harm in the process of providing that information.

Justifiable harm includes harm that is unavoidable in the process of meeting one's social function. Justifiable harm for a journalist includes such things as causing pain for a public official and the community by exposing corruption in government; it includes depriving people of pleasure by publishing accurate bad news that people need to have. Arguably it may even include breaking the law or deceiving people by going undercover to get a story that is vital to civic life when there is no other way to access the information. All of these activities are done in the name of providing the public with information that is pertinent to self-governance; that is, the harm caused is justified by the importance of the journalistic job.

Unjustifiable harm includes depriving ordinary citizens of opportunity and pleasure by revealing private information about them that does not advance the public's need for civic knowledge. It includes causing story subjects pain by publishing information that there is no particular need for the community to know.

Each socially required task brings special privileges and responsibilities. Causing pain is justifiable when journalists are providing citizens information that is necessary for self-governance. Causing pain is less justifiable when journalists are providing citizens with information of a more elective nature. For example, if a news organization were to write a story about how felons in the community have fared after their release from prison, people who have been rehabilitated and who now are serving as exemplary citizens would be harmed by the unwanted publicity. While it may be *of interest* to the community that felons can complete their sentences and then live productive lives, it is not *imperative* for self-governance. Furthermore, identification of those rehabilitated persons could cause extreme harm to them as well as to their friends and family who may not be aware of their past. If, however, a news organization published a story about a convicted felon who is likely to be a recidivist, the information could benefit the community significantly.

Methods of Analysis

Moral analysis consists of two phases: conceptualization and justification. The first step in journalistic ethics is determining if there is a potential ethical violation, if a journalist should be held blameworthy for the harm caused by a violation, and what that violation might be. Every journalistic situation has an ethical aspect, in that ethics concerns how we act in regard to one another.

Potential ethical violations are signaled by the realization that a person may be or is harmed by another's action. Sometimes no person is to blame for the harm, morally speaking, or the harm can be justified. Without purported harm, however, there is no claim of ethical violation. Actions that do, or are likely to, lead individuals to suffer harm are ethically questionable. Harm includes pain, death, disability, and deprivation of opportunity or of freedom. Actions that are likely to lead to individuals suffering harm include cheating, deception, breaking promises, and disobeying the law. In addition, individuals can be harmed when others fail to meet role-related responsibilities in regard to them (Gert 1988).

Let us examine a situation in which people suffer harm that is no one's fault. One can feel terribly disappointed (that is, suffer emotional pain) and be hungry (that is, suffer physical pain) when arriving too late to be seated immediately at a popular restaurant. The earlier arrivals are not morally blameworthy, although they constitute what Aristotle would call the proximate cause. Indeed, one could be shot and killed while standing in line waiting to get into the restaurant without the earlier eaters being blameworthy. They are a reason that the murder victim is standing outside, but they are not morally blameworthy for the fate that befalls the victim. Moral blameworthiness requires an intention to cause harm, a reasonable expectation that the actor should know that the action might cause harm, or a relationship between the actor and the person affected through which one incurs special responsibilities.

Journalists sometimes seek to excuse themselves when they cause harm by pointing out that all they are doing is reporting the story. The journalists are not responsible for the unethical or illegal action that brought the story subject to their attention, but publication of the story does cause harm for which the journalists can be held morally blameworthy. It is easiest to understand this concept by realizing that journalists and news organizations are more than willing to take credit for the good that they bring about through their work. One cannot, however, take responsibility for positive consequences without also taking responsibility for negative consequences. Journalists cannot claim to be the cause when the consequence of their reporting is positive and claim that they are *not* the cause when the consequence is negative. Journalists are both morally praiseworthy and morally blameworthy for the outcome of their work. Events happen without their involvement, but news is the creation of the journalist. While the production and presentation of a news story is an intentional act, it is reasonable to expect journalists to be sensitive to the unintended effects of their reporting.

It is expected in journalism that practitioners will act with the intent of telling citizens information that they should know. News organizations have tremendous power to impact the lives of individuals. Morally responsible actions by journalists entail judicious use of such power, including sensitivity to when one's professional actions might cause harm. Examining how well journalists have done this is the conceptual level of analysis. Ethical practice includes awareness of potential harm and awareness of what *kind* of harm might be caused through the professional action. Journalists should identify who might be harmed and how individuals might be harmed through their actions.

The next level of ethical analysis is justification. Justification is the process by which it is determined whether and to what extent an action in question is morally permissible. At the conceptual level, one might conclude that an individual is likely to be harmed. At the justification level, one would, in turn, consider whether it is morally permissible to cause that harm. In general, the closer the action is to the social function of journalism, the more morally permissible the action.

Major Issues in Journalism Ethics

Issues in journalism ethics can be divided into micro- and macroissues. Microissues involve the actions of individual practitioners or news organizations and their impact on individuals in the reporting and publication process. Macroissues involve the actions of news organizations or the industry as a whole and their impact on the society at large.

Microissues discussed later in this book include how information is gathered and how source material is presented. They involve how much truth a journalist has a responsibility to share with sources in developing a story and when leaving material out of a story counts as deceiving the readers.

Macroissues involve how media owners allow economics to impact the ability of journalists to do their work and how societal blinders and stereotypes affect the identification and presentation of what journalists call news. For example, if the budget that funds investigative reporting is cut to increase the news organization's profits, the business managers may be acting in a way that does not allow the news staff to meet their social responsibility.

Journalism Ethics and the Law

Constitutional law has been consistent in protecting freedom of the press. Even with such First Amendment protection, state and federal judgments have set some limitations on journalism. For example, in *Cohen v. Cowles* (111 S. Ct. 2513: 1991), the U.S. Supreme Court remanded to a Minnesota court a case in which reporters for two news organizations violated their promise to a source to keep his identity confidential. The Court said that a promise of confidentiality is a contract, upon which a source may sue if broken. In the same session, the Court, in *Masson v. New Yorker* (11 S. Ct. 2419: 1991), verified that a source has the right to sue if misquoted or misinterpreted. Furthermore, in more than half of the states, there is no state shield law that allows reporters to maintain confidentiality for their source if the courts believe that that information is needed in the investigation or prosecution of a crime.

The constitutional protections, however, give journalism more latitude than many other practices, which is why the practice of ethical journalism is so important. An increasing emphasis on preprofessional education in journalism and on the inclusion of ethics as part of that education indicates a hope that professional decision making will remain in the newsroom rather than the courtroom.

The Future

The practice of journalism will never be algorithmic. Advances in technology and simply the passage of time change how one interprets what it means for journalists to do their jobs. Predicting the future is thus one of those tasks that seems doomed from the start. The predictor makes statements that are either too predictable to be of interest or goes out on a limb that is neatly sawed off by the passage of time, but preserved as an embarrassing curio in the literature.

With that caveat in mind, it is likely that with the turn of the twenty-first century, the attention of ethics scholars, media critics, and concerned citizens will have turned from perceived media overcoverage to alarm over undercoverage. Rather than expressing disgust at the pain particular news organizations cause specific individuals, perceptive analysts and monitors of the industry may increasingly point out the problems caused by a more monolithic, yet fragmented, media monster that allows far too many relevant and important stories to slip through the cracks. The lens may turn from the microdissections of individual events to the wide-angle scrutiny of the systemwide failure of a crucial industry to meet its social responsibilities.

Again, journalists have a role-related responsibility to give people information that they need in order to function adequately in a self-governing society. The following four trends will make meeting this obligation more of a challenge in the future.

Trend #1: There is a continuing trend toward news organization ownership and control by nonmedia concerns. The effect that this trend has on the ability of a news organization to meet its social mandate is clear. If the purse strings are in the hands of those who are only economically invested in the news organization's mission, a tension is created between those trying to meet obligations to the public and those trying to meet obligations to stockholders. It creates a classic conflict of interests.

Ben Bagdikian (1987) said in his preface to the second edition of *The Media Monopoly* that he was surprised by four developments in the four years since publication of his first edition. A decade after his observation, his surprise is worth sharing. It has serious impact on what it means for journalists to do their jobs in the future.

Bagdikian (1987, ix) wrote that he was surprised by the "rapidity of enlarged corporate control, the naiveté, of so many working journalists about its impact, the degree to which students of communication have ignored the peculiarities of localism and local monopoly in American news, and the unconcern of the country's top editors with the extent to which mass advertising is changing the form and content of news itself."

In the third edition of *The Media Monopoly*, Bagdikian (1990) provides some illustrations of the control of news media:

- General Electric (GE) began bringing good news to light when it acquired NBC through its 1986 purchase of RCA. GE is the world's tenth largest corporation, a major defense contractor, producer of electric lamps, nuclear missiles, and locomotives.

- Times Warner is the largest media corporation in the world. It is the largest magazine publisher in the United States, the second largest cable company in the world, one of the largest book publishers in the world, and the world's largest video company.

- Rupert Murdoch's News Corp., Ltd., controls more newspaper circulation around the world than any other publisher including two-thirds of all newspapers in Australia, half of all in New Zealand, and one-third of Britain. Murdoch controls book publishing firms in Britain and the United States. He has the largest satellite television system in Europe and is the second-largest magazine publisher in the United States. He controls Fox Broadcasting Network and 20th Century Fox movie studies and is the world's largest distributor of videocassettes.

- Capital Cities/ABC owns the ABC network and the ABC O&O television stations, as well as a chain of American daily newspapers. In addition, it controls cable companies, Hollywood studios, the country's largest publisher of religious material, ESPN and Lifetime cable channels, and Fairchild Publications.

- Maxwell Communications of Britain owns newspapers, book publishing houses, magazines, databases, communication satellite channels, market services, and printing plants.

Consistent with Bagdikian (1990, 240), these media giants have, since 1990, consumed a larger market share of existing media including, almost incidentally, news organizations.

Ethical journalism in the future should include keeping careful vigilance over the industries that control news organizations. If corporate cuts are preventing news organizations from providing needed information to the community, someone has got to sound the alarm. Although this sacred cow may be looking in the window of the newsroom, nobody else in the community can tell people what they need to know about this conflict of interest in media ownership.

Trend #2: With a decreasing number of hands at the major national controls, there is an increasing diversity of news media outlets targeted for particular populations. This diversity of news outlets includes MTV News; news produced for Spanish-speaking readers, listeners, and viewers; news for African Americans, gays and lesbians, and Asian Americans; news for persons with disabilities; news for the business-oriented crowd; and news available on the World Wide Web.

This trend ought not to be viewed as a return to the many-voiced plurality press that existed before the telegraph and wire service started the trend toward homogeneity 100 years ago. There is an essential difference. The early–twentieth-century press was a multitude of different voices, backed by different funders with a diversity of agenda. The early–twenty-first-century press will consist of a few funders with a few financially correct agenda, controlling the production and dissemination of news to make their message as appealing as possible to as many different kinds of people as possible.

The trend toward fewer and less-diverse voices in the news media includes an even greater obligation to amplify the voiceless in society. Whatever the nature of the corporate owners, journalism is a profession of idealists, of people who are dedicated to open public discussion. Rather than being handed chestnuts like "two sides to a story," journalism students of the future need to be taught how to include the reality of many voices in every story.

Trend #3: In this growing global community, there will be more open windows in an ever more thickly settled town square. Increasingly, "we are there." Satellites—small cameras that carry their own power supply and easily movable equipment to broadcast what they pick up—create the sensation of instant news, which is not the same as real news. News is a creation of the journalist and the news organization. What comes out the end of the editorial process is a massaged, synthesized, encapsulated interpretation of an event or issue of importance to people in a self-governing society.

The open windows—the ability of media outlets to pick up and broadcast what is happening in our global community's town square—do not create news by simply being open. What comes in through those open windows is analogous to the honking horns and wisps of conversation and crying babies that one hears in a less virtual town square. Neither is news. News is what a profession, responsibly or not, creates for the community it serves.

The people at news organizations that use technology to put consumers on the scenes of selected events around the globe incur an obligation to self-consciously and purposefully select those items and events that people need to know. The question "What is news?" has an ever evolving answer. That answer has always been dependent, in part, on what information is accessible to journalists, but access is a necessary condition to something being news, not a sufficient condition. News without notice is a little like an unobserved tree falling in the forest. It still may make a sound, but who cares? Important, even vital, events are happening around the world all of the time, but until they get noticed and broadcast, their existence is irrelevant.

Unfortunately, the trend has been to make access a sufficient condition for calling something news. Can we follow a white Ford Bronco down Los Angeles freeways with a suicidal murder suspect inside? The fact that we can does not make it a special news report. Speaking of suicides, can we have a camera following a despondent minister waving a gun as he lurches through city streets? The fact that we can does not make it newsworthy for a nation.

The good thing about the continuing trend of greater and more instantaneous access is that there will be too much bleeding for it all to make leading news stories. News managers will have to use criteria other than just "we got it."

One of the bad things about the increasing trend toward access is the move toward pseudoaccess. Rather than admit a lack of access, news organizations are inclined to create the impression of access. Are journalists being kept backstage of the theater of operations in a war? If so, this lack of access should be starkly and repeatedly broadcast rather than being hidden by twirling trailers, fancy graphics, a golden rolodex of distant experts, and celebrity journalists center stage as it was in the Persian Gulf War.

Trend #4: The final (and finally not technical) trend is the trend toward holding news media more accountable for action and nonaction in both the courts and the court of public opinion. People are getting more subtle and sophisticated in their expectations of professional accountability, and the courts are beginning to recognize that the line between nonprotected commercial speech and that explicitly protected by the First Amendment is a line that is becoming more and more blurred. It is blurred on the corporate level and it is also blurred on the programmatic level. Increasingly, broadcast news reporters, who have earned credibility for presenting the truth, double as magazine show anchors, a division of the corporations' entertainment sections. The conventional expectations of what counts as documented news and what is broadcast as a magazine piece differ.

Media organizations want to blur the lines between news and entertainment to increase the profit margin for both. When people cannot tell which is which, however, they cannot be held responsible for using the wrong standards for judging the adequacy of one or the other. Media owners and managers are finding it difficult to have it both ways: they cannot purposefully confuse people and then be outraged when people respond to their product with obvious confusion.

This last trend is the one least likely to inform journalistic action in the future, but it is the one most important, that is, the trend toward greater accountability. Our society is one that is maturing, with citizens less and less willing to do what authority says, but at the same time that our citizenry is maturing, the enormity of private institutional power makes individuals increasingly powerless. It is as though our society were in an adolescent stage, with all of that stage's movement toward control and independence, but with the same adolescent tendency toward "couch-potato-ness."

Juries should be outraged at news media abuses, even if those juries are sometimes wrong. Rich corporate ownership will result in more news media victories in the courts, not because the news media are right, but because they have the most money to put forward. We only have to look as far as the O. J. Simpson trial to see what it means to have the best defense that money can buy. Few plaintiffs can afford a fight against one of the conglomerates that now own most news media. So there is a danger that the trend toward community outrage and demands for accountability will be stopped by the rich and powerful media owners convincing folks that it is fruitless to fight, so they might as well settle down and watch some television.

If our citizenry's social development is strong enough to withstand this type of persuasion, then news media, like government and other private industries, will be increasingly asked to justify itself. The result will be and should be self-conscious news media owners looking over their shoulders every step of the way.

The journalism that is ethical to do in this regard is the kind of journalism that encourages citizens to demand accountability of news media owners. In the best tradition of journalism, an ethical future of journalistic practice will involve the domino effect: when journalists do their jobs really well, they will be requiring others to do their jobs just as well.

References: Bagdikian, Ben. 1987. *The Media Monopoly.* 2d Edition. Boston: Beacon Press.
————. 1990. *The Media Monopoly.* 3rd Edition. Boston: Beacon Press.
Elliott, Deni. 1986. "Foundations for News Media Responsibility." In Deni Elliott. *Responsible Journalism.* Beverly Hills, CA: Sage, 32–46.
Gert, Bernard. 1988. *Morality: A New Justification for the Moral Rules.* New York: Oxford University Press.

CONTEMPORARY ETHICAL ISSUES

Chapter 2:
Chronology

Clifford G. Christians

1860s	The *Philadelphia Public Ledger* introduces its 24 Rules, which stress accuracy and fairness, during the Civil War. Other informal lists of moral guidelines appear at various times in the nineteenth century.
1889	The word *ethics* first appears in an essay on press criticism by W. S. Lilly, entitled "The Ethics of Journalism." As historian Hazel Dicken-Garcia notes, newspapers have been vigorously attacked in the British press since the early seventeenth century. Not until Lilly's article appears in *The Forum*, however, is the criticism directly connected to ethical principles. In the decade following, a

1889
cont.

coherent perspective takes shape within the industry, the dominant theory being utilitarianism (as demonstrated in a 1988 article on the period by ethicist John Ferre). Based on this ethical principle, moralists in the 1890s focus on the press' sensationalism and inaccuracy; they argue for education and economic pressure as the most effective strategies for reform.

1910

The Kansas Editorial Association officially adopts the first code of ethics for journalists, written by William E. Miller. Other statewide codes follow a decade later. This formal code activity is preceded by informal lists of moral guidelines that appear at various times in the previous century.

1912

The School of Journalism opens at Columbia University with a $2 million endowment from Joseph Pulitzer, publisher of the St. Louis *Post-Dispatch* and *New York World*. The provisions in his will for the Columbia endowment emphasize the importance of ethics in journalism education: "I desire to assist in attracting to this profession young men of character and ability, also to help those already engaged in the profession to acquire the highest moral and intellectual training.... There will naturally be a course in ethics, but training in ethical principles must not be confined to that. It must pervade all the courses."

1920s

Other state associations follow Kansas's lead in officially adopting codes of ethics for journalists: Missouri and Texas in 1921, South Dakota and Oregon in 1922, Massachusetts and Washington in 1923, and Iowa and New Jersey in 1924. Many newspapers, such as the *Brooklyn Eagle*, *Springfield Republican*, *Detroit News*, *Sacramento Bee*, *Seattle Times*, and *Kansas City Journal-Post*, also prepare their own codes of ethics during the 1910s and 1920s. Some codes are explicit ("always verify names"), and others moralistic ("be vigorous but not vicious").

1922

Casper S. Yost of the *St. Louis Globe-Democrat* organizes the American Society of Newspaper Editors (ASNE). Its purpose is to promote professional ideals among editors in chief, managing editors, and editorial-page editors of daily newspapers.

1923

A code of ethics called Canons of Journalism is adopted at the first annual meeting of the ASNE. The code empha-

1923
cont.

sizes public interest, impartiality, decency, truthfulness, and accuracy. The ASNE Canons of Journalism is the star of early codes. Several journalism associations—local, state, and national—copy or imitate its contents during the 1920s.

1924

The U.S. Senate begins investigating rumors that government oil reserves in the Teapot Dome are being sold to commercial oil companies. One ASNE member, Fred G. Bonfils of the *Denver Post*, is accused of accepting bribes to suppress information about the Teapot Dome scandal. Several ASNE members insist on expelling Bonfils for violating its code of ethics. The debate over code enforcement continues until 1929.

Nelson Crawford of Kansas State University publishes the first textbook on newspaper ethics in the United States, *The Ethics of Journalism*. He insists that the press is an instrument "of public accountability and public service." Crawford fosters ethics instruction in higher education and seeks to stimulate stronger codes in the profession. Leon Nelson Flint of the University of Kansas follows a year later with his *Conscience of the Newspaper*, beginning with actual cases and dealing with general issues in parts 2 and 3. William Gibbons's *Newspaper Ethics* (1926), Paul Douglas's *The Newspaper and Responsibility* (1929), and Albert F. Henning's *Ethics and Practices in Journalism* (1932) add more textbooks to a productive decade, helping establish an early version of social responsibility theory and contributing ethics instruction to the university training of journalists.

1926

The Society of Professional Journalists/Sigma Delta Chi (SPJ/SDX) adopts the ASNE Canons as its own code of ethics.

1929

ASNE members vote for voluntary obedience rather than disciplinary action. The concept of voluntary compliance with the ASNE code becomes standard policy for media codes of ethics from this point on.

In March, the National Association of Broadcasters (NAB) voluntarily adopts its own Code of Ethics. These voluntary regulations of program content and advertising are developed in more detail in terms of the NAB Radio Code in 1939 and the NAB Television Code in 1952.

1929
cont.

One of America's greatest twentieth-century journalists, Walter Lippmann, publishes *A Preface to Morals*. It becomes a best-seller with six editions printed in the first year. Lippmann identifies the basic problem with society as his generation's inability to discriminate right from wrong. Realizing that no progress is possible in a moral vacuum, Lippmann searches philosophy, theology, history, and sociology for values relevant to post–World War I conditions. He argues that underneath sound professional practice and a healthy public life are both an informed mind and a vital conscience.

1934

Congress establishes the Federal Communications Commission (FCC) to license broadcasters in "public interest, convenience, and necessity."

1944

In February, Robert M. Hutchins, president of the University of Chicago, announces the formation of a nine-member Commission on the Freedom of the Press. Funded by *Time* editor in chief Henry R. Luce and supplemented by a grant from the *Encyclopedia Britannica*, the commission issues its report in 1947.

1947

The Commission on the Freedom of the Press, including heavyweights such as Harold Lasswell of the War Communications Research Commission, Zachariah Chafee and William Hocking of Harvard, Charles Merriam and Robert Redfield of the University of Chicago, and Reinhold Niebuhr of the Union Theological Seminary, hears testimony from 58 members of the press, interviews 225 people from government and industry, holds 17 public meetings, and studies 176 documents prepared by its staff. The commission's 133-page published report is called *A Free and Responsible Press*.

Given the layers of a big-business media system establishing itself after World War II, the commission emphasizes five principles: (1) truthful accounts in their context of meaning, (2) a public forum of comment and criticism, (3) a representative picture of a society's various cultures, (4) clarification of goals and values, and (5) full access to the day's intelligence.

The commission publishes several books and monographs as background material for its report: the two-volume *Government and Mass Communications* by Zachariah Chafee, *Freedom of the Press: A Framework of Principle* by

1947
cont.
William Ernest Hocking, *Freedom of the Movies* by staff member Ruth Inglis, *The American Radio* by Llewellyn White, *Peoples Speaking to Peoples* by White and Robert Leigh, and *The American Press and the San Francisco Conference* by Milton Stewart.

1949
The FCC rules that since the airwaves are public property, broadcasters must make them accessible to many different viewpoints. All sides of controversial issues should be presented, according to the FCC, though balance ought to be ensured in overall programming as opposed to one program.

1960
The NAB Code Authority is formed, and it eventually grows into staffs in Washington, D.C., New York, and Los Angeles who hear complaints of violations. Broadcasters assume that active compliance helps protect them against government intrusion.

1967
Following weeks of firebombing, shooting, and looting in Detroit, Michigan, and Newark, New Jersey, President Lyndon Johnson appoints a National Advisory Commission on Civil Disorders, with Governor Otto Kerner of Illinois as chair. The Kerner Commission reviews nearly 1,000 sequences of television news coverage, newspaper stories, newsmagazine reports, and radio and wire service reports out of Detroit and Newark, preparing a report that will be released in the next year.

Mellett Fund for a Free and Responsible Press established six local news councils for one- to two-year experiments. Four are newspaper councils in Redwood City, California; Sparta and Cairo, Illinois; and Bend, Oregon. A press council in St. Louis directed by Earl Reeves involves both broadcasters and publishers. The Seattle Communication Council of media leaders and black citizens meets from June 1968 to December 1969.

1968
In March, the Kerner Commission issues its *Report of the National Advisory Commission on Civil Disorders*. Chapter 15 deals with the mass media's effect on the 1967 upheavals in Detroit and Newark. News coverage is found to be generally balanced and factual, although exaggerating property damage. It is also found to be occasionally sensational, and overly dependent on police information. The report severely indicts the communications media for tokenism:

1968
cont.

"Hiring one Negro reporter, or even two or three—is no longer enough. Negro reporters are essential, but so are Negro editors, writers, and commentators." The report finds no serious, long-term reporting of the black community. The largely white media do not communicate "a sense of the degradation, misery and hopelessness of living in the ghetto. They have not shown understanding or appreciation of Negro culture, thought, or history." A follow-up study in 1969 of newspapers in 16 of the largest U.S. cities confirms that only 2.6 percent of their staffs are black, including but one news executive among over 4,000 employees.

1971

Minnesota organizes a statewide news council in 1971, and by 1987 it alone survives on the state level. Hawaii also forms a press council in 1971, but it survives only in Honolulu.

1973

At the Society of Professional Journalists/Sigma Delta Chi convention in Buffalo, New York, the revision of its 1926 model becomes the flagship of contemporary codes and triggers a wave of code interest under way ever since. Consistent with code history since the inception of the ASNE codes of 1923, no enforcement provision is included.

The Twentieth Century Fund, a foundation endowed by Edward A. Filene in 1919, underwrites an independent nonprofit organization called the National News Council. Embracing print and broadcasting, it is patterned after the British Press Council established in 1953 and the Swedish Press Council of 1916. The newly formed council receives complaints about ethical lapses in the press, calls on the responsible editors and reporters for explanation, and then pronounces judgments that publicly clear or condemn the media organizations involved. The council has 18 members—10 from the public and 8 from the media—with William B. Arthur as executive director and Norman Isaacs as chair. Beginning in 1977, it publishes its findings, first in the *Columbia Journalism Review* and later in *Quill*. While 30 media organizations contribute money to its expenses, the *New York Times* and the Associated Press lead many other news organizations in opposing it as infringing on their First Amendment freedom.

1973
cont.

The United Nations Educational, Scientific, and Cultural Organization (UNESCO) declares that the New International Economic Order depends on a new communication order. By this time, UNESCO has already developed a Declaration of Principles for satellite broadcasting (1972). Also in 1973, the Non-Aligned Countries meeting in Algeria insist on every nation's right to communicate and condemn existing media channels as a legacy of the colonial past.

1974

John C. Merrill publishes a landmark book on the philosophical roots of journalism ethics, *The Imperative of Freedom*. It argues for journalistic autonomy in terms of a libertarian worldview; therefore, duties cannot be imposed from outside. Merrill's follow-up study in 1989, *The Dialectic in Journalism*, integrates freedom with responsibility. The foundation on which he unifies opposites is the dialectical tradition from Heraclitus (sixth-century B.C. Greece) to Georg W. F. Hegel (nineteenth-century Germany). In the living moments of history we are able to reconcile the people's right to know with journalistic freedom, duties and consequences, absolutes, and situationalism.

1975

Nelson Poynter of the *St. Petersburg Times* and *Evening Independent* founds the Modern Media Institute as a nonprofit teaching and research center for improving journalism education and practice.

1976

In October, the General Assembly of UNESCO at Nairobi appoints a 16-person International Commission for the Study of Communication Problems. Sean MacBride, Ireland's former minister for foreign affairs and winner of both the Nobel and Lenin Peace Prizes, is made chair.

The programming sections of the NAB Radio Code and NAB Television Code are suspended when a federal judge rules that "family viewing" standards violate the First Amendment.

1977

The Hastings Center of New York initiates a systematic study of ethics instruction and curricula in American higher education. Funded by the Rockefeller Brothers Fund and the Carnegie Corporation of New York, the project focuses on professional and undergraduate teaching. Through con-

1977
cont.

ferences, papers, empirical analyses, and monographs over two years, the Hastings Center Project on the Teaching of Ethics in Higher Education outlines a central and significant role for practical and applied ethics in the curriculum. Law, journalism, medicine, business, social work, engineering, and government policy making are included, with five instructional goals common to all of them: (1) stimulating the moral imagination, (2) recognizing moral issues, (3) developing analytical skills, (4) eliciting moral obligation, and (5) tolerating disagreement and ambiguity. The monograph *Teaching Ethics in Journalism Education*, by Clifford Christians and Catherine Covert, is published in 1980 as part of this Hastings Center project. Also as part of the project, the instructional practice in journalism ethics is surveyed. This first comprehensive survey of the 247 schools belonging to the Association for Education in Journalism and Mass Communication (AEJMC) identifies 68 programs with freestanding courses in ethics. This number increases to 117 media ethics courses in a 1985 follow-up study, and to 183 courses in 158 schools teaching media ethics in 1995 (21 of these schools taught two or even three courses).

1980

Anne Vander Meiden of the State University of Utrecht (the Netherlands) finishes an international reader, *Ethics and Mass Communication*. He publishes this anthology for the Professional Education Section of the International Association for Mass Communication Research. For the first time, ethical issues and professional codes are addressed cross-culturally in book form, with contributions from Korea, Belgium, England, Germany, the United States, Finland, and the Netherlands.

On 28 September, the *Washington Post* carries a story headlined "Jimmy's World." In over 2,000 words, starting on the front page, reporter Janet Cooke gives an eyewitness account of eight-year-old Jimmy mainlining heroin from the dope-dealer boyfriend of his mother. Washington officials demand information to find the boy, but the *Post* refuses on the grounds of its First Amendment protections and its pledge of confidentiality to Jimmy's mother and the drug pusher.

A few weeks later, the *Post* submits the story for a Pulitzer Prize and wins, but on the day the prize is announced, information on Cooke's background is found to

1980
cont.

be false. Within 24 hours, the *Post* returns the prize, announces that the story is fabricated, and accepts Janet Cooke's resignation. Bill Green, the *Post*'s ombudsman, releases a 17,000-word review of the Jimmy story on 19 April 1981. He details the breakdowns at the *Post* from idea stage to Cooke's resignation. The case becomes a cause célèbre at professional meetings and in journalism ethics classrooms.

UNESCO's International Commission for the Study of Communication Problems addresses communication rights issues in its report, *Many Voices, One World: Communication and Society, Today and Tomorrow*. The 1980 U.N. General Assembly in Belgrade adopts many of its principles for reform toward a just and balanced New World Information and Communication Order.

1980–1990

International conferences on media ethics are held in Kristiansand (Norway), Stuttgart (Germany), and at Villa Cavalletti in Rome during the 1980s.

1982

On 20 September, Richard Cole of the University of North Carolina, president of the Association for Education in Journalism and Mass Communication (AEJMC), appoints a nine-member AEJMC Ad Hoc Committee on Ethics. Its mission is to stimulate interest in ethics by the pervasive approach, that is, working across AEJMC as a whole rather than isolating concerns into a standing committee. In 1985, the AEJMC at its annual convention in Memphis adopts ethics officially and explicitly as one of the five primary obligations of its Standing Committee on Professional Freedom and Responsibility. Ethics activities in teaching, research, and public service begin to appear by 1987 in the various divisions of the organization.

1982–1983

In March 1982, a U.S. district court judge rules that NAB code provisions regulating commercial advertising artificially increase prices and lessen competition. On 17 January 1983, the NAB's board of directors officially dissolves the Code Authority.

1983

After processing more than 1,000 complaints about inaccuracy, unfairness, and irresponsibility, the National News Council closes its doors.

1984	In March, the Poynter Institute for Media Studies (the renamed Modern Media Institute) holds its first seminar in applied ethics for reporters and editors.

In May, Edmund Lambeth of the University of Kentucky launches the first annual Workshop on the Teaching of Journalism Ethics. The Association for Education in Journalism and Mass Communication (AEJMC) supports this weeklong training for professors who are newly involved in teaching ethics, and the Freedom Forum underwrites it financially. Syllabi and the latest textbooks and teaching materials for the freestanding course are introduced. Participants work through ethical theory, case studies, moral development models, instructional goals, and learning theory.

1985	By the mid-1980s, the networks and leading journalists argue for abolishing this Fairness Doctrine so they can cover issues without the fear of government intervention. By August 1985, the FCC itself assails the regulation as violating First Amendment guarantees of free speech.

In May, the Society of Professional Journalists/Sigma Delta Chi board of directors unanimously denies expulsion procedures and affirms its long-standing commitment to awareness and voluntary self-regulation.

James Jaksa and Michael Pritchard of Western Michigan University, and their colleagues, begin the Commission on Communication Ethics (COCE). As a subunit of the Speech Communication Association (SCA), the COCE sponsors research papers and activities at the SCA's annual convention. They deal with ethical issues in interpersonal and organizational settings to and in the mass media. As of 1990, the COCE cosponsors (with Western Michigan University) the National Communication Ethics Conference every two years at Gull Lake, Michigan.

In the fall, Jay Black of Utah State and Ralph Barney of Brigham Young begin publishing the *Journal of Mass Media Ethics (JMME)*. After establishing the need during discussions with the Association for Education in Journalism and Mass Communication (AEJMC) and the Society of Professional Journalists, the editors have their own univer-

1985
cont.

sities underwrite *JMME* as a biannual (now quarterly) refereed journal.

JMME aims to bridge the gap between academics and professionals. While focusing on news in print and broadcasting, it also deals with ethical issues in advertising, public relations, and entertainment. It devotes special issues to such topics as photojournalism ethics, journalism moral philosophy, privacy, and codes of ethics. Deni Elliott of the University of Montana is "Book Review" editor, and Louis Hodges of Washington and Lee edits the "Cases and Commentaries" section. With volume 5, Lawrence Erlbaum takes over publication of *JMME* as a quarterly.

1986

In May, the Poynter Institute for Media Studies introduces a four-day seminar for teachers of journalism ethics. This seminar, along with the institute's seminar in applied ethics for reporters and editors, is then held annually as part of Poynter's Ethics Program, directed by Bob Steele.

1987

Congress votes to renew the legal base of the FCC Fairness Doctrine, but President Reagan vetoes the bill. The FCC subsequently abolishes the fairness provision.

1988

In the spring, Professors Thomas Cooper and John M. Kittross of Emerson College edit a new biannual newsletter. Cosponsored by Emerson, the Silha Center at the University of Minnesota, and the United Church of Christ, *Media Ethics Update* serves as a general news and issues umbrella for the many programs, groups, and individuals involved in mass communication ethics. (The "News and Events" section continues, but analysis and commentary expand as the publication's name changes to *Media Ethics* and it develops into magazine format in 1993.)

The Association for Education in Journalism and Mass Communication Ad Hoc Committee on Ethics outlines an ongoing ethics agenda for the AEJMC, issues its final report, and goes out of existence, as planned from the beginning.

1989

At the end of the decade, Thomas W. Cooper of Emerson College edits a comprehensive treatment of ethics by an international network of scholars, *Communication Ethics and Global Change*.

1989
cont.

Surveys of media ethics in 13 countries find three areas of worldwide concern: truth, social responsibility, and free expression.

Beginning in 1989 in Harare, Zimbabwe, MacBride Round Tables are held annually around the world to address changing international and media conditions and to issue statements on policy and professional action in light of the 1980 U.N. General Assembly principles.

Distressed with the lack of attention given to ethics concerns in the trade magazines, Barry Bingham Jr. creates *FineLine* in April. A 12-page monthly newsletter, *FineLine* carries cases written by reporters and editors that demonstrate the kinds of moral concerns and ethical reasoning that surface in the electronic and print newsrooms. *FineLine* also includes a monthly analysis column, "P.S. Elliott," written by Deni Elliott. Although *FineLine* is intended as a corporate newsletter, with a corporate newsletter price tag, its avid readers are reporters and professors, those least able to afford it. The newsletter folds after 33 months due to low subscription.

1990

On the tenth anniversary of the publication of "Jimmy's World," the Poynter Institute for Media Studies hosts an ethics conference in St. Petersburg, Florida, entitled "The Search for a Green Light Ethic." A preoccupation with scandals is said to promote a red-light ethics of restraint and a timid press. Participants seek instead an ethics of courage and vision inspired by journalism excellence.

1990–1996

Michael Traber, editor of *Media Development*, hosts a series of colloquia from 1990 to 1996 on media ethics for the World Association of Christian Communications. Calling together academics in ethics in Slovenia, São Paulo, Seoul, Dar es Salaam, Colombo, and Munich, discussions are held on the transcultural foundations of ethics in various cultures. The results of this project in comparative ethics are published in *Communication Ethics and Universal Values* (edited by Clifford Christians and Michael Traber), with contributors representing 14 societies on four continents.

1994

Ed Lambeth and others form the Civic Journalism Interest Group (CJIG) within the Association for Education in

Journalism and Mass Commmunication (AEJMC). The CJIG sponsors research papers, workshops, reports, and networking on civic journalism, including ethics. It emphasizes both teaching and scholarship and includes professionals as well as academics. The CJIG is an association-wide response to the growing interest in public journalism and press responsibility.

1996   Paul Martin Lester of California State–Fullerton establishes a web site on media ethics (http://www5.fullerton. edu/les/ethics_list.html). It provides links to the associations and institutes that specialize in professional ethics generally. In addition, resources specifically on journalism ethics are available. Lester's web site is linked to the Society of Professional Journalists (SPJ), the Freedom Forum, the Poynter Institute, the Organization of News Ombudsmen, the Minnesota News Council, the Nieman Foundation, European Journalism Ethics Codes, and others.

The Society of Professional Journalists (SPJ), a 17,000-member association of reporters, editors, and journalism faculty and students, adopts a completely revised Code of Ethics at its September annual convention. The code is based on four guiding principles: journalists should (1) seek and report the truth; (2) minimize harm caused by the reporting process; (3) act independently—remaining free from conflicts of interest and not bowing to pressures from those who would distort the news; and (4) remain accountable to their sources, audiences, and fellow professionals. Specific guidelines and standards of practice are listed under each principle. This version takes into account new technologies and the expanding arena in which journalism takes place.

CONTEMPORARY ETHICAL ISSUES

Chapter 3: Biographical Sketches

Deni Elliott

Many people have contributed to the growth and development of journalism. Some have been visionary in their understanding of what the field needed so that it could progress. Others have demonstrated the need for attention to particular issues through actions that raised the ire of practitioners or critics. People of both types are included here; the selection was made from lists supplied by journalism ethics educators. This set of biographies is not all-inclusive. Some important figures may have been inadvertently omitted. In addition, many of the people who have had significant impact on the growth of journalism ethics in the United States and abroad have done so quietly, remaining behind the scenes, facilitating the work of others. It is to those important people not included here that this section is dedicated.

Material for each sketch was provided by the subject unless otherwise noted: Deni Elliott (*DE*), John Ferre (*JF*), and Louis Hodges (*LH*).

Ralph Barney (b. 1931)

Ralph Barney, founding coeditor of the *Journal of Mass Media Ethics*, is a student of media ethics and international/intercultural communications. A former newspaper reporter and editor, he is also a longtime educator. On the National Ethics Committee of the Society of Professional Journalists, he was an author of the society's book *Doing Ethics in Journalism: A Handbook with Case Studies* (2nd edition 1995). He has also been a Fulbright lecturer at the University of South Pacific in Fiji (1981–1982), a book editor in Beijing (1987–1988), and a media adviser in the newly democratic African nation of Malawi (1995). Barney was professional-in-residence in applied ethics at Ohio University in 1995. He is now professor emeritus at Brigham Young University.

Carl Bernstein (b. 1944)

As a young reporter at the *Washington Post*, Carl Bernstein, along with Bob Woodward, inspired a generation of reporters by exposing the corruption in the Nixon administration. The series of stories on Watergate ultimately resulted in the president's resignation. In addition to illustrating the power of good investigative reporting, Woodward and Bernstein raised a host of ethical questions for analysis. They addressed such topics as how one verifies information when documentation is unavailable, the use of anonymous sources, and the threat of breaking a promise of confidentiality as a way of extracting further information. Bernstein's work in uncovering Watergate is documented in *All the President's Men* (1974) and *The Final Days* (1976). Carl Bernstein is now a freelance writer living in New York City.—*DE*

Barry Bingham Jr. (b. 1933)

Barrry Bingham Jr. was editor and publisher of the *Courier-Journal* and *Louisville Times* in Louisville, Kentucky, from 1971 to 1986, when the properties were sold. During his tenure, he took an early stand on banning "freebies" (special favors and gifts) for journalists. He was acknowledged in 1974 by the *Wall Street Journal* as a "Mister Clean" of the newspaper industry. Bingham published *FineLine*, a newsletter on media ethics, from April 1989 until December 1991. That newsletter was known for bringing lively discussions of ethics into the newsroom through the publication of real-life dilemmas of practicing journalists. Bingham continues to be active in the arts and community service nationally and in Kentucky.

Jay Black (b. 1943)

Jay Black is Poynter-Jamison chair in media ethics and press policy at the University of South Florida–St. Petersburg and a professor of mass communication. He is founding coeditor of the *Journal of Mass Media Ethics* (since 1985) and coauthor of *Doing Ethics in Journalism: A Handbook with Case Studies* (2nd edition 1995). His most recent book project is as editor of *Mixed News: The Public/Civic/Communitarian Journalism Debate* (1997). More than 300 items in his vitae indicate wide involvement in research, writing, and consulting on professional ethics, media ethics, professionalism, values, moral development, and press criticism. Since 1996, he has been national ethics chair for the Society of Professional Journalists.

Sissela Bok (b. 1934)

Sissela Bok is a writer and philosopher who is currently a distinguished fellow at the Harvard Center for Population and Development Studies. Bok's many publications, while intended for a mass or broad applied ethics audience, have attracted a strong following among scholars and practitioners in the journalism ethics field. In particular, *Lying: Moral Choice in Private and Public Life* (1978) and *Secrets: On the Ethics of Concealment and Revelation* (1982) have led generations of journalism students through the complexity of journalism ethics debates. She was a member of the Pulitzer Prize Board from 1989 to 1997, and chair this last year. Her work-in-progress is *Mayhem: Violence as Public Entertainment*, due to be published in early 1998.

Joann Byrd (b. 1943)

Joann Byrd is editor of the editorial page of the *Seattle Post-Intelligencer*. From 1992 to 1995 she served as the first woman ombudsman of the *Washington Post*. Byrd served at the *Post* after 36 years' experience in newsrooms. Byrd has also taught journalism ethics at the University of Washington (1995–1996) and the Poynter Institute for Media Studies in St. Petersburg, Florida (1996–1997). She received a fellowship at the Freedom Forum Media Studies Center at Columbia University to develop a decision-making model for newsrooms dealing with ethical problems on deadline (1988–1989).

Clifford G. Christians (b. 1939)

Clifford G. Christians is research professor of communications at the University of Illinois, Urbana-Champaign, and director of the Institute of Communications Research. Along with Catherine Covert, he represented journalism ethics in the Hastings Center Project on the Teaching of Ethics in Higher Education (1977–1980) and served as the first chair of the Ad Hoc Committee on Ethics for the Association for Education in Journalism and Mass Communication (1982–1986). He is coauthor of several significant books in media ethics, including *Good News: Social Ethics and the Press* (1993), with John Ferre and Mark Fackler; *Media Ethics: Cases and Moral Reasoning*

(5th edition 1997), with Kim Rotzoll and Mark Fackler; and *Communication Ethics and Universal Values* (1997), with Michael Traber.

Roy Peter Clark (b. 1948)

Roy Peter Clark is senior scholar at the Poynter Institute for Media Studies in St. Petersburg, Florida. Known primarily for his work with writers, he created and conducted the first journalism ethics seminars for practitioners, students, and professors at the Poynter Institute in 1983. That program has grown into one of national and international influence. A critic of ethical studies based on scandal and gross misbehavior, what he calls "red light ethics," Clark has promulgated a set of positive journalistic attitudes and behaviors, "green light ethics." He has conducted conferences on privacy, race, public journalism, and the Hutchins Commission on Freedom of the Press.

Janet Cooke (b. 1955)

In 1980, Janet Cooke authored "Jimmy's World," a 2,000-word front-page story in the *Washington Post* that documented the life of an eight-year-old heroin addict. The story raised ethical concerns first when Cooke honored her pledge of confidentiality by refusing to tell police where to find the child and then months later when the *Post* returned Cooke's Pulitzer Prize after discovering that the story had been fabricated. Jimmy simply did not exist. Cooke has been an object lesson to students of journalism ethics since that time. Currently, she is not working as a journalist.—*DE*

Thomas Cooper (b. 1950)

Thomas Cooper is associate professor of mass communication at Emerson College. He edited *Television and Ethics: An Annotated Bibliography* (1988) and *Communication Ethics and Global Change* (1989), and he continues to copublish *Media Ethics*, a biannual commentary and newsmagazine initiated in 1986. Cooper assisted speechwriters in the White House during the Carter administration, was an assistant to Marshall McLuhan, initiated U.S./Soviet space bridges (audio and video hookups between U.S. and Soviet counterparts—i.e., doctors with doctors, youth with youth), and taught at Harvard, Temple, the University of Maryland, and the University of Hawaii.

Nelson Crawford (1883–1963)

Nelson Crawford wrote the first book devoted entirely to the subject of journalism ethics, *The Ethics of Journalism* (1924), which presented journalism practices in terms of professionalism. Foreshadowing social responsibility theory, Crawford argued that the press is an instrument of service to the public, to which it is accountable.—*JF*

Richard P. Cunningham (1926–1996)

Richard P. Cunningham, professor of journalism at New York University, played a major role in the ethics of journalism beginning with his coverage of civil rights in the South during the 1960s for the *Minneapolis Tribune*. Recognizing his special talent and his concerns for issues of ethics in the profession, the *Tribune* appointed him its first reader representative in 1972. For three years he served as associate director of the National News Council until its demise in 1984. New York University was able to attract him to its faculty in 1986, specifically to teach ethics. Cunningham wrote an ombudsman/ethics column for the *Quill* from 1984 until his death on 21 November 1996.—*LH*

Everette Dennis (b. 1942)

Everette Dennis is an educator, author, and foundation administrator who has promoted cooperation between the academy and industry as founding director of the Media Studies Center at Columbia University (1984–1996) and currently as head of an international university consortium funded by the Freedom Forum, a media foundation. In 1977, he became Distinguished Professor of Communications at Fordham University's School of Business Administration and president of the American Academy in Berlin. He has authored and edited some 30 books as well as various monographs and more than 200 scholarly articles.

Deni Elliott (b. 1953)

Deni Elliott is director of the Practical Ethics Center, professor in the Department of Philosophy, adjunct professor at the School of Journalism, and University Professor of Ethics at the University of Montana–Missoula. She wrote the first dissertation on the teaching of journalism ethics, for Harvard University in 1984, and remains interested in how ethics can be taught to professionals and preprofessionals. She is now directing the nation's first M.A. program in philosophy with an emphasis on the teaching of applied and professional ethics. Elliott has worked since 1985 as an ethics coach in newsrooms and wrote the analysis column "P.S. Elliott" in *FineLine*, a journalism ethics newsletter published from 1989 to 1991. She has written dozens of articles, book chapters, and pieces for the lay press on journalistic ethics. She also serves as the book review editor for the *Journal of Mass Media Ethics* and produces video documentaries on topics in practical ethics.

Mark Fackler (b. 1947)

Mark Fackler is professor of communications at Wheaton (Illinois) College. His professional experience includes writing for magazines, radio, and public relations. He has been guest lecturer at the Poynter Institute for Media Studies in St. Petersburg, Florida, and in 1996 taught media ethics and law at Daystar University in Nairobi, Kenya. He has contributed to several books and reference works and is coauthor of *Media Ethics: Cases and Moral Reasoning* (5th edition, to be published in 1998) and *Good News: Social Ethics and the Press* (1993).

Fred W. Friendly (b. 1915)

Fred Friendly began his journalistic career as a writer and producer for radio programs in 1938. His collaborations with Edward R. Morrow led him to produce the television series "See It Now" and "Small World." From 1959 to 1964, he was executive producer of "CBS Reports," then served as president of CBS News from 1964 to 1966. He has written numerous books, including *Minnesota Rag: The Dramatic Story of the Landmark Supreme Court Case That Gave New Meaning to Freedom of the Press* (1981), in which his argument against government censorship of the press is particularly poignant. Among his many accolades, Friendly has received ten George Peabody Awards.—DE

Michael Gartner (b. 1938)

Michael Gartner is editor and co-owner of the *Daily Tribune* in Ames, Iowa. In 40 years of journalism he has been page-one editor of the *Wall Street Journal* (1970–1974), editor and president of the *Des Moines Register* (1974–1985), editor of the *Courier-Journal* (Louisville, Kentucky, 1986–1987), general news executive of *USA Today* and Gannett Company (1987–1988), and president of NBC News (1988–1993). He has been an op-ed columnist for the *Wall Street Journal* and *USA Today* and is a past president of the American Society of Newspaper Editors and former chairman of the Pulitzer Prize Board (1991–1992). Gartner has a long history of promotion and discussion of ethics in the industry. He was among the first to welcome an ethics coach-in-residence into his newsroom (at the *Courier-Journal*, 1986–1987) and was an outspoken critic of the practice of withholding the names of accusers in sex crimes. He stepped down as president of NBC News in 1993 after an on-air apology for a staff member's mistake in the production of a segment on fire hazards in General Motors pickup trucks.

Loren Ghiglione (b. 1941)

Loren Ghiglione, James M. Cox Jr. professor of journalism at Emory University in Atlanta, edited *The News* in Southbridge, Massachusetts, from 1969 to 1995. He served as a founding officer of the National News Council from 1973 to 1981. He directed the *New England Daily Newspaper Survey* in 1973; the resulting 386-page book, *Evaluating the Press* (1973), critically examined the ethical and news performance of the region's dailies and won the national Sigma Delta Chi Award for research about journalism. He has edited or written six other journalism books, most raising questions about press ethics, and he has contributed to *Drawing the Line* (1984) and other books on media ethics. He founded the Task Force on Minorities in the Newspaper Business in 1985. As 1989–1990 president of the American Society of Newspaper Editors, he focused on issues of diversity and pushed for the first study of gays and lesbians in U.S. newsrooms. His 1990 Library of Congress exhibit, "The American Journalist: Paradox of the Press," raised questions about journalism ethics and the portrayal of those ethics in fiction and film.

Theodore Glasser (b. 1948)

Theodore L. Glasser has been on the faculty of the Department of Communication at Stanford University since 1990. Before that he served as the associate director of the Silha Center for the Study of Media Ethics and Law at the University of Minnesota. His work on press responsibility has appeared in a variety of periodicals and books, and he has lectured extensively abroad and in the United States on the subject. Glasser's research focuses on the norms of practice among American journalists. He approaches questions of ethics both normatively and empirically. He has argued against a narrow conception of "professional ethics," which he believes runs counter to efforts to promote public accountability in journalism. Glasser's most recent book, *Custodians of Conscience* (coauthored with James Ettema of Northwestern University), deals with investigative journalism and moral discourse. It will be published in early 1998 by Columbia University Press.

David Hawpe (b. 1943)

David Hawpe is executive editor of the *Courier-Journal* in Louisville, Kentucky. A veteran with more than 30 years of newspaper experience, Hawpe began lecturing on the importance of ethics in the early 1970s. He has served as a model practitioner, one who notices morally relevant characteristics of the reporting and presenting of news and one who is ready to think carefully about those issues, sharing the problem with others in the newsroom. Hawpe's newsroom is a community in which journalists at all levels are encouraged to initiate and engage in deliberation about ethics. Hawpe chaired a successful two-year effort to rewrite the ethics code for the Associated Press Managing Editors Association in the mid-1990s.

Louis Hodges (b. 1933)

Louis Hodges is Knight Professor of Journalism at Washington and Lee University. He is former director of Washington and Lee's program in Society and the Professions: Studies in Applied Ethics. He created one of the first programs in academic journalistic ethics to bring together practitioners and students for sustained dialogue (1974). Hodges is a founding board member for the *Journal of Mass Media Ethics*, an editorial board member of the *Newspaper Research Journal*, a contributing editor for *Media Ethics*, and an at-large member of the National Ethics Committee of the Society of Professional Journalists.

John Hulteng (b. 1921)

John Hulteng produced some of the foundation for current work in journalistic ethics with *The Messenger's Motives* (1976) and *Playing It Straight* (1981), in which he annotated the American Society of News Editors Code of Ethics. Though retired, Hulteng holds an office in the Department of Communication at Stanford University.—*DE*

Norman Ellis Isaacs (b. 1908)

When he was 15, Norman Ellis Isaacs became a school sports correspondent for the *Indianapolis Star*. When the *Star* soon offered him a full-time job, he dropped out of high school and went to work "on a sports staff run by a sports editor on the 'take,'" as he later wrote. In 1938, Isaacs became managing editor of the *Indianapolis Times*. In 1961, he became executive editor of the *Courier-Journal and Louisville Times*. He created the nation's first newspaper ombudsman there in 1967. He retired early, in 1970, to become editor-in-residence at the Graduate School of Journalism at Columbia University.

Isaacs's was a consistent voice for ethical behavior in the news business over 40 years. Among other things, he attempted to overhaul the ethics codes of the Associated Press Managing Editors (when he was the association's president in 1953) and of the American Society of Newspaper Editors (when he became its president in 1969). In the early 1970s, he was instrumental in the founding of the National News Council. He served as the council's chair for five (1977–1982) of the ten years of its existence. Later, he wrote a book on newspaper ethics—rather, the lack of them—called *Untended Gates: The Mismanaged Press* (1986). He retired to Santa Barbara, California, in 1996.

Francis P. Kasoma (b. 1943)

Francis P. Kasoma is professor of journalism and mass communication at the Department of Mass Communication at the University of Zambia.

IIis first book in journalism ethics, *Journalism Ethics in Africa*, published in 1994 in Nairobi by the African Council for Communication Education, remains the only book on journalism ethics in Africa as of early 1997. Kasoma has published more than 20 papers on journalism ethics, including "Media Ethics or Media Law: The Enforcement of Responsible Journalism in Southern Africa" in *Equid Novi, Journal for Journalism in Southern Africa* (Vol. 15, No. 1, 1994) and "Ethical Issues in Reporting Politics" in *Reporting Politics and Public Affairs*, edited by Charles Okigbo (1994).

Edmund Lambeth (b. 1932)

Dr. Edmund Lambeth of the University of Missouri created the National Workshop on the Teaching of Ethics in Journalism and has directed that annual, six-day learning experience for educators since it was first held in 1984. The *Library Journal* described his book *Committed Journalism: An Ethic for the Profession* (1986, 1992) as a "bold effort to look at old questions of journalism ethics in a new light by linking journalism's issues to classical philosophical ones." A *Journal of Communication* review said that "no other book on journalism ethics to date demonstrates as much concern for educational philosophy, for cultivating those cognitive skills that enhance the reporters' stewardship of free expression."

Paul Martin Lester (b. 1953)

Paul Lester is a professor in the Department of Communications at California State University, Fullerton. Once a newspaper photojournalist, he has written and edited some of the most innovative textbooks in the field of mass communication, including *Photojournalism Ethics: An Ethical Approach* (1991) and *Visual Communication Images with Messages* (1995). His most recent work, *Images That Injure, Pictorial Stereotypes in the Media* (1996), is a valuable contribution to the dialogue concerning stereotypes and the media. The book illustrates the many ways that media can provide negative representations.

John C. Merrill (b. 1924)

John C. Merrill is professor emeritus of journalism at the University of Missouri, Columbia. With 20 books in the field to his credit, Merrill is the most prolific author in journalism ethics. His writings and 45 years of teaching at institutions of higher learning around the globe have affected generations of journalists and journalism scholars. Merrill's merging of philosophical principles with journalistic issues has expanded both the problems and the solutions facing journalists in a capitalist society. Merrill has been a Senior Fellow at the Freedom Forum Media Studies Center at

Columbia University and is a member of the Journalism Hall of Fame at Louisiana State University.—DE

Philip Meyer (b. 1930)

Philip Meyer is a Knight Professor in the School of Journalism and Mass Communication at the University of North Carolina at Chapel Hill. Using an empirical approach, he follows the effects of technological and economic pressures on media ethical behavior, using his 1982 study of moral values in the newspaper business as a baseline. A recent response to those pressures has been a movement that some media managers call "public journalism," and Meyer is one of a small group trying to evaluate it. Meyer is coauthor (with Edmund Lambeth and Ester Thorson) of *Assessing Public Journalism*, to be published by the University of Missouri Press in 1998. His baseline study was published as *Ethical Journalism* in 1987.

Nelson Poynter (1903–1978)

For four decades, from 1939 to 1978, Nelson Poynter was the editor and owner of the *St. Petersburg* (Florida) *Times*, which he converted into a newspaper known internationally for journalistic innovation, quality, and public service. In 1945, he founded *Congressional Quarterly*, respected as the fairest and most objective monitor of the workings of Congress. In 1947, he promulgated his Standards of Ownership, a declaration of responsibility for which he, and his company, could be held accountable. Upon his death in 1978, he left the stock of his publishing company to the Modern Media Institute in St. Petersburg, now known as the Poynter Institute for Media Studies. The Poynter Institute is a leading center for journalism research and practice, known for its provocative and topical seminars on ethics and values in the industry.

Cornelius B. Pratt (b. 1952)

Cornelius Pratt helps make journalism ethics a global discourse through his work on Africa. His book chapters and journal articles include "A Developing-Region–Based Model of Proto-Norms for International and Intercultural Communications" in *Ethics in International and Intercultural Communication* (Lawrence Erlbaum 1997) and "Multinational Corporate Social Policy Process for Ethical Responsibility in Sub-Saharan Africa" in *Journal of Business Ethics* (July 1991). Pratt is professor in the College of Communication Arts and Sciences at Michigan State University.

Joseph Pulitzer (1847–1911)

Joseph Pulitzer, a newspaper publisher at the turn of the nineteenth century who was notorious for his publication of sensationalized tidbits and rumor, started the now respected Journalism School at Columbia University. Initially, Columbia's trustees were suspicious of Pulitzer's stated motives of wanting to raise journalism to professional levels so that the practice and its products would be respected by the community. The school was concerned about its own credibility if it had the infamous Pulitzer name attached to it. Eventually, in 1912, Columbia accepted Pulitzer's $2 million posthumous endowment, began the school, and instituted the most coveted journalism prize in the United States for excellence in reporting and news presentation.

Oliver (Bill) Sipple (1942–1989)

Oliver (Bill) Sipple died in a rundown apartment in San Francisco, his brief claim to fame—a note from ex-President Gerald Ford—tacked to his wall. Sipple inspired years of discussion concerning privacy and journalism beginning in 1975, when he saved President Ford from a potential assassin's bullet. Sipple eschewed publicity and was devastated to find that, despite his request for privacy, he and his sexual orientation were placed in the public forum. Sipple created an early case for media to ponder whether closeted homosexuality was a matter for public discussion.—*DE*

Bob Steele (b. 1947)

Bob Steele has been the director of the Ethics Program at the Poynter Institute for Media Studies in St. Petersburg, Florida, since 1989. A former television news reporter and producer, Bob is frequently consulted on ethics issues by journalists from around the country. He has presented ethical decision-making workshops at nearly 40 television stations and newspapers. He coauthored *Doing Ethics in Journalism: A Handbook with Case Studies*.

Ida Tarbell (1857–1944)

Ida Tarbell did not start out as an investigative journalist interested in ethics; rather, she hoped to be a historian of the French Revolution. However, her painstaking exposé of the Standard Oil Company and John D. Rockefeller, serialized in *McClure's Magazine* during 1902–1904, earned her the reputation as the first practitioner of contemporary documents-based, nonbiased investigative reporting. She illustrated how accurate journalism is a basis for ethical journalism.

Steve Weinberg (b. 1948)

Steve Weinberg is a book author, freelance magazine writer, book reviewer, and editor. He is also a part-time teacher at the University of Missouri School of Journalism. Since Weinberg left newspaper and magazine staff work in 1978, his freelance work has appeared throughout the industry. From 1983 to 1990, Weinberg served as executive director of Investigative Reporters and Editors (IRE), an international association. He remains editor of the *IRE Journal*, a bimonthly magazine. Weinberg writes and lectures about the ethics of investigative journalism.

Robert (Bob) Woodward (b. 1943)

Robert (Bob) Woodward, along with Carl Bernstein, brought down Richard Nixon and a score of officials in his administration through investigative work on the Watergate affair. The series of stories on Watergate ultimately resulted in the president's resignation. In addition to illustrating the power of good investigative reporting, Woodward and Bernstein raised a host of ethical questions for analysis, including how one verifies information when documentation is unavailable, the use of anonymous sources, and the threat of breaking a promise of confidentiality as a way of extracting further information. Woodward's work in uncovering Watergate is documented in *All the President's Men* (1974) and *The Final Days* (1976). He is currently an editor at the *Washington Post*.

CONTEMPORARY ETHICAL ISSUES

Chapter 4:
Issues in Journalism Ethics

The main function of the press within a democratic society is to keep the public informed. However, just what shape this information takes, what it includes, and how it is presented can be a product of several factors of news organizations, including business interests, views about the nature of truth and reality, confidence in newspersons as purveyors of information, and the definition of news itself. This section will discuss such factors as they apply to the general problem of news selection.

The Shape of the News
News and the Newsworthy
Elliot D. Cohen
Physical limitations of space, time, money, etc., make it inevitable that the amount of information that is published by news organizations is only a small fraction of available information. For example, most daily newspapers have room for less than one-fifth of the daily information provided by their own news staffs (McCombs, Danielian, and Wanta 1995). As such, news organizations must sift

through available information in an effort to distinguish that which is newsworthy from that which is not, and that which is more newsworthy from that which is less. The responsible exercise of such judgment requires standards of news selection. These standards, in turn, presuppose an even broader understanding of the nature and function of a news organization and of news itself.

How the term *news* is defined places constraints on the newsworthy, since only news can ever be newsworthy. According to Joshua Halberstam (1992), there are three conditions that standardly restrict the meaning of news and hence of newsworthiness. First, as it typically functions in journalistic discourse, *news* implies that which is new in the temporal sense of current. For example, the report that Nixon has died is "old news" or "no news" and hence no longer newsworthy. It is noteworthy, however, that even ancient artifacts may be the subject of news when they are newly discovered. For example, the recent discovery of an ancient Egyptian tomb may be grist for the news.

Second, news is typically anchored to concrete events. Although Halberstam does not define what he means by an event, the relevant sense appears to be that of a temporal occurrence. That is, all events have dates and durations and often (although not always) have spatial locations (Woozley 1969, 131–132). For example, the events of the *Challenger* exploding and the attempted exhuming of the *Titanic* occurred at specific times and places; and certain superstrains of bacteria resistant to antibiotics have gradually developed over time in certain regions of the world. On the other hand, water freezing at 32 degrees Fahrenheit and two plus three adding up to five do not qualify as events since they lack dates, durations, and spatial locations.

Third, *reports* of events constitute news, not the events themselves. For example, the fact that a fireman was killed trying to rescue a small child is not news. Rather, this fact becomes news when reported. On this view, therefore, it is reports or stories about events that are the newsworthy items, not the events themselves. The practical result seems to be that news organizations must consider what the report of an event would say *before* they can decide if it would be newsworthy.

Insofar as it is the presentation of the event (that is, the report or story) that is being assessed for newsworthiness, the manner in which the event is framed must also figure into the assessment. Thus, an interesting or unusual slant to the description of an event may arguably make the story more or less newsworthy. For example, some news organizations might consider "Man bites dog" to be more newsworthy than "Man defends himself against dog attack" even though both descriptions may refer to the same event.

Basing his view on an intensive study of "CBS Evening News," "NBC Nightly News," *Newsweek*, and *Time*, Herbert Gans (1980, 80) has described news as "information which is transmitted from sources to audiences, with journalists—who are both employees of bureaucratic commercial organizations and members of a profession—summarizing, refining, and altering what becomes available to them from sources in order to make the information suitable for their audiences." In Gans's view, news arises out of the interplay between journalist, source, and audience. Journalists choose sources that suit their specific audiences, and sources themselves choose to selectively speak to certain journalists. Since audiences are not only recipients of information but also subscribers ("sources of income"), journalists seek to maintain their audiences' allegiance, which may even affect the choice of sources as well as the content of their stories. It is in this context of a "tug-of-war" between the journalistic triad—journalist, source, and audience—that the news is fashioned and refashioned, "bought" and "sold," and finally determined to be newsworthy or not. In the process, events may be highlighted to exaggerate selling features of a story that may sometimes bear little resemblance altogether to the observed event (*see also* Forms of News Bias). News thus emerges as "the exercise of power over the interpretation of reality" (Gans 1980, 81).

In Gans's view, the newsworthiness of a story is thus determined by a number of subjective "considerations," including political, commercial, and value considerations. Such interests that shape the news are relative, and there are no absolute standards of newsworthiness. What is newsworthy for one system of journalists, sources, and audiences is not so for another. This would seem to suggest that a report of a sporting event would be, within a given system in which athletics was valued above all else, more newsworthy than a report about a newly discovered cure for diabetes or even HIV.

According to Gans, no perspective on reality can claim any more "objectivity" than the next. Instead, there are simply a number of different ways of looking at reality. For example, the way the poor perceive America and the way the middle class or wealthy do will be significantly different. Since perspectives on reality are many, there cannot be just one news perspective. "Different perspectives lead to different questions and different answers, requiring different facts and different news" (Gans 1980, 310).

Gans's answer to the news selection problem is accordingly to include as many different perspectives in the news as possible. Such multiperspectival news would add to the current news approach more perspectives representing various sectors of society, including people of different ages, incomes, educational levels, ethnicities, and religions. By avoiding partiality and favoritism toward one group perspective over another, making news more representative of the entire population, Gans thinks that journalists can help further the ideal of democracy (Gans 1980, 332).

Gans realizes, however, that the number of different perspectives that can be included in any news package will be limited by time, space, and budget. Consequently, Gans proposes a "modest degree of multiperspectivism" in which the perspectives of currently neglected groups (for example, poor, elderly, and adolescent) would be allotted a more representative share of scarce news resources (Gans 1980, 319–322).

Given, however, that not all groups can feasibly be included, which of the less popular perspectives should be given more coverage? Should as much time be devoted to the perspectives of the Nazis, the Ku Klux Klan, adulterers, and pedophiles as that devoted to the perspectives of their victims? Does the satanic slant on reality truly deserve as much attention as, say, the views of Mothers Against Drunk Driving?

Answers to such specific questions presuppose answers to other more general questions: Are there any *objective* standards of newsworthiness, that is, standards that determine what perspectives people *ought* to take irrespective of those that they may actually take? Are there *universal* standards, that is, standards that transcend individual groups of people and regard all of us?

In arguing against Gans's relativism, Jay Newman, following a lead from the ancient Greek philosopher Plato, has suggested that there are certain objective ideals—"justice, wisdom, and other ideals of civilization"—that can and should guide journalists in their selection and presentation of the news. Thus, he states that "to be a citizen of a nation or a member of the human race is to have certain rights and responsibilities. When gross injustice is committed by or against our fellow nationals or our fellow human beings anywhere in the world, the fact is newsworthy, regardless of our individual and cultural biases and perspectives" (Newman 1989, 128). According to Newman, the journalist may function as an educator to help advance civilization. Even sports reporting can transcend statistics and trivial gossip in an effort to promote audiences' appreciation of distinctively human values such as personal achievement, the overcoming of adversity, strategic reasoning, cooperation, sportsmanship, and self-discipline (Newman 1989, 132).

Anticipating the criticism that "high-minded journalism" may inevitably turn into media propaganda and manipulation of the masses, Newman reminds us that there is a recognizable distinction between education on the one hand and manipulation on the other (for instance, propagandizing, indoctrinating, conditioning, and brainwashing). While the latter—"flashy rhetorical images," force, pity, and "clever half-truths"—appeals to emotions of easily manipulated recipients, the former tries "to help those being educated to think critically and analytically for themselves instead of relying exclusively on the unchallenged testimony of self-professed political experts" (Newman 1989, 130).

Newman's faith in the educative powers of news reporters can, however, be contrasted with the less optimistic view espoused by Walter Lippmann in his classic work *Public Opinion*. According to Lippmann (1946, 271), the function of news is to "signalize an event," that is, to record the reports of sources upon which the accuracy of news rests. It is not, therefore, generally the function of news to determine the truth, or in other words, to "bring to light the hidden facts, to set them into relation with each other, and to make a picture of reality on which men can act." According to Lippmann, most areas of knowledge require specialized ability and training outside the purview of journalistic training. For the most part, a journalist's perspective is constructed "out of his own stereotypes, according to his own code, and by the urgency of his own interest" (Lippmann 1946, 272). Further, "there is an inherent difficulty about using the method of reason to deal with an unreasoning world" (Lippmann 1946, 312). Thus, even if journalists possessed great wisdom, it cannot be supposed that audiences in a position to be enlightened by them would seize the opportunity.

Nevertheless, placing the power of shaping reality in the hands of official news sources, for which the press is to be a mouthpiece, encounters its own risks. For example, according to Theodore Glasser (1992), doing so can undermine the press' ability to safeguard democracy—its so-called "watchdog" function—by placing it under the control of the elite and prominent sector of society; and it can stifle journalists' independence and creativity.

In a democratic society, the press has a primary responsibility to support an informed and independent public comprised of individuals who can, at least collectively, think rationally and make enlightened decisions about matters of great importance. Yet, in deciding what is newsworthy, the path toward promoting democracy may not always be clearly lighted, and journalists may not easily avoid tension between alternative, sometimes discordant, objectives. As can be gleaned from the foregoing, these objectives include making money (since news organizations are private businesses) versus fostering an enlightened public (since they are also public servants); catering to group interests versus seeking a more "objective" news stance; and merely describing what news sources say versus independently interpreting reality. Whether and how journalists can satisfactorily resolve these and related conflicts in addressing story selection remains a challenge for the future of news organizations and, indeed, for the future of the democratic principles with which these organizations are entrusted.

References: Gans, Herbert J. 1980. *Deciding What's News. A Study of CBS Evening News, NBC Nightly News, Newsweek, and Time.* New York: Random House.

Glasser, Theodore L. 1992. "Objectivity and News Reporting." In Elliot D. Cohen, editor. *Philosophical Issues in Journalism.* New York: Oxford University Press, 176–185.

Halberstam, Joshua. 1992. "A Prolegomenon for a Theory of News." In Elliot D. Cohen, editor. *Philosophical Issues in Journalism.* New York: Oxford University Press, 11–21.

Lippmann, Walter. 1946. *Public Opinion.* New York: Penguin Books.

McComb, Maxwell, Lucig Danielian, and Wayne Wanta. 1995. "Issues in the News and the Public Agenda: The Agenda-Setting Tradition." In Theodore L. Glasser and Charles T. Salmon, editors. *Public Opinion and the Communication of Consent.* New York: Guilford Press, 281–297.

Newman, Jay. 1989. *The Journalist in Plato's Cave.* Rutherford, NJ: Fairleigh Dickinson University Press.

Woozley, A. D. 1969. *Theory of Knowledge.* London: Hutchinson University Library.

Ethics of the News Story

Carole Rich

Every time a journalist writes a news story, he or she confronts ethical choices. In many cases, the writer is not even aware of the ethical reasoning involved because the writing process and the structure of a news story can become automatic.

In this age of burgeoning information from print, broadcast, and online sources, however, selectivity is becoming a cornerstone of the journalist's craft. Such selectivity requires ethical reasoning. Writing is not an unbiased action. By selecting the focus, words, facts, quotes, and sources for a news story, the writer consciously or subconsciously makes decisions governed by journalistic values. Consider the following two stories about the same event:

> Hundreds of thousands of black men answered Nation of Islam leader Louis Farrakhan's call for a march on Washington yesterday with a historic rally that washed them in a warm sense of brotherhood and challenged them to return home with a new sense of purpose (Fletcher and Harris 1995, 1A).

This *Washington Post* article uses words such as *warm*, *brotherhood*, and *new sense of purpose*, which create a positive tone that is reflected throughout most of the story. The second paragraph interprets the event for readers this way:

> The huge assembly—estimated by police at 400,000 people and clearly the largest civil rights demonstration in U.S. history—created the sheltering atmosphere of a family reunion. An array of speakers sternly charged participants to take more responsibility for their lives and condemned white racism.

Compare the difference in word choice and tone in this story by the *New York Times*:

> Heeding a call for personal atonement and racial solidarity, hundreds of thousands of black men gathered from across the nation in the heart of the capital today to vow stronger leadership in protecting their communities from violence and social despair (Clines 1995, 1A).

Although the message in the lead is positive, the emphasis at the end of the sentence on the negative words *violence* and *social despair* sets the stage for a more critical tone, which the rest of the story reflects. In the third paragraph, the writer interprets the event as follows:

> The rally was marked by a spirit of individual resolve as much as dramatic protest, with speeches by many prominent blacks, including the poet Maya Angelou and the Rev. Jesse Jackson. But it wound down in something of an ambivalent mood as Mr. Farrakhan delivered a booming, rambling keynote speech that threatened to eclipse the occasion.

From the hundreds of quotes, facts, and comments of participants in a day-long event called the "Million Man March" in Washington, D.C., the writers of these stories carefully selected those facts, quotes, and comments that served their purpose in setting the tone and interpreting the event for readers.

Is it the journalist's duty to interpret the news? How does the writer decide what to include in the story? What guidelines can the journalist follow to adhere to ethical standards? These are some of the ethical issues facing journalists in an era of multimedia delivery of news and information overload.

The Law

Legally the First Amendment to the U.S. Constitution gives journalists in the United States the right to freedom of expression. Ethically, journalists exercise that right by practicing certain moral principles.

The Issues

Ethics is often defined as what one "ought" to do. Philip Patterson and Lee Wilkins, authors of *Media Ethics: Issues and Cases*, define ethics as rational choices one makes between what is good and bad, what is morally justifiable action and what is not. "Ethics is less about the conflict between right and wrong than it is about the conflict between equally compelling (or equally unattractive) values and the choices that must be made between them," the authors write (Patterson and Wilkins 1991, 3).

Journalists often believe that ethical reasoning is limited to difficult dilemmas involving privacy matters, anonymous sources, conflicts of interest, or issues that could cause harm to sources. Ethical principles, however, apply to every news story.

Few journalists would dispute that it is their duty to serve the public. How they should do that ethically is more debatable. To that end, many media organizations have devised codes of ethics citing values and standards of practice; however, these codes lack enforcement and serve only as guidelines.

Most media organizations espouse these values cited by the American Society of Newspaper Editors in its code of ethics: "Every effort must be made to assure that the news content is accurate, free from bias and in context, and that all sides are presented fairly."

Several versions of the Society of Professional Journalists Code of Ethics, originally adopted in 1926 and revised several times, stress objectivity as a goal, but is objectivity possible or even desirable? Furthermore, what other values should guide the journalist in writing a news story?

Elliot D. Cohen, editor of *Philosophical Issues in Journalism*, questions the conviction that journalists should just report the facts, not create them. "In the first place," he asks, "to what extent is it possible for journalists, or human beings generally, to transcend their own subjectivity in accounting for

'the facts'? . . . And if journalistic objectivity is attainable, is it something journalists ought to pursue?" (Cohen 1992, 156).

No, insists Theodore L. Glasser, a Stanford University professor of media
ethics. "Objective reporting is biased against what the press typically defines
as its role in a democracy—that of a Fourth Estate, the watchdog role, an
adversary press," he writes in Cohen's book. "Objective reporting is biased
against the very idea of responsibility; the day's news is viewed as something
journalists are compelled to report, not something they are responsible for
creating" (Glasser 1992, 176).

If the responsibility of journalists is to serve the public by providing information that will empower readers and viewers to form opinions and make
decisions about issues, the writer must interpret the news. It is not sufficient
to present a news story as a collection of facts and quotes without substance
and meaning. A news story should include context, background, and significance to the reader or viewer—all dependent on the writer's interpretation
and organization of sources, facts, and observations.

Nevertheless, interpretation does not preclude values. At issue is what values should guide the journalist in presenting news.

"The principles of accuracy and fairness stand at the very heart of journalism," according to *Doing Ethics in Journalism*, a Society of Professional
Journalists handbook by Jay Black, Bob Steele, and Ralph Barney (1995, 53).
"Accuracy and fairness speak to the obligation of providing meaningful
information to citizens who depend on its quality, authenticity, and lack of
bias to understand issues and to make important decisions" (Black, Steele,
and Barney 1995, 17). Other guiding principles the authors cite include the
need to seek truth, act independently, and minimize harm.

Achieving these ethical principles, particularly fairness and balance, is not
always easy. Journalists must also strive to make the story interesting. If the
story is ethical but unreadable, the writer has not served the public anyway.

Cases

Stephen Martino experienced a difficult ethical dilemma as editor of his campus newspaper, the *University Daily Kansan*, when he tried to apply values of
truth, accuracy, and fairness to a news story. A Kansan reporter conducting
background checks of candidates for student senate positions discovered public records that revealed one candidate had served two years in prison for indecent solicitation of a child. The night before the story was scheduled to run,
the student resigned from his candidacy and from his office as president of the
university's gay and lesbian organization. He claimed it was because he had
contracted the AIDS virus, but three weeks earlier when the student learned
he was HIV-positive, he told another reporter that he would not resign from
either position because of his illness. Was it in the public's interest to reveal the
student's criminal background if he was no longer a candidate?

The student's friends urged Martino not to mention his criminal background in the story about his resignation. They claimed he had already paid his debt to society and the information would cause him great harm when he was already suffering from his HIV-positive condition.

Martino decided to include the information in the story because he believed it was relevant to the reason the candidate resigned. In an editorial that ran the same day as the news story, Martino wrote, "To my way of thinking, omitting the truth is the same thing as lying. Had the *Kansan* not reported the full story as it knew it, it would have been accused of a cover-up, and its credibility would have been destroyed." Angry students protested the next day by dumping the newspapers on the lawn in front of the University of Kansas journalism school.

Editors at the *Wichita Eagle* seeking fairness and balance in controversial news stories also experienced ethical dilemmas one summer when protesters waged massive demonstrations against a clinic that performed abortions in the city. More than 2,000 protesters on both sides of the abortion issue converged on Wichita for weeks. The newspaper tried so hard to give fair and balanced coverage that copy editors actually measured the number of inches of type given to the pro-choice and anti-abortion sources in stories to make sure they received equal treatment. That approach was taking ethical values to extremes. Not all sources were equally newsworthy. Despite the newspaper's efforts, the sources on each side of the issue did not consider the news reports fair.

The journalist's mission is not to please the public, but to serve it. That is a hard and often unpopular task.

Looking Ahead

Journalists will continue to debate standards that should guide the profession to serve changing needs. New technologies create new ethical problems for the media. Much of the information available on the Internet, for example, is unsubstantiated and inaccurate. The journalist's role in synthesizing and interpreting news for the public, therefore, will become even more important as consumers are bombarded with a plethora of information from many sources. Problems change; values do not.

From the best-written stories, guidelines emerge for analyzing the ethics of the story.

- Focus: Does the focus, the main idea, accurately reflect the most important point of the news and set a fair tone for the story?
- Lead: Does the lead entice the reader or viewer? Does it avoid sensationalism? Is the lead substantiated? Does it stress an accurate and fair interpretation of the news?

- Lead quote: Does the first quote in the story support the lead? Is the source quoted central to the story? Is the quote relevant?
- Organization: Is the story arranged to balance different points of view? Does the order give fair coverage to the sources and issues?
- Word choice: Does the story avoid judgmental adjectives that reflect the writer's opinions? Is the word choice sensitive to preferences of diverse groups?
- Context and significance: Is the purpose or news value of the story clearly explained? Does the story explain how readers or viewers are affected?
- Background: Does the story clarify what led up to this issue or event? Is this perspective based mainly on facts, not the writer's opinion?
- Supporting facts and quotes: Does the body of the story present divergent sides of an issue? Are sources in the story credible? Are their quotes crucial for information or interest? Are the quotes used in proper context? Does the story contain comments from people affected or harmed by the news?
- Ending: Does the ending quote or statement reflect the tone in the focus or offer the lasting impression the writer is attempting to create in the story?
- Can the writer justify his or her choice of information on the basis of interest, accuracy, and fairness? Is there any information that could be deleted without affecting the credibility of the story? Has the writer considered the interests of the public paramount instead of the interests of the sources?

The time-honored ethical values of accuracy, fairness, and truth provide an ethical foundation that sets the media apart from other purveyors of information. Without adherence to values, journalists cannot gain the public's trust. Without that credibility, journalists cannot fulfill their mission of enlightening the public in a democratic society.

References: Black, Jay, Bob Steele, and Ralph Barney. 1995. *Doing Ethics in Journalism: A Handbook with Case Studies.* 2d Edition Greencastle, IN: Society of Professional Journalists, 17, 53.

Clines, Francis, X. 1995. "Black Men Fill Capital's Mall in Display of Unity and Pride." *New York Times* (October 17): 1A.

Cohen, Elliot D., editor. 1992. *Philosophical Issues in Journalism.* New York: Oxford University Press, 156.

Fletcher, Michael A., and Hamil R. Harris. 1995. "Black Men Jam Mall for a 'Day of Atonement.'" *Washington Post* (October 17): 1A.

Glasser, Theodore L. 1992. "Objectivity and News Bias." In Elliot D. Cohen, editor. 1992. *Philosophical Issues in Journalism.* New York: Oxford University Press, 176.

Martino, Stephen. 1995. *University Daily Kansan* (April 6).

Patterson, Philip, and Lee Wilkins. 1991. *Media Ethics: Issues and Cases.* 2d Edition. Madison, WI: Brown & Benchmark, 3.

Rich, Carole. 1997. *Writing and Reporting News: A Coaching Method.* 2d Edition. Belmont, CA: Wadsworth, 400.

Computer Technology and the News

Elliot D. Cohen

Computer technology has had considerable impact upon news and its delivery, and it is likely to continue to do so in the future. With the rapid growth of computer network technology in the past decade, news organizations can now electronically send and receive information in an instant from remote parts of the globe with just a click of the mouse. Online access to information available on the Internet has made it possible for reporters to do inexpensive investigative reporting without leaving their desks. For example, electronic bulletin boards set up by government agencies, private organizations, and individuals can provide pertinent, downloadable information, contact lists, and facilities for exchanging messages as well as requesting information (Landau 1992).

New computer technology has also been developed that permits digital manipulation of photographs, thereby allowing news organizations to quickly alter photographs to eliminate features they deem undesirable (Reaves 1991).

Online news services have begun to appear. For example, NBC recently connected with the Microsoft Network to provide online news. In addition to its 24-hour television broadcasts, CNN also provides news on the Internet. Utilizing multimedia technology, such services provide color photos and sound clips as well as text.

Newspapers such as the *New York Times, Boston Globe, Philadelphia Inquirer*, and Baltimore *Sun* have now moved into cyberspace with their own paperless, online news services. Readers on the World Wide Web can scan through the latest news as well as link to archival articles. Some papers also provide information that is only available online. The *New York Times* has a special section called "CyberTimes," which features original columns and articles on Internet and computer technology information.

Online newspapers have also begun to develop an interactive approach to media presentation, such as the *New York Times'* "Send a Letter" feature in the editorials section, which permits readers to E-mail their own views. The *Philadelphia Inquirer's* "Daily News Heartnet" provides the facility for specifying criteria for searching the personals section and for responding by E-mail.

Circulation problems among newspapers in recent years appear to be one factor influencing newspaper executives to develop electronic news sources (Caragata 1996; Underwood 1993). Pressures of declining newspaper sales may also explain recent trends toward a reader-driven approach to newspapering (Underwood 1993). Amidst the already uncertain future of newspapers in an era of multimedia technology expansion, the new Federal Telecommunication Bill has been signed into law. This law aims at creating greater competition within telecommunication markets by breaking down partitions between such services as telephone and cable television. It is intended that the law will stimulate mergers throughout the telecommunication industry, stimulate development of new multimedia products and services, and permit American companies to emerge as "supercompetitors" in the global market (Carney 1996).

Given the concern of newspaper executives that increased competition in the telecommunication industry may render newspapers obsolete, it is understandable that they might seek out a new form in which to cast the news. It can be questioned, however, whether this new form will inevitably sacrifice news content. Is there any harm in a reader-driven, high-tech approach to the news?

Some cynics about technology are wary of "technological totalization," a self-proliferating process in which technology seizes social control, eliminates moral values, and imposes its own "technicized amorality." According to this view, once technology is set in motion, it has a tendency to keep itself in motion and to proliferate at increased rates. Thus, "electronic technology expands from the Atlantic cable to communication satellites, from seven TV channels to forty, from specialized companies to multinational conglomerates." Moreover, at the roots of this technological progression is the principle of expedience, which casts aside all other values in favor of faster and cheaper ways of calling up unlimited quantities of news and entertainment (Christians 1996).

According to Alan Drengson (1995, 87–88), technological totalization includes the following key characteristics:

- The creation of *objective measures* of progress defined as increasing efficiency and quantity of output, using common denominators
- The *accumulation of technical gains* used to further other technological gains
- An intensifying *systematization of technological process* that produces greater standardization and uniformity, including an operational definition of qualities such as sound and sight in terms of abstract formulas and digital codes
- Ongoing *refinement of research and development methodology* with increasing emphasis on forms of methodical innovation and development to yield new technological processes
- A *redefinition of basic concepts and legal codes* to allow the patenting even of living substances for the purposes of exclusive market rights (exploitation)

Given the adequacy of these standards, it appears that a convincing argument might be advanced for the trend toward such technological control of our social fabric and especially of our media. While the "newness" of news has always been a defining mark of news delivery, computer technology has taken speediness of delivery and time saving to unprecedented heights. From photographic technology to E-mail, a prime mark of progress has become rapidity of delivery in terms of measurable units of time. In general, the faster a computer delivers information, the higher marks it receives. While 50 MHz was once considered state of the art, 200 MHz is now considered more respectable. While a 2,400-bps modem used to be "fast," it is now outdated. Similarly, the *larger* the information storage area, the better. Thus, the question is no longer "How many megabytes is your hard drive?" Instead we have graduated to gigabytes. Journalism has now become "digital" through its storage of documents, images, and sounds on computers using numerical codes. Giant corporations that dominate the information technology market have provided conditions for ever increasing increments of efficiency. Consideration of emerging computer technology even in the past decade can attest to the dominion of technology over information storage and delivery, and to technological progress in these areas as measured purely in terms of objectifiable units of efficiency.

In confronting technological totalization, Drengson (1995, 86) proposes a "balanced technology practice" in which we are guided not merely by what is technologically possible but by what is "vitally necessary given overall values and spiritual meaning." Insofar as technology absorbs us in an endless quest for efficiency, we may lose sight of what intrinsic values motivate us in the first place.

A central question is thus efficiency for what end? The possession of speedy, inexpensive tools for accessing large amounts of information is at most a means, not itself an end, and it matters what we dredge up when we do so with great rapidity and thrift. While it is a truism that all that glitters is not gold, in a technological era where technology reins supreme it may become increasingly difficult to distinguish the glitter from the gold.

While one virtue that may be claimed for the technological explosion is the provision of a bottomless newshole in cyberspace filled with an endless stream of information, a balanced media technology practice will presumably need to be selective in what it pours into that hole. Inundating the public with information may self-defeatingly "produce not informed citizens but those whose self-perceptions and basic attitudes have become crystallized" as though being entranced by a "ceaseless kaleidoscope consisting of thousands of pictures, each following the other at an extraordinary pace" (Christians 1996, 163; Ellul 1957, 75). A challenge for journalists in an age of high technology may thus be that of sitting through such a kaleidoscope, without themselves getting carried away by its spectacle, in an effort to call the public's attention to what is important and to help it to maintain perspective.

References: Caragata, Warren. 1996. "News, One Byte at a Time." *Maclean's Magazine* 109 (January): 34–35.

Carney, Dan. 1996. "Congress Fires Its First Shot in Information Revolution." *Congressional Quarterly Weekly Report* 54 (3 February): 289–292.

Christians, Clifford G. 1996. "Propaganda and the Technological System." In Theodore L. Glasser and Charles T. Salmon, editors. *Public Opinion and the Communication of Consent*. New York: Guilford Press, 156–174.

Drengson, Alan. 1995. *The Practice of Technology: Exploring Technology, Ecophilosophy, and Spiritual Disciplines for Vital Links*. Albany: State University of New York Press.

Ellul, Jacques. 1957. "Information and Propaganda." *Diogenes: International Review of Philosophy and Humanistic Studies* (June): 61–77.

Landau, George. 1992. "Quantum Leaps: Computer Journalism Takes Off." *Columbia Journalism Review* (May/June): 61–64.

Reaves, Sheila. 1991. "Digital Manipulation of Photos with New Computer Technology." In Philip Patterson and Lee Wilkins, editors. *Media Ethics: Issues and Cases*. Dubuque, IA: William C. Brown, Publishers.

Underwood, Doug. 1993. "The Newspapers' Identity Crisis." In Shirley Biagi, editor. *Media/Reader: Perspectives on Mass Media Industries, Effects, and Issues*. 2d Edition. Belmont, CA: Wadsworth, 17–21.

Objectivity and News Bias

Journalistic Objectivity

Mike W. Martin

Journalists are often criticized for failing to be objective, and the tone of the criticisms calls into question their competence, honesty, fairness, and integrity. For example, they are blamed by conservatives for having a liberal slant, by liberals for permitting distortions caused by business interests, and by politicians for being overly negative to current government officials. Exactly what is objectivity, is it possible, and how much of it is desirable?

The legal context for discussing objectivity is set by the First Amendment to the U.S. Constitution, which apparently prohibits all restrictions on the press: "Congress shall make no law...abridging the freedom of speech, or of the press." In fact, the phrase *freedom of speech* has been construed by the courts as referring to a right that, like virtually all rights, has some limits, including restrictions against libel and slander. There have been additional restrictions, most notably the Fairness Doctrine imposed by the Federal Communications Commission on the electronic media, which required that important issues be aired, opposing views on controversial topics be represented, and political candidates criticized in the media be given the opportunity to respond. In defending these restrictions, Justice Byron White argued that because the airwaves are public property, government can require balanced representation of community views (*Red Lion Broadcasting Co. v. FCC*, 395 U.S. 367: 1969).

Turning to the moral issues, objectivity in reporting and interpreting events implies being truthful, unbiased, fair, and balanced. What this means may vary according to whether objectivity is ascribed to individual journalists, news reports, commentaries, news organizations, general media coverage of an event, or trends in the entire media. Moreover, there are different senses of objectivity depending on the intended contrast—objectivity versus what? Four contrasts have special interest: partisanship, unbalanced partisanship, value judgments, and, cognitive distortion. Thus, objectivity might mean: (1) being nonpartisan, in the sense of not advocating a position on controversial issues; (2) maintaining balanced partisanship, as when a newspaper provides a fair representation of opposing partisan viewpoints, either in general or regarding particular issues; (3) maintaining value neutrality, in the sense of stating facts without making value judgments; or (4) not distorting facts and understanding. With regard to each of these senses we can ask exactly what is meant, is it achievable, and is it desirable?

First, to be nonpartisan is to avoid taking a stand on controversial issues. Certainly an individual reporter can strive to avoid both overt and covert advocacy on contentious political, moral, and economic issues. Although complete success may be rare, substantial degrees of neutrality and impartiality are possible. But is nonpartisanship desirable? As a rule, news reporters assigned to provide a chronicle of events and opinions should strive to maintain "professional distance" by setting aside their personal views on issues about which reasonable persons disagree. Nevertheless, in setting a context for the story, as well as in providing in-depth understanding, they are easily drawn into advocacy. By contrast, commentators and editorial writers both may and often should take stands, while seeking to be accurate about facts, fair in representing alternative viewpoints, and unprejudiced (nonracist, nonsexist, nonbigoted).

Second, the idea of balanced partisanship is applicable to an entire news forum (newspaper, media program, etc.) and to news organizations. Here objectivity means avoiding one-sidedness in the range of partisan positions represented, either in general or regarding particular issues. A newspaper reveals unbalanced partisanship when it prints primarily conservative or liberal editorials. Doing so may be objectionable or permissible, depending on the stated mission of the forum or organization. Some magazines and electronic media programs have an explicit political commitment, while others offer forums for presenting diverse views, both in general and on specific issues. Extensive diversity is desirable within and made possible by democracies.

Third, objectivity as value neutrality is possible to some extent but, more importantly, is often undesirable. Value judgments are made both in (a) choosing topics to report and (b) determining the content of the reports. Concerning the choice of topics, the paramount criterion is newsworthiness, which implies value judgments about what is important, socially significant, and of sufficient interest to a targeted audience. Concerning the content of reports, journalism requires selecting questions to ask, sources to query, information to put in or leave out, space or time allocations, and choice of emphasis in headlines and graphics. All such decisions are made on the basis of value judgments about what is most newsworthy (important and of interest to a targeted audience). Even word choice and paragraph structure are shaped by values. Imagine how dull and colorless reports would become if journalists had to avoid calling a philanthropist "generous" or a murderer "brutal."

Fourth, objectivity as the absence of all cognitive distortions may be impossible and perhaps unclear in meaning. To be sure, the ideal of a perfectly rational person guided Western thought from Plato to the eighteenth-century Enlightenment, but the "unmasking" trend began during the nineteenth century with thinkers like Friedrich Nietzsche and Karl Marx and was intensified by twentieth-century postmodernists. It debunked the ideal of complete rationality as a ruse used to serve the interests of dominant groups. Without falling into postmodernists' skepticism about the possibility of finding truth, we can acknowledge that all cognitive schemas—structured sets of ideas, perspectives, and values—impose some limitations and biases.

Consider three cases. First, Janet Cooke was forced to return the 1981 Pulitzer Prize she had won for a story in the *Washington Post* on an eight-year-old drug addict. The alleged child, she confessed, was a composite of several children. Some might say that because the case involved sheer fabrications, more nuanced questions about objectivity are irrelevant. The case, however, is especially interesting in light of Walter Lippmann's distinction between news (description) and truth (understanding) (1946). Although Cooke did not attempt to be objective in stating the facts about one actual child, her interpretive account of drug addition ironically provided considerable understanding through an objective interpretation of the issues (which was recognized by the awarding of the Pulitzer Prize).

Second, the opposite excess occurred during the 1950s in reports on the McCarthy anti-Communist hearings, as well as a decade later in coverage of the Vietnam War. In both instances, journalists adopted the tendency to report the available facts by relying on government sources for information, context, and opinion. The upshot was a serious distortion of understanding. Worse, reporters who uncritically reported Senator Joseph McCarthy's unfair charges against alleged Communists inculpated the press in harming innocent persons.

Third, as a positive example, Edward R. Murrow aspired to the highest standards of unbiased reporting throughout his career, but his most memorable contributions involved advocacy in analyzing problems and even recommending solutions. His 1954 expose of McCarthy is often credited with initiating the downfall of that demagogue. Of equal importance, though ultimately of less influence, was his 1960 documentary on the desperate plight of migrant farmworkers. From its title *Harvest of Shame* to its compassionate and respectful interviews and its culminating call for reform, the documentary used objective reporting of fact mixed with appeals to conscience. Clearly partisan in favoring labor interests over the farmers' lobby, it was also brilliant investigative reporting.

How far, and how best, to prevent "the intrusion of personal beliefs and values into news coverage" is "the single most intractable problem in journalism," according to Stephen Klaidman and Tom L. Beauchamp (1987, 59). They urge journalists to avoid partisanship. H. Eugene Goodwin (1987, 12) adds that even though "the word 'objective' has fallen into dispute," if not disrepute, professional journalists continue to endorse the aims of being unbiased, balanced, and fair. Donald McDonald (1971) also expresses cautious optimism: "Objectivity as meaning a substantially truthful account of contemporary public affairs is well within the possibility of the mass-communications media despite many practical difficulties."

Robert Miraldi affirms the value of partisan journalism when it is guided by the values of compassion and justice. He challenges the limitations imposed by "the routines of journalism" aimed at balance, documentation, close attribution of sources, and the structuring of reports within media conventions of time, space, and headlines (Miraldi 1990, 16–17). David E. White (1985) challenges the usual contrast between objectivity and partisanship, urging that partisanship can be objective in the sense of being honest and fair.

Representing postmodernist doubts about the existence of truths independent of particular cognitive perspectives, Herbert J. Gans (1992) suggests that reporters set aside personal values and concentrate on greatly increasing the range of views reported, and Theodore L. Glasser (1992, 176) renounces the search for objectivity as an "ideology" that favors the status quo, "emasculates the intellect by treating it as a disinterested spectator," and undermines the personal integrity of journalists who are required to set aside their consciences." By contrast, Andrew Edgar (1992) uses a hermeneutic (interpretive) approach to distinguish between good and bad forms of bias. Bruce Wayne McKinzie (1994) explores the connection between practical standards of journalistic objectivity and beliefs in a reality independent of human cognition. In a more wide-ranging critique of the excesses of some forms of postmodernism and feminism, Louise M. Antony (1993) champions the value-laden search for "good biases" that should guide reasonable persons.

Debates about journalistic objectivity, at both practical and theoretical levels, will and should continue. The search for journalistic excellence is accompanied by perennial concerns about how to distinguish factual reporting from reform-oriented advocacy, illuminating analysis from concealed bias, and honest from dishonest forms of partisanship. At the practical level, more worrisome than occasional abuses by individual reporters is the erosion of objectivity at the institutional level, especially given increasing economic pressures favoring entertainment over elucidation of complex issues. Scholarly work on journalistic objectivity may benefit from attention to related debates in epistemology, philosophy of science, and feminism. At the same time, the need for a rough consensus about the practical standards for journalistic excellence—confirming sources, balanced range of opinions cited, fairness, etc.—should not be confused with the more theoretical philosophical issues about what counts as knowledge.

References: Antony, Louise M. 1993. "Quine as Feminist." In Louise M. Antony and Charlotte Witt, editors. *A Mind of One's Own: Feminist Essays on Reason and Objectivity*. Boulder, CO: Westview Press.

Edgar, Andrew. 1992. "Objectivity, Bias and Truth." In Andrew Belsey and Ruth Chadwick, editors. *Ethical Issues in Journalism and the Media*. New York: Routledge, 112–129.

Gans, Herbert J. 1992. "Multiperspectival News." In Elliot D. Cohen, editor. *Philosophical Issues in Journalism*. New York: Oxford University Press, 190–201.

Glasser, Theodore L. 1992. "Objectivity and News Bias." In Elliot D. Cohen, editor. *Philosophical Issues in Journalism*. New York: Oxford University Press, 176–185.

Goodwin, H. Eugene. 1987. *Groping for Ethics in Journalism*. 2d Edition. Ames: Iowa State University.

Klaidman, Stephen, and Tom L. Beauchamp. 1987. *The Virtuous Journalist*. New York: Oxford University Press.

Lippmann, Walter. 1946. *Public Opinion*. New York: Macmillan.

McDonald, Donald. 1971. "Is Objectivity Possible?" *The Center Magazine* 4 (September/ October). Reprinted in Anthony Serafini, editor. 1989. *Ethics and Social Concern*. New York: Paragon House, 632–657.

McKinzie, Bruce Wayne. 1994. *Objectivity, Communication, and the Foundation of Understanding*. New York: University Press of America.

Miraldi, Robert. 1990. *Muckraking and Objectivity*. New Haven, CT: Greenwood Press.

White, David E. 1985. "Objectivity as a Journalistic Virtue." *Journal of Social Philosophy* 16 (Fall): 13–19.

White, Justice Byron. 1969. *Red Lion Broadcasting Co. v. Federal Communications Commission*. Cited by Marc A. Franklin, editor. 1982. *Mass Media Law*. 2d Edition. Mineola, NY: Foundation Press, 658–659.

Forms of News Bias

Elliot D. Cohen

The term *bias* broadly understood signifies a favorable or unfavorable bent, or leaning, toward something. In the context of journalism, such a leaning may on the one hand simply refer to a certain perspective among other equally respectable ones (Blair 1988). It is in this sense that Herbert Gans (1980) once argued that all news is biased since it always ultimately reflects somebody or another's perspective.

On the other hand, bias in the context of journalism often signifies unfair, dishonest, self-serving, unbalanced, or misleading slanting of news. It is in this normative sense that the American Society of News Editors (1975) has declared that "every effort must be made to assure that the news content is accurate, free from bias and in context, and that all sides are presented fairly." Insofar as such news bias interferes with the central journalistic purpose of keeping the public adequately informed, journalists have a professional responsibility to avoid and prevent it.

Such (objectionable) news bias can come in different forms. These forms of bias include biases arising from faulty thinking, devices of news slanting, and organizational biases.

Biases of Faulty Thinking

S. H. Stocking and P. H. Gross (1992) have suggested a number of faulty thinking errors that can lead to news bias and that appear to represent human tendencies to misuse or misinterpret empirical data. Some examples of these faulty thinking errors are briefly reviewed below.

One error, dubbed "the eyewitness fallacy," amounts to a naive acceptance of eyewitness testimony. It is assumed that "seeing is believing" and that reality is given in perception exactly as it really is. The flaw here is failure to realize that individual observations can be colored by such personal aspects as the perceiver's prejudices, stereotypes, past experiences, expectations, and stress. Memory of such observations can, of course, fade with time, and it may also be affected by what transpires after witnessing an event. Thus, a reporter's memory of the details of an event may be altered by having heard someone else's account of the same event. Insofar as reporters assume that their own perceptions are incorrigible, they may prematurely curtail their investigations. For example, a reporter whose perception is slanted by racial stereotypes may rely on such faulty perception instead of seeking out further information. (*See also* Images and Stereotypes.)

A second error is a "confirmation bias," in which a reporter may slant an investigation in favor of a preferred outcome. For example, a journalist who is already committed to the theory that there is a crime wave against the elderly may unwittingly seek out and interview only those sources likely to confirm the crime wave, such as elderly victims, elderly people who live in the "bad" part of town, crime prevention officials, etc. (Stocking and Gross 1992). In this regard, it is also worth noting how stereotyping can support a confirmation bias. For example, a reporter who preconceived all or most elderly people as weak and vulnerable may be inclined toward committing the confirmation bias in testing the theory that there is a crime wave against the elderly.

A third error is a "biased sample" error, in which generalizations are (consciously or unconsciously) inferred from unrepresentative samples. For example, different journalists covering the Watergate hearings in the 1970s, starting with different samples, came to opposite generalizations. One journalist who generalized from letters supposedly sent to Senator Ervin's committee concluded that audiences appreciated televised hearings, while another journalist using television station call-ins as a sample concluded the opposite (Stocking and Gross 1992).

According to Association of Public Opinion Research, in order to avoid misleading the average person, news media should include all of the following information when publishing or broadcasting the results of polls:

> (1) who sponsored the survey, (2) the exact wording of the question asked, (3) a definition of the population actually sampled, (4) the sample size (for mail surveys, include both the number of questionnaires mailed out and the number returned), (5) an indication of what allowance should be made for sampling error, (6) which results are based on part of the sample rather than the total sample, (7) whether interviewing was done personally, by mail, or on street corners, and (8) the timing of the interviewing in relation to the events (Johnson 1988, 165).

Ralph Johnson (1988) maintains that very few newspapers actually observe these standards, often omitting such information as margin of error and exact wording of questions asked.

A fourth error is that of an "illusory correlation," in which a connection between two events or characteristics is claimed without adequate evidence. In one form, this fallacy involves assuming a causal relationship to exist between two events simply because one event came after the other. For example, the Clinton administration, as part of its campaign strategy, claimed responsibility for economic improvement. While it is possible that certain of Clinton's policies contributed to positive economic growth, economic change is a notoriously complex phenomenon. Independent evidence is required, and temporal succession alone proves nothing.

Devices of News Slanting

In his book *Logic and Contemporary Rhetoric*, Howard Kahane (1995) points to further "devices used to slant the news." A fundamental difference between these devices and the errors noted by Stocking and Gross is that the latter in contrast to the former are largely committed unintentionally.

Stories can be "played up or down" depending on where they are placed and how much space is devoted to them. A story can be played down by placing it at the back of the newspaper, or in television news, toward the end of the program. For example, the *Canton* (Ohio) *Repository* (28 July 1974) devoted most of its front page to football and relegated to a bottom corner the decision by the House Judiciary Committee to recommend Nixon's impeachment (Kahane 1995).

Similarly, information *within* an article can be played down by placing it at the back of the article where readers are less likely to read it, and it can be played up by placing it in the front.

Media may also use headlines that are "misleading, sensationalized, or opinionated" as in the following August 1997 headline from the *Philadelphia Daily News*: " 'You're Out of Here!' It's Revenge: Daddy Fred Goldman on Doing In O. J."

The article discusses the recent book by Fred Goldman and family, in which Fred Goldman admits to having fantasies about putting a gun to O. J. Simpson's head. The reference to "Daddy" Fred Goldman makes a mockery of his having entertained such thoughts.

A headline from the *San Francisco Chronicle* reads "Chiapas Peasants Start Big Land Grab," notwithstanding the article's admission that the Mexican Chiapas Indians had retaken land that was still lawfully theirs (Kahane 1995).

The latter example illustrates the general problem of lifting out of context. Knowing the background conditions under which a claim is made can affect its meaning. For example, a headline stating "Israeli Missile Injures and Kills Innocent Iraqi Women and Children" takes on new import (without mitigating the tragedy) when it is learned that the missile was electronically programmed to seek out and destroy Iraqi weapons that happened to be deployed from an area populated by civilians. Ross Perot's statement "I'm the wrong man," lifted from its actual context in the 1992 presidential debate, takes on new meaning when it is seen as the consequent clause of the larger conditional statement "If there's more time for gridlock and talk and finger pointing, I'm the wrong man." The statement "When I awakened from sleep

I was still sleeping" sounds contradictory until we learn that it is a description of a dream within a dream.

There is a sense in which any attempt to describe a particular event involves dislodging it from the broader context in which it is imbedded. Indeed, each event is related to further events, which are related to further events, and so on. Nevertheless, not providing *enough* context can be misleading. This problem can easily occur in photojournalism as well as print media. For example, former President Gerald Ford once complained, "Every time I stumbled or bumped my head or fell in the snow, reporters zeroed in on that to the exclusion of almost everything else. The news coverage was harmful.... [This] helped create the impression of me as a stumbler. And that wasn't funny" (Smoller 1992, 148).

A video of Ford hitting someone in the head with a golf ball and a photo of him stumbling as he stepped down from a plane were damaging insofar as they were made to represent the rest of his life. What Ford was hoping to see from the press were more articles and photographs revealing him in the act of doing something right. Because media coverage of his presidency highlighted his stumblings to the exclusion of his successes, it was biased.

Journalists can also slant the perception of reality through their choice of words. (*See also* Ethics of the News Story.) Highly emotionally charged language can be used to help create a misleading appearance of reality, especially when these words are applied to aspects of reality lifted from their contexts. For example, in the following, William A. Dorman (1988) describes the results of a study he conducted on how the press contributed to a negative view of the former Soviet Union and, in particular, one of its leaders, Leonid Brezhnev:

> *Newsweek's* 20-page treatment, insofar as Brezhnev the man—is concerned, can be summed up by the headline: "The Cautious Bully"... United Press International found the Soviet leader to be "canny," "burly," and "beetle-browed," a favorite description in much of the media. The *New York Times* also described Brezhnev as "canny," "burly," "gregarious and talkative," with a reputation as a lover of good food and drink, fast cars....

Time magazine, Dorman reports, summed up Soviet history since the Bolshevik Revolution as follows:

> Tsarist autocracy quickly gave way to the "dictatorship of the proletariat," and the United States began sixty-five years of trying with a great variety of tactics and theories but with notable lack of success, to find some way of ameliorating the more maddening, sometimes murderous aspects of Soviet tyranny.

In these examples, there is use of pejorative language—"burly," "murderous," etc.—to slant perception against the Soviet Union with no attempt to *balance* this with anything positive. There is no attempt at putting Soviet history in a context that would also reflect favorable dimensions of Soviet society. Instead, the whole Soviet Union or the whole person of Brezhnev is dominated and represented by the negative portrayal. As Dorman suggests, an anti-American journalist could equally have degraded the United States through a negative portrayal of its politics by painting only the dark side of the Nixon years. Journalists can thus slant reality by illuminating only one side of a story, using strong emotional language to cast the light.

This device can also be used to support popular stereotypes. For example, in the local section of the *Philadelphia Daily News* (14 February 1997), a story appeared under the headline "Gem of a Contradiction: Slain Jeweler, Wife Apparently Were Quite Wealthy." It described the double murder of Richie Zimmerman, a jeweler and his wife, Patricia, who apparently had a million dollars "stashed" in a bank safe-deposit box. The lead reads:

> They were an odd couple, the beauty and the beast, she a curvaceous blonde with the face of an angel, and he a pudgy and rumpled man with a limp, as shrewd and stingy and disliked as she was naive and warm-hearted and desirable.

Extreme language like "beauty" and "beast," "curvaceous blonde," and "pudgy and rumpled" is juxtaposed to highlight the negative qualities of Mr. Zimmerman, just as a large coffee stain would be all the more apparent on a clean white shirt. The article includes statements such as these:

> Richie Zimmerman was so tight with a buck that he exploded at his wife for paying somebody $10 to change a flat tire during a snowstorm, said the jeweler... In a business where haggling over price was expected, Zimmerman was king... To him, no price was the right price. Even at the Jeweler's Row Diner on Sansom Street, where the Zimmermans often dined on chicken soup, Zimmerman would put $4 on the counter for a $6 tab....

In these terms Mr. Zimmerman emerges as a symbol of a cheap, haggling, underhanded, chicken-soup-drinking, rich jeweler—a characterization supportive of a popular Jewish stereotype. Indeed, reporting on what Mr. Zimmerman often ordered at the Row Diner (chicken soup) served no apparent purpose save for an ethnic slur.

Organizational Biases

Edward Jay Epstein points to still another set of news biases that depend on the structure of news organizations and not on individual reporters who work for these organizations. According to Epstein, while the importance of personal biases of reporters is undeniable, emphasis on these biases serves to distract attention from a far more important type of bias, "organizational bias." Epstein (1992, 244) writes:

Indeed, if the organization is "tilted" in its preferences in one direction, news will tend to be distorted regardless of the fairness—or unfairness—of the individual newsman. Just as a roulette wheel mounted on a tilted table tends to favor some numbers over other numbers no matter how fair the croupier might be, a news organization that is tilted in a certain direction because of the way it is structured will also tend to favor certain types of stories over others.

According to Epstein, the clearest cases of such organizational bias occur in television news. Network news organizations, claims Epstein, are subject to certain pressures—pressures of time, advertisers, audiences, and affiliated stations. Network news organizations are inevitably led to "tilt" the structure of news in responding to these pressures.

First, enforced constraints on the amount of time allotted to network news (23 minutes to present several filmed news stories) make it impossible to provide sufficient attention to context, including explanations and causes of events. The result is an oversimplified presentation of the issues, leading to "a picture of society as unstable" wherein "any institution is capable of foundering, collapsing, or being overthrown without evident cause" (Epstein 1992, 246).

Second, network news organizations are under pressure from advertisers to maintain their audiences so that advertising revenues are not lost. This prompts news organizations to adjust the nature of news to fit the capacities of their average viewers, who, it is assumed, are likely to be attracted when images are clear and easily recognized but distracted when images are unfamiliar and confusing. The result is oversimplified or stereotypical images—for example, shabbily dressed children standing for poverty. (*See* Images and Stereotypes.)

It is also assumed that these viewers, whose attention spans tend to be short, will most likely remain engaged through action figures in conflict. This leads producers to look for clear images depicting opposition—for example, black against white, military against civilian. The result is again an oversimplified portrayal of reality.

It is also assumed that these viewers' attention will most likely be held when stories play out with a clear beginning, middle, and end. Since the reported events do not necessarily follow this course in terms of available footage, the result is an editing of reality to fit this fictive form.

Third, network affiliates require that local news be distinguished from national news. While reports on the president, Capitol Hill politics, and the state of the economy may be about national events, these stories are not usually sufficient to carry the flow of national news. Satisfying this demand may require that local stories be made to *look* like national ones. This illusion may be accomplished by piecing together local events around some national theme, for example, discussing urban crime by interviewing residents in different cities about how they are coping with crime. Such a "process of nationalizing the news yields a constant agenda of national crises in place of local happenings" (Epstein 1992, 248).

Epstein queries, "Given these constraints, do the media present a picture of reality upon which rational men can make decisions?" His own response is to suggest that the news be viewed as a map is viewed. Although the map does not provide a literal geographical depiction, it can still be useful. Similarly, realizing the ways in which the news "systematically distorts reality" can help us in using the news as a decision-making vehicle. Unfortunately, he charges, the media typically try to conceal these distortions from their audiences unlike topographers who provide mileage keys.

Epstein's map analogy, however, may be challenged. While maps represent quantifiable distances drawn to scale, most news content is not similarly quantifiable. For example, failing to provide important facts about the conditions that led to the Beijing student massacre or exactly why there has been so much tension between the Serbs and the Croats cannot be compensated mathematically. What is required is the provision of empirical facts, which the average person cannot be presumed to know.

If the news is to serve the function of accurately informing the public, then it must take heed of the fundamental ways in which biases can thwart this goal. Since news organizations are also private enterprises in a capitalist society, it is unlikely that they will turn a blind eye on news biases that pay; yet, they can justify their existence only by keeping the public adequately informed.

References: American Society of Newspaper Editors. 1975. Statement of Principles.

Blair, Anthony. 1988. "What Is Bias?" In Trudy Govier, editor. *Selected Issues in Logic and Communications*. Belmont, CA: Wadsworth, 93–103.

Dorman, William A. 1988. "Mass Media and International Conflict." In Trudy Govier, editor. *Selected Issues in Logic and Communications*. Belmont, CA: Wadsworth, 65–72.

Epstein, Edward Jay. 1992. "Organizational Biases of Network News Reporting." In Elliot D. Cohen, editor. *Philosophical Issues in Journalism*. New York: Oxford University Press, 244–249.

Gans, Herbert J. 1980. *Deciding What's News: A Study of CBS Evening News, NBC Nightly News, Newsweek, and Time*. New York: Random House.

Johnson, Ralph. 1988. "Poll-ution: Coping with Surveys and Polls." In Trudy Govier, editor. *Selected Issues in Logic and Communications*. Belmont, CA: Wadsworth, 163–177.

Kahane, Howard. 1995. *Logic and Contemporary Rhetoric: The Use of Reason in Everyday Life*. 7th Edition. Belmont, CA: Wadsworth.

Smoller, Fred. 1992. "Network News Coverage of the Presidency: Implications for Democracy." In Elliot D. Cohen, editor. *Philosophical Issues in Journalism*. New York: Oxford University Press, 223–236.

Stocking, S. Holly, and Paget H. Gross. 1992. "Understanding Errors and Biases That Can Affect Journalists." In Elliot D. Cohen, editor. *Philosophical Issues in Journalism*. New York: Oxford University Press, 223–236.

Diversity

Keith Woods

The call for the U.S. media to understand and embrace diversity found one of its earliest expressions in the Hutchins Report of 1947. This report, *A Free and Responsible Press*, underscored the moral obligation for mass-market journalism to listen and speak to all segments of the population. The Commission on Freedom of the Press, which drafted the report, said that society needs truth that is kept in context and massaged by a vigorous exchange of comment and commentary, truth that is strengthened by connecting the public to itself, and truth that is transmitted evenly throughout society. The commission, led by University of Chicago chancellor Robert M. Hutchins and funded by magazine publisher Henry R. Luce, assumed that the standards they proposed would not be new to the managers of the press, as they were drawn largely from the profession and its stated practices. Nevertheless, caricatures of minorities continued. In that year *Editor and Publisher*, the oldest journal serving the press, ran an advertisement featuring a cuddly Eskimo and a white-lipped, spear-carrying savage, the latter presumably from Africa.

Five decades after the Hutchins Report, the dissonance between what media organizations say they stand for and what they do still remains pronounced when the subject is cultural diversity. Diversity is often thought of as existing outside the fundamental mission of excellent journalism. It is often monitored by separate committees, covered by separate reporters, and tacked on as something new and different to think about when the facts have been gathered and the headlines written. Yet it is only through mining diversity that we make possible the most complete and responsible telling of the truth and, therefore, the most ethical and excellent journalism.

The Law

The law has a small part in the debate that has gotten smaller as the country has crawled and lurched away from mandated diversity. The Federal Communications Commission (FCC) requires that broadcast stations hire a proportion of minorities equal to one-half of the proportion that that minority represents in the regional workforce. If 8 percent of the region's workforce is Latino, the station must show that 4 percent of its workforce is Latino. Stations must also keep a detailed accounting of their efforts to achieve these goals. Failure to do either can result in anything from a fine to loss of license.

Several American newspapers bound by Equal Employment Opportunity Commission (EEOC) consent decrees after settling discrimination lawsuits must show equal diligence in chronicling efforts to achieve some measure of workforce diversity, but there exists no formula equivalent to that of the FCC. In either case, enforcement is reserved for the most egregious offenses and does not alone ensure great strides in improving newsroom diversity.

The Issues

Journalistic diversity, like objectivity, is an ideal at the end of a continuum, with homogeneity and exclusion at one end, and maximum representation and affirmative inclusion at the other. It is easier, then, to know when a newsroom is not diverse than it is to know when it can justifiably declare itself so. The value of diversity extends beyond the achievement of fairness in opportunity and maximum representation to embody the "truth" that journalists tell.

In the world of journalism, the goal of diversity is often described in three ways:

1. As social responsibility: There is a duty-based notion that newspapers and broadcast stations ought to hire from and cover communities beyond the norm of white men because that is the fair and equitable thing to do.
2. As good business: A more diverse staff will lead to more diverse coverage, which will lead to a broader customer base and a better bottom line.
3. As legal responsibility: The FCC dictates that broadcasters achieve minimum standards of pursuing and achieving diversity (newspapers already hit by—or living in fear of—lawsuits from the EEOC have hired and promoted based on that fear).

Critics and proponents alike often speak of each motivation to the exclusion of the others, and rare is the argument that diversity speaks to the foundation of journalism—accuracy, fairness, and some level of objectivity. The biases of journalists are the obstacles that litter the path to the goal of objectivity. Those who study organizational diversity recommend recognition of and vigorous examination of those biases as a necessary first step toward fairness. Lee Gardenswartz and Anita Rowe (1994, 32) wrote, "Without examining and understanding the layers of diversity that form our filters, we are apt to be victims of our differences, making unconscious assumptions and encountering unexplained and frustrating barriers. From that self-appraisal might come an understanding of both the individual contributions one has to offer and the biases and limitations each brings to a group effort (Gardenswartz and Rowe 1994, 18). It might also inspire people to become more educated and seek greater diversity where they work, play, and pray.

In journalism, as everywhere, unexamined biases—particularly assumptions about intelligence and aptitude—can determine who is hired and assigned. They can determine who is covered and how. All determine how much "truth" is told. Carol Liebler's (1994, 127) research revealed a unique twist on that issue:

> As newsroom diversity increases, perceived autonomy decreases, especially for minority journalists. The reason for this remains unclear, but some possible explanations can be considered. As the work force diversifies, uncertainty in the newsroom regarding job assignments, capabilities, experience and other similar factors may increase. Under such conditions, an editor may be inclined to hold

a tighter rein on all reporters. Furthermore, the belief that a reporter's race may affect the nature of news content seemingly conflicts with a primary news value—objectivity. Thus greater newsroom diversity may result in a perceived new threat to personal bias. Less autonomy may be granted if editors feel that they are defending traditional definitions of newsworthiness against a putative threat from diversity.

The opportunities are many for personal biases to ultimately affect the truth journalists tell by determining who does the telling and from what forum. That may be the strongest argument for more contributors to the marketplace of ideas. Many contemporary studies have found that which Hutchins found in 1947: News told from a narrow perspective tends to pervert judgment. The media, the commission contended, have a moral responsibility to mitigate that perversion, a responsibility commensurate to the substantial power and influence news organizations command in American society.

Cases

News organizations often find themselves in turmoil after telling a truth without making the fullest use of the diversity in their midst.

When a southwestern newspaper decided to do a special report about juvenile delinquency in 1994, it wound up with an internal problem. Several staffers, particularly those who were black, complained that the project was poorly reported, unfairly focused on black children, and rushed into the newspaper before it was ready. The report, a white editor said, seemed to imply that juvenile crime occurred only in minority communities. Very few local minority leaders were interviewed. Nearly all of the photographs selected for use depicted minorities.

The complaint contained echoes of the 1968 Kerner Commission's indictment of media. Appointed by President Lyndon Johnson, this was a commission formed to study the civil uprisings in the mid-1960s. An entire chapter was devoted to problems with news media. The commission wrote, "[The news] repeatedly, if unconsciously, reflects the biases, the paternalism, the indifference of white America" (Kerner Commission 1968, 366).

In early 1996, a southeastern newspaper published the story of a lesbian couple who decided to have a wedding ceremony to formally, if not legally, declare their commitment to one another. The negative response from many in the community, and some on the staff, was overwhelming. Having admitted that the organization did not fully appreciate the views of some conservative Christians who were opposed to the story, the publisher wrote a column apologizing to readers who were offended. The apology left some in the newsroom feeling that the newspaper did not value people who were gay or lesbian, people whose views were not sought as the apology was being written.

Could the American media have better handled the 1996 controversy involving the Clinton administration's affiliation with foreign investors if the reporting had been informed by the views of more Asian Americans? Story after story spoke of the "Asian Connection," a reference that exhumed images of the so-called yellow peril of the Pearl Harbor era. The story had as its core not the ethnicity of campaign contributors but the possibility that non-Americans were influencing domestic and foreign policy. Yet, ethnic references saturated the news. The references prompted the Asian American Journalists Association (AAJA) to send out an advisory to the major television and radio networks as well as to the nation's largest newspapers.

"In some stories relating to the questionable contributions, race identifiers unfairly paint all members of that ethnicity as unethical or illegal," AAJA president Benjamin Seto wrote. "The connections of Asian Americans to Asians living outside of the United States continue the long-standing stereotype that Asian Americans are foreigners who do not follow U.S. laws. Perpetuating such stereotypes undermines the fair and accurate coverage of Asian Americans" (Asian American Journalists Association 1996).

Seto's concern hinged on a notion advanced by Robert Entman (1994, 517), which holds that white American media consumers, the majority racial group in the country, are likely to allow the limited depiction of another racial group to represent all members of that group "in a way singular whites do not stand for all whites."

Looking Ahead

In 1978, the American Society of Newspaper Editors (ASNE) announced its "Goals 2000" project, designed to bring newsroom diversity in line with the communities ASNE members served by the end of the millennium (e.g., in a community made up of 10 percent Hispanic residents, the makeup of the newspaper serving that community should reflect that population). The organization now concedes that for an overwhelming majority of newspapers, the goal is unreachable. The issue of diversity, however, has made it to the agendas of the ASNE and the Radio-Television News Directors Foundation (RTNDF) in ways that might make the Hutchins and Kerner authors feel some optimism. While the ASNE retools and refocuses "Goals 2000," the RTNDF has published its *Minority Recruitment Directory* to help women and ethnic minorities find work in broadcast newsrooms. Each organization has made some effort to monitor and adjust the way it reports on people who are not white men. As the nation grows ever more diverse, with an ever more complex truth to tell, such efforts are a crucial step toward journalism that is more ethical.

References: Asian American Journalists Association. 26 December 1996. Online information. World Wide Web: http://www.aaja.org/.

Entman, Robert. 1994. "Representation and Reality in the Portrayal of Blacks on Network Television News." *Journalism Quarterly* (Autumn): 517.

Gardenswartz, Lee, and Anita Rowe. 1994. *Diverse Teams at Work: Capitalizing on the Power of Diversity*. New York: Irwin, 32.

Kerner Commission. 1968. *Report of the National Advisory Commission on Civil Disorders*. New York: New York Times Company, 366.

Liebler, Carol. 1994. "How Race and Gender Affect Journalists' Autonomy." *Newspaper Research Journal* (Summer): 127.

Images and Stereotypes

Paul Martin Lester

The list is endless and always injurious: African Americans play sports. Latinos are gang members. Native Americans are alcoholics. Wheelchair-using individuals are helpless. Gay men are effeminate. Lesbians wear their hair short. Older adults need constant care. Anglos are racists or rednecks. Homeless people are drug addicts. These and other stereotypes are perpetuated by visual messages presented in print, television, motion pictures, and computers—the media (Lester, 1996).

The media stereotype because humans stereotype. Since our brains naturally classify what we see, we cannot help but notice the differences in physical attributes between one person and another. As with the printing term used to describe multiple stampings from a single mold, a stereotype is a shorthand way to describe a person with collective, rather than unique, characteristics. It is easier and quicker for a photojournalist to take a picture of an angry African American during a riot than to take the time to explore in words and pictures the underlying social problems that are responsible for the civil disturbance.

Because visual messages are products of our sense of sight, pictures are highly emotional objects that have long-lasting staying power within the grayest regions of our brain. As Walter Lippmann wrote in his 1965 book *Public Opinion*, "Whether right or wrong,...imagination is shaped by the pictures seen.... Consequently, they lead to stereotypes that are hard to shake."

The media messages that stereotype individuals by their concentrations, frequencies, and omissions become a part of our long-term cultural memory. One of the chief reasons for this phenomena is that the media typically portray members of diverse cultural groups within specific content categories—usually crime, entertainment, and sports—and almost never within general interest, business, education, health, and religious content categories (Lester 1995, 380–394). Such stereotypical coverage is a concern because history has shown that stereotyping leads to scapegoating, which leads to discrimination, which leads to segregation, which leads to physical abuse, which leads to state-sponsored genocide.

The Law

Although there is little in case law concerned with visual stereotyping, an argument can be made that the false-light branch of privacy law may be an outlet for those who feel they have been harmed by a negative stereotype.

Although nowhere in the U.S. Constitution is the word *privacy* even mentioned, the First Amendment protects to a great extent what a media organization can publish (Christians, Fackler, and Rotzoll 1995, 115–131). The amendment, however, does not offer absolute protection. Unfortunately for journalists, neither do the courts. Civil courts hear complaints from individuals regarding violations of privacy. The result can be a tort—a civil wrong against another that results in injury. Because a privacy tort happens against a single individual (not a group), journalists sued in civil courts are subject to the whims of jurors and judges and may be forced to pay damages to a wronged party.

Courts have recognized four major branches of privacy law: (1) unreasonable intrusion, (2) unreasonable revelation of private facts, (3) unreasonable placement of another person in a false light before the public, and (4) misappropriation of a person's name or likeness (Christians, Fackler, and Rotzoll 1995, 115).

For this discussion, the false-light provision is the most appropriate. It is a violation of the false-light branch to place another before the public if the false light in which the other was placed would be highly offensive to a reasonable person and if the actor had knowledge of or acted in reckless disregard of the falsity of the publicized matter and the false light in which the other would be placed (*Photographers' Guide to Privacy* 1994, 4).

False light includes embellishment (adding false material) and distortion (arranging images or words to give a false impression). For example, in Maryland a false-light claim was lodged by a man whose photograph was used to illustrate an article about murders, drug abuses, and economic hardships of teenagers in Baltimore. Meanwhile, in Michigan, a woman shown walking down a Detroit street successfully sued a television station that aired her image in connection with a story about prostitution in the area (*Photographers' Guide to Privacy* 1994, 13–14).

The Photographers' Guide to Privacy, published by the Reporters Committee for Freedom of the Press, outlines the variations of privacy laws for each U.S. state. Although false light is invoked the fewest times against journalists in the cases reviewed for the publication, it is nevertheless an area of law that can result in a judgment for an individual pictured as an unflattering stereotype.

The Issues

Most media experts come up with several reasons why the media stereotype: advertisers that demand quickly interpreted shortcut pictures, lazy or highly pressured reporters who do not take or have the time to explore issues within their multifaceted and complex contexts, limited diversity in news organizations, journalists' presumption that readers and viewers only accept images of diverse members within a limited range of content categories, and—regrettably and often denied—culturism. *Culturism* is a term that describes the belief that one cultural group—whether based on ethnicity, economics, education, etc.—is somehow better or worse than some other cultural group. Culturism may explain why mainstream media are slow to cover human catastrophes in remote sections of the world such as Rwanda, Somalia, and South-Central Los Angeles.

Cases

Since its beginning in 1971, the Minnesota News Council has received over 1,560 complaints against news outlets about coverage that raises ethical concerns. Of the more than 100 complaints reviewed by a hearing of 12 members from the media and 12 from the public, 9 complaints have involved issues of racism, sexism, and stereotyping. The Minnesota News Council is an organization that "promotes media fairness through public accountability" (Minnesota News Council 1997). One of its services is to conduct public hearings after complaints of media coverage are received from individuals or organizations. Although the council has no authority in its actions, and those who bring a complaint must waive the right to sue, its purpose is "to help the public and the media create a moral force for fairness."

Complaints relating to images included news sources who thought they were misquoted, resulting in racist or derogatory statements that were untrue; a newspaper that failed to give adequate coverage in a sex discrimination lawsuit; and a newspaper survey that was thought to be biased by the way the questions were worded. Three of the cases—case numbers 35, 39, and 75—involved visual material.

Case 35 A high priest of the Church of Wicca (also known as the religion of witchcraft) complained that "...artwork, photographs, and articles perpetuated negative and erroneous stereotypes about the occult." Included with the two articles was a picture of an ex-occultist, Conlith Christensen, in artwork illustrating a book on satanic practices "depicting demons torturing a man." The complaint was upheld as it was the opinion that "...the placement of the photograph of Christensen was unfair and misleading." The layout appeared to associate her with the book account and the satanic activities described in it

Case 39 Ben Sternberg, a professional boxing promoter complained that "the use of inflammatory graphics...falsely implied...that he was a racist and somewhat of a Mafia figure." His complaint was upheld as it was concluded that "...a photograph of Sternberg at ringside wearing dark glasses created the impression that he was some sort of a sinister 'Mafia figure.'"

Case 75 A Sunday edition of the Minneapolis *Star Tribune* featured an eight-page story with "25 photographs on teenage pregnancy, told as the personal story of one teenager, Makela Scott, a 16-year-old Black girl...." The United Black Front claimed that the story "[is] unfair both to the young girl and to the Black community, and, indeed, promotes racial prejudice...

[because it] uses photographs which are insensitive to community values...."
Although the grievance was denied by the council, the newspaper's managing editor Tim McGuire noted, "We listened to complaints that we don't present Blacks in a positive light often enough and that we don't show Blacks just being average folks. We have raised consciousness among our staffers on that issue and have made some policy changes, such as urging our people to roam the minorities of our communities more to look for news and photo opportunities" (Minnesota News Council 1997).

Perhaps these cases would have had successful hearings in a court of law had the complainants used the false-light provision of privacy law.

Looking Ahead

Because most readers and viewers only have contact with those from diverse cultural groups through media representations, editors should make an assessment of the pictorial coverage of underrepresented groups for their own newspaper or television station. If biases are found, photographers, reporters, and editors should attend sensitivity training workshops with members of the public in order to promote fairer and more balanced images. Members of diverse cultural groups should be depicted in media presentations in everyday life situations.

References: Christians, Clifford G., Mark Fackler, and Kim B. Rotzoll. 1995. *Media Ethics and Moral Reasoning.* White Plains, NY: Longman, 115–131.

Lester, Paul Martin. 1995. *Visual Communication Images with Messages.* Belmont, CA: Wadsworth.

———, editor. 1996. *Images That Injure: Pictorial Stereotypes in the Media.* Westport, CT: Praeger.

Lippmann, Walter. 1965. *Public Opinion.* New York: The Free Press.

Minnesota News Council. 1997. Online information. World Wide Web: http://www.mtn.org/-newscncl/.

Photographers' Guide to Privacy. 1994. Arlington, VA: Reporters Committee for Freedom of the Press, 4, 13–14.

The Free Press and Democracy
Freedom of Speech and Press
Martin Gunderson

Journalism flourishes only when there is freedom of speech, but journalism is not the only reason for protecting speech. Scholars have offered a variety of justifications, although they tend to be of three main types. One is that free speech is necessary to find truth. John Stuart Mill (1859) argued that we cannot be certain the opinion we suppress is false, and even if it is false, it may contain a portion of the truth or at least be useful in challenging those who have true opinions to defend them and thereby make their beliefs more vital. The underlying assumption of the truth argument is that there is a kind of marketplace of ideas in which true opinions will eventually prevail. In the United States, the most prominent defender of this justification of free speech was Oliver Wendell Holmes (*Abrams v. U.S.*, 250 U.S. 616: 1919) (Holmes dissenting).

This justification has been criticized on the grounds that we do not have a genuine marketplace of ideas because the powerful dominate the forums of expression so that little genuine competition takes place (Baker 1989, chap. 1). Also, the truth justification is narrower than current First Amendment interpretations that protect political demonstration and artistic expression whether or not they are attempts to state truths.

A second prominent justification is that free speech is necessary for a democracy (Fiss 1996, chaps. 1 and 2; Meiklejohn 1960, 27, 35–36). Free speech enables citizens to have enough information to make appropriate decisions and allows exposure of government activity so that citizens can take corrective action. It also enables citizens to attempt to persuade one another. Some have argued that this rationale especially emphasizes freedom of the press, since the press functions like a fourth branch of government to check the operation and expose abusive practices of the judicial, legislative, and executive branches (Baker 1989, chap. 10). This defense of free speech is broader than the truth defense in that it covers such activities as political parades and artistic expression insofar as they can be seen as influencing democratic processes.

The democracy argument presupposes both political equality and the availability to citizens of relevant information and appropriate diversity of views. These presuppositions could be undermined by powerful individuals dominating the forums of communication (Sunstein 1993, 20–21). In this way the democracy defense is vulnerable to the same concerns as the truth defense. The truth and democracy justifications will be ineffectual to the extent that a few major players control the media.

Defenders of the truth or democracy rationale could reply that although there is not currently a genuine marketplace of ideas or sufficient equality among speakers, it is a goal worth seeking through regulations such as guaranteeing access for those whose voice is currently not heard (Fiss 1996, chaps. 1 and 2; Sunstein 1993, chap. 2).

The third prominent justification is that free speech is necessary for individual flourishing and individual autonomy. People benefit from using their capacities, which sometimes requires freedom of speech. Communicating with others helps one to develop understanding (Schauer 1982, 54–55). It has also been argued that individual autonomy requires that individuals decide for themselves what their beliefs will be and what choices they will make, including the choice of whether to obey the law. If the government restricts freedom of speech, then these individuals will not have the information they need to make wise choices. Moreover, the freedom to express oneself is a part of one's individual autonomy (Schauer 1982, 67–72).

The defense of free speech based on individual autonomy and individual flourishing is much broader than the previous two defenses. Forms of expression having nothing to do with truth or democratic discourse may be important to individuals, in which case political equality is less important. Critics claim it does not provide a justification of a principle of free speech that differs from a general defense of liberty (Schauer 1982, 56–58). They also object that it is not clear why individual autonomy should be more valued than the sorts of social welfare considerations that might require restricting freedom of speech (Schauer 1982, 55). In particular, the individual autonomy rationale may sanction speech such as hate speech and obscenity, which actually impoverish democratic discourse.

The justification of free speech is important in determining both the strength and scope of the right. Strength is a matter of what, if any, competing consideration can override the right to free speech. In its strongest version, the right to freedom of speech is absolute. In its weakest version, the freedom of speech is simply one value that must be balanced against other values. In the middle, one could adopt a weighted balancing approach or a category approach in which some kinds of speech are given more protection than others. Scope is a matter of what sorts of speech are protected by the right to free speech. Typically, the stronger the right, the more narrow the scope (Schauer 1982, 134).

The U.S. Supreme Court has adopted a middle ground in interpreting the free speech and press clause of the First Amendment. While in some early cases the Supreme Court adopted a weighted balancing approach, its more recent cases use a category approach in which some speech is given more protection. At the core of First Amendment protection is political speech, but other types of speech are given full protection as well. Fully protected speech includes entertainment (even nonobscene nude dancing) as well as political, philosophical, and religious speech (*Schad v. Borough of Mount Ephron*, 452 U.S. 61, 65: 1981; *Southeastern Promotions, Ltd. v. Conrad*, 420 U.S. 546: 1975). Government restrictions on the content or subject matter of fully protected speech are constitutional only if there is a compelling state interest for the restrictions and they are drawn as narrowly as possible (*Board of Airport Comm'rs of Los Angeles v. Jews for Jesus*, 482 U.S. 569, 572–573: 1987; *Boos v. Berry*, 485 U.S. 312, 321: 1988; *Sable Communications of Cal. v. FCC*, 492 U.S. 115, 126: 1989). Some other categories of speech are given significant protection, though not as much protection as entertainment, political, philosophical, and religious speech. For example, the content of defamatory speech may be restricted, although the Supreme Court has adopted various First Amendment safeguards. Public figures who bring defamation suits must show actual malice in the sense of reckless disregard of the truth or knowing falsity (*New York Times v. Sullivan*, 376 U.S. 254: 1964). Similar limitations are applied in the case of privacy suits that rest on publication placing plaintiffs in a false light (*Time, Inc. v. Hill*, 385 U.S. 374: 1967). (*See* chapter 5 for specific defamation and privacy cases.)

At the other extreme, the Supreme Court has interpreted the First Amendment to permit significant content regulation of speech that contains a clear and present danger of imminent lawless action, fighting words, obscenity, and/or false or deceptive advertising. The major concern with regulating speech that is not given significant First Amendment protection is the difficulty of designing regulations that are not so vague or overly broad that they also restrict protected speech. This difficulty can be seen in the recent controversy over hate speech. While many would argue that hate speech should not be given constitutional protection, colleges and universities have had a hard time drawing regulations that are not overly broad or vague, and several hate speech codes have been struck down by the courts (*John Doe v. University of Michigan,* 721 F. Supp. 852: E.D. Mich. 1989). For example, a loosely worded regulation designed to forbid racial epithets directed at individuals may also restrict the academic expression of unpopular racial views.

Such restrictions on the types of speech protected by the First Amendment make sense with regard to the democratic and truth justifications. It is difficult to see how obscenity, fighting words, and deceptive advertising contribute to democratic discourse or truth. These types of expression might be defensible, however, if the right to free speech is justified in terms of individual autonomy.

The strong protection of speech from content-based regulation contrasts with the lesser standard of protection for content-neutral regulations based on the time, place, and manner of the speech. Such regulations do not violate the First Amendment so long as they are not based on the content or subject of the speech, they further a significant state interest, and they provide for alternative forums (*Metromedia, Inc. v. City of San Diego,* 453 U.S. 490, 516: 1981; *Virginia Pharmacy Board v. Virginia Citizens Consumer Council,* 425 U.S. 748, 771: 1976).

The different justifications for freedom of speech can lead to different policies regarding access to the media as well as to differences over what sort of speech should be protected. Consider the Federal Communication Commission's (FCC) Fairness Doctrine, which was in place for roughly 30 years before it was repealed by the FCC in 1987. The Fairness Doctrine required broadcasters to provide coverage of vitally important controversial issues and to provide reasonable opportunity for the presentation of contrasting viewpoints. The doctrine was upheld by the Supreme Court, in *Red Lion Broadcasting Co. v. FCC* (395 U.S. 367: 1969), on the grounds that the number of broadcast frequencies were limited and that the airwaves are public. When the FCC abandoned the Fairness Doctrine, it did so in part on the grounds that new technologies such as cable and satellite television had greatly expanded channel availability and diversity in programming.

Attempts to extend similar fairness regulations to the print media were struck down as unconstitutional by the Supreme Court's ruling in *Miami Herald v. Tornillo* (418 U.S. 241: 1974). The majority argued that requiring access for diverse viewpoints would interfere with newspapers' editorial discretion. They also reasoned that having more abundant print media outlets reduces the need for regulation.

Debate over the Fairness Doctrine did not end in 1987. Defenders of the democracy justification continue to claim that fairness regulations are important to encourage the diversity of viewpoints necessary for democratic discourse (Fiss 1996, chaps. 1 and 2; Sunstein 1993, chap. 2). The regulations can also be justified in terms of providing a more adequate marketplace of ideas. While some would argue that technological developments such as cable television and computer networks provide sufficient diversity, defenders of the democracy argument claim that programming diversity is insufficient because many people still do not have such technology (Sunstein 1993, 67–77).

The individual autonomy justification provides a reason for not regulating access to the media because access and fairness regulations restrict the editorial autonomy of broadcasters. If *Red Lion Broadcasting*'s support of the Fairness Doctrine is most easily justified in terms of a democracy rationale of free speech, *Miami Herald*'s rejection of the Fairness Doctrine for print media is most easily supported on the basis of individual autonomy.

Issues regarding access also arise in a quite different context. Effective journalism requires freedom to engage in news gathering as well as freedom from restrictions on speech. The Supreme Court has not, however, interpreted the First Amendment to provide a right to engage in news gathering, with the exception of a right to attend trials (*Press-Enterprise v. Superior Court*, 478 U.S. 1: 1986; *Richmond Newspapers v. Virginia*, 448 U.S. 555: 1980). (*See* chapter 5 for further discussion of media access to information from the government.) Such news gathering rights that exist have been created by statutes such as the Federal Freedom of Information Act (5 U.S.C., sec. 552), the Federal Government in the Sunshine Act (5 U.S.C., sec. 552b), and their state equivalents. The statutes have exemptions to protect privacy, however, and must be interpreted with care to balance the right to free speech against the need to protect private information in government files. (*See* Privacy and Journalism.)

How conflicts between the various justifications of free speech play out in the future will depend in part on technological development. If cable television with public access channels and networks such as C-Span and CNN becomes more widely available and if journalists make use of online computer services that become widely available and more interactive, then access and fairness regulations may not be needed. In that case, the justifications based on democracy, the search for truth, and individual autonomy may be, at least in part, complementary.

References: Baker, C. Edwin. 1989. *Human Liberty and Freedom of Speech*. New York and Oxford: Oxford University Press.
Fiss, Owen M. 1996. *Liberalism Divided: Freedom of Speech and the Many Uses of State Power*. Boulder, CO: Westview Press.

Meiklejohn, Alexander. 1960. *Political Freedom. The Constitutional Powers of the People*. Westport, CT: Greenwood Press.

Mill, John Stuart. 1859. *On Liberty*. Edited by Elizabeth Rapaport, 1978. Indianapolis: Hackett Publishing.

Schauer, Frederick. 1982. *Free Speech: A Philosophical Enquiry*. Cambridge: Cambridge University Press.

Sunstein, Cass R. 1993. *Democracy and the Problem of Free Speech*. New York and Toronto: Macmillan.

Privacy and Journalism

Martin Gunderson

The legal enforcement of privacy rights is a mixed blessing for journalists. On the one hand, it sometimes limits news gathering and publishing. In such cases privacy conflicts with freedom of speech. On the other hand, it sometimes enables journalists to protect sources and work product. When this type of protection occurs, privacy supports freedom of speech.

Federal and state statutes protect government-held private data and create exceptions to freedom of information acts and open meeting laws to protect privacy. Most states also protect privacy through tort law. Torts are injuries or harms, other than those arising from contracts, that create legal liability for damages. The four major privacy torts are (1) disclosure of private facts, (2) placement of another in a false light, (3) intrusion into solitude, and (4) appropriation of name or likeness for commercial purposes. The first three are of special concern to journalists, while the fourth is of concern primarily to advertisers. Although the torts have different elements, the plaintiff's consent, either explicit or implicit, is a defense against all of them.

Perhaps the most obvious privacy tort is disclosure of private facts. The plaintiff must show that the defendant publicized private information about the plaintiff that a reasonable person would find highly offensive and that is not of legitimate public concern (i.e., not newsworthy) (American Law Institute 1977, sec. 652D). Although the U.S. Supreme Court has not dealt with the disclosure of purely private facts, it did hold that the publication of rape victims' names is not a violation of privacy when the names are legally obtained from court or police records (*The Florida Star v. B.J.F.*, 491 U.S. 524; 1989).

A plaintiff may also complain that published information placed him or her in a false light. The plaintiff must show that the publication placed him or her in a false light that would be highly offensive to a reasonable person under the same circumstances and that the defendant knew that the publication was false or acted in reckless disregard of the truth (American Law Institute 1977, sec. 652E). (*See* the discussion of *Time, Inc. v. Hill* in chapter 5.)

In both of these torts a crucial concept is legitimate public interest, which unfortunately is difficult to define. If legitimate public interest is characterized simply as what the public takes an interest in, then tort law does not offer adequate protection of privacy, since the public often takes an interest in private matters. If, on the other hand, it is interpreted as having significant value for the public, then tort law offers at least some protection for privacy, but the concept of legitimacy is so vague that the court's interpretation may be arbitrary and difficult to predict. These problems are compounded by the fact that the courts often rely on the interpretation of journalists in determining what is to count as newsworthy.

A third privacy tort involves intrusion into private places. The plaintiff must show that the defendant intentionally intruded upon the plaintiff's solitude, seclusion, or private affairs in a manner that a reasonable person would find highly offensive (American Law Institute 1977, sec. 652B). This tort poses a problem for investigative reporters who may need to use subterfuge to enter private areas in order to obtain information needed for their stories. In *Dietemann v. Time, Inc.* (449 F.2d 245: 9th Cir. 1971), for instance, two reporters who pretended to be patients in order to expose a medical quack working in a home office were held liable for the tort of intrusion. Tort law, however, does not restrict journalists from photographing people and recording what they do in public so long as the journalists do not harass their subjects (*Galella v. Onassis*, 353 F. Supp. 196: S.D.N.Y. 1972, aff'd in part and rev'd in part, 487 F.2d 986: 2d Cir. 1973).

In the fourth privacy tort, the plaintiff must show that the defendant appropriated the plaintiff's name or likeness for the defendant's benefit (American Law Institute 1977, sec. 652C). This tort does not, however, include merely using a plaintiff's name or likeness in a magazine story even if the motive is to sell more magazines, since this would unduly restrict freedom of speech. The tort, therefore, is of more concern to advertisers than journalists.

Privacy torts have been criticized because of their conceptual vagueness. Terms like *reasonable person, legitimate public interest, private affairs,* and *offensiveness* make it difficult for a person to predict whether free speech or privacy would weigh more heavily if the matter were to be judged by a court. The problem is that there is not sufficient agreement on the underlying norms that give these concepts meaning (Bezanson 1992, 1158–1163).

The conflict between freedom of speech and privacy also occurs in the context of statutes designed to provide access to records that may be important for news gathering. While there is no constitutional guarantee of access to documents or public meetings, various state and federal statutory rights of access have been created with freedom of information acts and various sunshine laws. The federal Freedom of Information Act (FOIA) provides a right of access to documents and records in the hands of government agencies (5 U.S.C., sec. 552). There are, however, nine exemptions, two of which concern privacy. Subsection 6 exempts from disclosure "personnel and medical files and similar files the disclosure of which would constitute a clearly unwarranted invasion of personal privacy." Subsection 7(C) exempts from disclosure "records or information compiled for law enforcement purposes, but only to the extent that the production of such law enforcement records or information ... could reasonably be expected to constitute an unwarranted invasion of personal privacy...." Under FOIA these exemptions permit, but do not require, the government to refuse to release private information. The Federal Privacy Act of 1974 makes them mandatory, although there are exceptions. In addition, the act gives people access to their personal records upon request and limits the type of information an agency may collect and the manner in which it may be collected. The Supreme Court has held that in determining whether a disclosure of private information is justified, the individual's right to privacy must be balanced against the FOIA's policy of subjecting government agencies to public scrutiny (*U.S. Dept. of Justice v. Reporters Committee for Freedom of the Press*, 489 U.S. 749, 772: 1989; *U.S. Dept. of State v. Ray*, 502 U.S. 164: 1991).

Access to information enhances the role of the press and the effectiveness of speech in general whether free speech is justified in terms of producing truth, making democracy possible, or enhancing individual well-being and autonomy. (*See* Freedom of Speech and Press for more detail on these justifications.) The main objection to access laws is based on privacy. Since the government collects a great deal of information about individuals and private organizations, a concern with freedom of information laws is that they might threaten privacy, notwithstanding the exemptions.

In considering the conflict between free speech and privacy, the underlying philosophical and policy issue is how to balance the right to privacy with the right to free speech. Such balance requires a consideration of the various reasons why privacy is thought to be important as well as the justifications given for freedom of speech. Most obviously, privacy protects us from the prejudice and intolerance of others. Privacy is also necessary for people to carry out various activities because it limits social pressure and coercion. If journalists were not able to protect the privacy of their sources, it would be difficult to gather information relevant to a range of important news stories. Privacy may even be essential to the formation of personal identity. It creates the space necessary for forming one's own thoughts and desires in a way that differentiates oneself from others (Bloustein 1984, 188; Goffman 1961, 3–48). Privacy also enables people to function as members of associations (e.g., families and groups of friends) that have a role in forming personal identity (Schoeman 1992, chaps. 1, 7, and 9).

The factors to be balanced also depend on the justifications of free speech. If free speech is justified in terms of enhancement of individual well-being or autonomy, then speech and privacy have, in part, the same justification. If, however, free speech is defended on the grounds that it leads to truth, the value of the truth gained by the violation of privacy must be weighed against the degree of harm done to the individual who claims his privacy has been violated. The value of seeking truth will grow insofar as it affects democratic choice and is a matter of legitimate public interest, but as this occurs, privacy protection afforded by the law will shrink.

The situation is more complex if free speech is defended on the grounds that it is necessary for democracy. Purely private information is not likely to be relevant to democratic discourse. When private information is relevant, it is arguable that it is of legitimate public interest and therefore should be given less protection. As was noted, however, it is difficult to specify the scope of legitimate interest with sufficient precision.

Privacy and free speech are not always competitors. Freedom of speech requires the protection of the journalist's work product and the identity of sources. If sources and work product cannot be protected, then an important source of information will be closed or limited to reporters.

The classic Supreme Court case on this subject is *Branzburg v. Hayes* (408 U.S. 665: 1972), in which Justice White writing for the majority held that the First Amendment provides no reporter's privilege against testifying before a grand jury about confidential sources. In a concurring opinion, Justice Powell stated that the Court must balance the duty of the citizen to testify against the requirements of freedom of the press. In his dissenting opinion, Justice Stewart offered a three-pronged test. To require a reporter to testify regarding confidential sources the state must (1) show that there is probable cause to believe the reporter has information that is clearly relevant to a specific law violation, (2) demonstrate that the information sought cannot be obtained by alternative means less likely to undercut the First Amendment, and (3) "demonstrate a compelling and overriding interest in the information." Most federal courts have interpreted *Branzburg* narrowly as applying only to criminal cases and have adopted a balancing approach for civil cases, sometimes even adopting a version of Justice Stewart's test. They have thereby created a qualified reporter's privilege. (*See* chapter 5 for further discussion of *Branzburg*.)

The privilege does not, however, extend to defamation cases in which a reporter is the defendant. Since a defamation plaintiff who is a public figure must prove reckless or knowing falsity, it would not be possible for the plaintiff to establish his or her case without testimony of the reporter regarding how the story was researched and written (*Herbert v. Lando*, 441 U.S. 153: 1979).

The majority of states have also adopted shield laws protecting reporters from testifying about their sources. Most of these statutes apply to news media employees and exclude freelance writers and academics. A few, however, cover anyone who gathers information for dissemination to the public. Some of them protect only the confidentiality of reporters' sources, while others cover the work product as a whole. Although there is no federal shield law, there is at least some federal protection. The Department of Justice has guidelines for when journalists can be subpoenaed. The attorney general must approve all subpoenas issued to journalists on the basis of the following principles: there must be reasonable grounds to believe that the information is relevant and essential, alternative sources of the information must be sought, the subpoena must be narrowly drawn, and care must be taken to avoid claims of harassment (28 C.F.R., sec. 50.10).

Apart from subpoenas to testify or produce documents, journalists also need to worry about search warrants. The Federal Privacy Protection Act of

1980 strictly limits the circumstances under which search warrants can be issued to obtain a reporter's work product. The state must show that the materials relate to a crime that has been or is being committed by the journalist or that the seizure is necessary to prevent death or serious injury. Documents other than the journalist's work product are protected to a lesser extent (42 U.S.C., sec. 2000).

In the future, computer databases with wide accessibility, coupled with private information collected by the government and sometimes available through freedom of information acts, will increasingly raise troubling issues for the protection of privacy while providing opportunities for enterprising journalists. How the scope of privacy and free speech is determined will depend ultimately on which justifications of free speech and privacy prevail as well as on the technological developments that provide greater access to private information.

References: American Law Institute. 1977. *Restatement of the Law, Second: Torts*. St. Paul, MN: American Law Institute Publishers.

Bezanson, Randall P. 1992. "The Right to Privacy Revisited: Privacy, News, and Social Change, 1890–1990." *California Law Review* 80 (October): 1133–1175.

Bloustein, Edward J. 1984. "Privacy as an Aspect of Human Dignity." In Ferdinand David Schoeman, editor. *Philosophical Dimensions of Privacy*. Cambridge: Cambridge University Press, 156–202.

Code of Federal Regulations. 1996. Washington, DC: United States Government Printing Office.

Goffman, Erving. 1961. *Asylums*. New York: Doubleday.

Schoeman, Ferdinand David. 1992. *Privacy and Social Freedom*. Cambridge: Cambridge University Press.

United States Code, 1994 Edition. 1995. Washington, DC: United States Government Printing Office.

Journalism Ethics and the Coverage of Elections

Marty Linsky

Throughout American history, the media have been part of the election story. Until the late nineteenth century, most American newspapers were partisan organs, published to further the aims of particular candidates, issues, parties, and ideologies. With the emergence of the ethos of an independent press, the role and responsibility of news organizations in the electoral process have understandably undergone considerable and continual revision.

The relationship between the press and the election process is not independent of the constantly evolving relationships between the media and other institutions, or of broader societal trends. Given the centrality of elections to the nurturing and maintenance of democracy, ethical issues around campaign coverage take on a special significance. These questions, however, are not confined to national elections. They are just as relevant and as applicable to a local school board contest as they are to a presidential campaign. Furthermore, while the dilemmas are sharpened in election coverage, they are not fundamentally different questions than those that a news organization must consider when covering politics and public affairs between election cycles.

There is one core threshold ethical question distinctively about election coverage: "Do the media have a responsibility for the nurturing and maintenance of the election process?" Most of the microethical decisions involving reporting on campaigns flow from the way a news organization implicitly or explicitly answers this question.

What is the news organization's responsibility to the electoral process itself, as an institution of democracy? The media continue to wrestle with this one, and do not speak with one voice (Linsky 1996, 7–9). On the one end are those First Amendment purists who say that an independent press has no responsibility to the institutions of democracy, only a responsibility to report freely and independently what is happening to them. For these folks, a press that does that is by definition fulfilling its democratic responsibilities. This view recalls the old line attributed, perhaps apocryphally, to Werner Von Braun, "I send the bombs up. Where they come down is someone else's business."

Others in news organizations worry more about where the bombs land. Their view is that everyone in a democracy has an obligation to nurture and maintain democratic institutions; the media, which play a central role in covering elections and making government both transparent and accountable, have a special obligation. The implications of this view are considerable.

Such a view means, to take an obvious example, worrying about voter turnout and thinking about what coverage would increase citizen participation. It means making judgments about what a good, democratic election campaign would be like, and then using their power to try to make it happen. It probably means providing more than typical coverage to lesser candidates—those behind in the polls and those from minor political parties. It most surely means breaking the convention of not doing repetitive stories, by republishing issue-oriented pieces about where the candidates stand. In short, it means taking an active and aggressive responsibility for the quality of the election campaign on the theory that ensuring good democratic elections is too important a task to be left to self-interested politicians.

Once a newspaper, radio station, or television station decides that it has some obligations to nurture sound democratic elections, it must face a series of dilemmas relating to coverage, but all of these dilemmas have analogs in nonelection coverage as well. Whether covering elections, government, politics, business, or any other aspect of public life, news organizations struggle with the tension between the aspiration of objectivity and distance, and the reality of impact and consequences. In thinking about election coverage, the media must resolve five basic strategic questions, each of which has ethical implications. The first is about the allocation of resources.

Bodies, Space, and Time

The news organization must decide on resource allocation. How much money to spend, on what, and with what commitment to publication space or broadcasting time are all issues that will have considerable consequences for the nature of the campaigns. It will help determine whether lesser-known candidates can raise money and otherwise get their messages out. It will determine whether the campaign will be experienced by the voters for months or only for weeks. It will answer the question of whether reporters are going to specialize and build up expertise on certain campaigns, candidates, issues, or parties, or whether coverage will shift from reporter to reporter, with candidates not knowing who is going to cover them next. It will also signal to the news consumers whether they can expect regular coverage in the same place or at the same time, or whether coverage will be episodic.

The second strategic issue is also about allocation of resources but focuses on the nature of the coverage. It is generally framed as covering the horse race versus the issues.

Horse Race versus Issues

Like most of the issues of campaign coverage, how much space and time to allocate to the horse race aspect—who is ahead and who is behind—and how much to allocate to the issues has its roots in a basic ethical journalistic dilemma: do you give consumers what they want or what they need? In this case, there is usually a great desire on the part of the politically interested consumers at least to find out about the horse race aspects of the campaign. This type of information not only involves who is ahead but also the campaign strategies and decisions. Such a consumer demand is often an incentive for news organizations to invest heavily in their own polling so they can have exclusive snapshots of how the race is going and not have to report on competitors' or candidates' polls. As clear as is the demand for horse race coverage, equally clear is the view that what people need in order to be informed voters is an understanding of the issues and the candidates' views on them. Do you give them what they want or what they need? Do you tease them with the commercially powerful poll on the front page and hope that will engage them enough to read the issue coverage inside, or do you bury the poll, as a kind of dessert for those who have waded through the issue coverage to find it? Does substantial coverage of the horse race devalue the process and increase cynicism about campaigns or increase interest, however shallow and uninformed? If there is more coverage of the issues, what issues do you cover? That brings us to the strategic question for news organizations about the nature of the campaign conversation itself.

Who Sets the Agenda?

Looking at the post–World War II period, during the 1950s and 1960s, the governing press ethic was to cover campaigns in a largely passive way, reporting what candidates had to say when the candidates said it. The politicians rarely complained about the quality of coverage, although since politics was much more of a participatory rather than a spectator sport than it is today, there were concerns about not enough coverage.

Watergate and the Vietnam War changed all that, bringing to public affairs journalism not only a new kind of journalist, more educated and more aggressive, but also a new ethic of campaign coverage. This ethic involved the press assuming some responsibility for deciding what the politicians should talk about during the campaign. The change is not surprising. Coverage of Vietnam, Watergate, and the civil rights movement as well could be understood to indicate that the press was slowly and reluctantly, but steadfastly, moving toward pursuing what it thought was important regardless of the views of those in high political office. Election coverage in the 1970s and 1980s was characterized by media initiatives to impact the campaign agenda. There were many manifestations of this new strategy: long takeouts on issues in newspapers, snap quizzes of candidates on live television, and news organizations' sponsorship of debates. The politicians, at first caught unaware, became more aggressive themselves in developing techniques to keep control of the campaign conversation. In the 1990s, some news organizations, motivated by a combination of commercial and ethical considerations, developed a new response to the agenda-setting dilemma: Bring in the voters. "Citizen-based campaign coverage" is the generic label for a range of coverage experiments carried out in the 1992, 1994, and 1996 election cycles. The idea was to broaden the campaign conversation to go beyond journalists and candidates and include average voters. News organizations, sometimes working in cross-media partnerships, devised several techniques, such as polling on issues and then asking candidates to respond to the issues voters were most interested in, or having average voters ask questions of the candidates directly, that were aimed at engaging more readers, viewers, and listeners in the process. These techniques presumably created a better-informed electorate and a higher turnout. Apart from questions of how to measure success, these experiments met with a mixed response from some candidates, who felt that under this system they were not able to get their message out. The partnerships among news organizations came under particular attack, with some candidates feeling that the result was homogeneous coverage, which shut out certain issues, ideas, and perspectives.

Who should set the agenda? Why should the media not leave it to the politicians to decide what the issues are going to be, report what they say, and let the voters decide? Do the news organizations have an obligation to try to force the candidates to address issues that voters or the news organizations themselves deem to be most important? That question is one of accountability, whether the news organization is going to take responsibility to try to ensure that someone's version of the "most important" issues are addressed by the candidates.

The question of taking on that responsibility leads to the third strategic issue, namely, whether to leave it to the other candidates, their supporters, and interest groups to hold the candidates accountable for the veracity of what they say or to do it for them.

Accountability: Ad Watch, Fact Checking, and Consistency Mavens

Taking on the task of holding candidates accountable is a huge responsibility. It has the virtue of having a patina of objectivity and of pushing the candidates to a higher level of internal scrutiny before they go forward with facts or allegations. Like most of the strategies under discussion here, however, it takes away from other candidates and interest groups the opportunity to make those facts and allegations part of the core dialogue of the campaign. News organizations have been experimenting with three types of accountability mechanisms. The most visible are ad watches. News organizations cover the campaign ads, assessing their accuracy and their probity. With most of campaign budgets going into advertising, paying some attention to the ads is a logical extension of coverage. Some news organizations have gone further, assigning reporters to assess the accuracy and consistency of speeches and then reporting on what they have found. This is, of course, one of those situations where only the bad news is news. If a candidate delivers the same message to the old folks' home as to the baby boomers' coffee klatch, and the facts, including the credit taking, are accurate, then there is no story. The prospect of getting into an argument with the local newspaper about a strategic inconsistency, a shading of the facts, or an exaggerated degree of credit taking is enough to make candidates be much more careful than they would be if they were not being watched so closely. Being untruthful or inconsistent is a double-barreled problem, for it not only undermines the message, but it also raises questions about the candidate's values and character.

The Character Issue

One of the most vexing strategic-ethical issues for news organizations is the extent to which they are going to be interested in or even seek out information about the candidates' character, personal values, lifestyle, and characteristics that are manifest in their private lives rather than in their public behavior. The presidencies of Lyndon Johnson, Richard Nixon, and Jimmy Carter all evidenced some flaws, which were conventionally attributed to personal qualities and characteristics that had not been adequately reported in their campaigns. So, it is not surprising that coverage of candidates' character subsequently became a growth industry in campaign coverage at all levels, but the issue is still open. Those favoring more of such coverage make two arguments: first, that a person's personal qualities and personality quirks affect their decision making, particularly under pressure. The nature of the people a candidate associates and feels comfortable with will influence priorities and perspectives. In short, the private and personal seeps into the public life.

Second, they say that we are electing a whole person, not just the public portion of a person, and that voters have a right to know how the candidate behaves in private, with family, free time, and oldest, dearest friends. These qualities are part of the reason people vote for or against a candidate, so the news organization has a responsibility to make them known.

The countervailing considerations are significant as well. Candidates often argue that coverage of family, personal finances, and charitable contributions is an invasion of privacy and discourages many people from running for office, people who are willing to subject their public record to the most intense and critical scrutiny but want to protect their family and friends. Some more disinterested observers suggest that it benefits both the public and democracy to preserve a zone of privacy for candidates and elected officials because everyone needs some time offstage in order to be a whole person. Keeping mental health might require the opportunity to relieve the pressure of public scrutiny from time to time.

The dilemmas for a news organization in thinking about campaign coverage are significant because elections are such a central aspect of the democratic process. Democracy cannot survive without the engagement of a critical mass of ordinary citizens. Like it or not, and Internet or not, the press is a primary mediating institution between the governors and the governed. How it thinks about and carries out its democratic responsibilities will have consequences far beyond rating points and circulation, but the right answers to the questions may be different for different news organizations in different circumstances in different times. The ethical responsibility may lie more in their sheer wrestling with these issues, in a thoughtful, deliberate, and visible way, than in whether they come down on one side or the other.

> Reference: Linsky, Marty. 1996. "Optimism, Pragmatism, and Journalism." In *The Poynter Report*. St. Petersburg, FL: Poynter Institute for Media Studies.

Morality and Professionalism
Journalistic Ethics and Ordinary Morality
Mike W. Martin
Like all professionals, journalists are guided by a role morality—the responsibilities, rights, ideals, and virtues especially germane to their role as professionals. How is this role morality related to ordinary morality, that is, to common moral standards that are more widely (if not universally) applicable to people in general? Is there a unique ethic for journalists that applies only to them? Or is there just one set of moral values that has particular implications when applied to the circumstances in which journalists work and that serves to establish and justify the particular moral standards applicable to them? More generally, how is journalism related to morality? Are the ideas of good (competent, excellent) journalists and good (morally decent, admirable)

persons largely unrelated, or do moral values partly define journalistic excellence? These questions draw us into the most theoretical aspects of journalistic ethics, but they also have practical implications.

The legal context for these issues is provided by the First Amendment, which prohibits restrictions on freedom of the press. This prohibition gives journalists sweeping legal protection in pursuing their work, although they are governed by laws against libel and slander. A legal right, however, does not automatically make actions "all right." Morally responsible journalism is a far richer idea than legally protected freedom of expression.

The most fundamental theoretical task concerning morally responsible journalism is to clarify how journalistic ethics is related to ordinary morality. In turn, that task requires clarifying the ideas of professional ethics, ordinary ethics, and morality itself. As applied to journalism, "professional ethics" might mean: (1) the discipline or activity of studying the moral issues raised in journalism, (2) the standards officially endorsed by the profession, especially those set forth in codes of ethics promulgated by professional societies, (3) the standards actually acted on by most journalists, or (4) the justified (valid) moral standards (duties, rights, virtues) that journalists ought to abide by. Similarly, "ordinary ethics" might mean: (1) the discipline or activity of studying moral issues in general, (2) the standards professed by groups or individuals, (3) the standards that groups or individuals actually act on, or (4) the justified moral standards that apply more widely than merely to journalists (Martin 1981).

The primary theoretical issue contrasts the fourth definitions: How do the justified moral standards that journalists ought to abide by relate to more widely applicable justified moral standards? Are valid journalistic standards implied and justified by general moral principles? Or do journalistic standards constitute a domain of their own, insulated from ordinary morality? More generally, how intimately should ordinary (justified) moral values permeate journalistic practice, and why?

Answers to these theoretical questions have practical implications concerning the moral psychology of professionals. For one thing, if journalists believe that their professional roles and standards are substantially isolated from wider morality, they may be more tempted to do things that the general public finds offensive, such as using deception and invading privacy when conducting investigations. Worse, they may lapse into thinking of ethics as entirely relative to the profit-driven demands of their particular organizations. They may also feel little personal accountability in terms of wider moral principles: "I was only doing my job and following orders."

From another angle, like all professionals, journalists may sometimes do things they find personally offensive or that threaten their integrity. This is the problem of "dirty hands": when does a professional role require or permit doing unsavory things that would not be acceptable outside the role? The ambiguities involved in identifying such actions are reflected in the two meanings of "compromise." When do journalists make reasonable compromises (desirable accommodations) within their organizations, and at what point have they compromised (betrayed) their integrity? Grasping how professional ethics relates to wider morality helps journalists maintain moral perspective in situations raising dirty-hands issues.

There is much disagreement and unclearness about the idea of a "special ethic" for journalists and for other professionals. All sides to the dispute grant that professionals have especially strong responsibilities, such as to maintain confidentiality, obtain informed consent, and zealously pursue the distinctive goods served by their profession. In various ways, these responsibilities intensify some ordinary moral requirements (for example, "keep confidences") and downplays others (for example, "respect privacy"). The controversy arises when these responsibilities, together with any accompanying rights and virtues, are labeled "special" and regarded as creating a moral universe not existing elsewhere. J. O. Urmson (1978, 65) finds this suggestion misleading and insists there is only one system of justified moral values combined with "fascinating problems about how journalists can best discharge their common human duties of honesty and sincerity." Anita Silvers (1985, 27), by contrast, finds the suggestion illuminating: "journalists' special obligations and concomitant rights derive from the special capacity of the institution of journalism to secure and disseminate truths." Stephen H. Daniel (1992, 55) goes further in suggesting that "the standards of ordinary morality and journalistic excellence embody characteristics of two different language games."

Perhaps both sides to this dispute make valid points. Professionals do have distinctive responsibilities and rights linked to the particular public goods that society authorizes them to pursue. At the same time, those responsibilities and rights do not exist in a vacuum. Urmson is correct to highlight continuities with the full spectrum of moral values by viewing professional responsibilities as implied by more widely applicable values. Silvers and Daniel are equally correct to accent discontinuities by emphasizing how professional standards depart in certain respects from parallel standards outside the profession. As an analogy, consider parental responsibilities and their accompanying rights and virtues. In a straightforward sense, parents have special responsibilities to care for their children; however, it might be more misleading than helpful to insist there is only the universal principle "If one becomes a parent, then one acquires new responsibilities." Parental ethics is not a world unto itself. Parental responsibilities are justified by wider moral principles, such as "Commitments generate responsibilities" and "One is accountable for the foreseeable effects of one's actions." Similarly, journalists acquire special responsibilities, but ones that are rooted in more widely applicable moral values.

Having invoked this parental analogy, we should note that ordinary morality is not limited to the ethics of everyday personal relationships such as family, friendship, and love. Instead, it refers to all nonprofessional morality and includes wider principles of social justice and community involvement. As Thomas Nagel (1978) suggests, the ethics of the professions is not derivable from the ethics of everyday personal relationships; both have a common foundation in wider moral values.

Needless to say, ordinary morality is notoriously difficult to characterize. The search for a comprehensive ethical theory that captures our most carefully considered and sound moral convictions is essentially the entire history of moral philosophy. The "our" belies enormous disagreement, and no one theory has won a consensus. Is it then futile to seek a foundation for journalistic ethics? Certainly we must fully acknowledge the legitimate differences in how reasonable persons interpret, weigh, and apply moral values to particular situations. We can embrace moral pluralism (the view that moral values are open to more than one valid interpretation) without lapsing into ethical relativism (the view that morality is reducible to whatever standards a group endorses). Nevertheless, the application of contrasting ethical theories promises a variety of interesting perspectives, which are largely mutually reinforcing and, when they clash, shed light on areas of disagreement among reasonable persons.

To cite a few contrasting viewpoints on the foundations of journalistic ethics, Edmund B. Lambeth (1992) applies duty ethics in identifying journalists' duties of truth telling, justice (fairness), respect for liberty, humaneness, and stewardship of community resources (most notably, a responsible free press). John Merrill (1990) defends a libertarian version of rights ethics that makes paramount the rights to freedom of the press. An opposing communitarian perspective, emphasizing what people owe to one another within communities, is set forth by Clifford G. Christians, John P. Ferre, and P. Mark Fackler (1993). Jeffrey Olen (1988) develops a social-contract framework centered on the idea of an implicit agreement between the media and the public it serves.

Of special interest, Stephen Klaidman and Tom L. Beauchamp (1987, 23–27) explore virtue ethics, presenting a compelling argument for understanding journalistic competence as entailing moral values—commitments to accuracy, fairness, and honesty. One cannot be a competent or excellent journalist unless one is honest in accurately reporting the facts, checking and citing sources, and avoiding bias. Also necessary for journalistic competence is fairness in presenting a balanced range of views. Competence is itself a moral virtue, in that without it one is liable to sloppiness and carelessness that can cause great damage to the reputations of individuals affected by what one writes. At least in these general terms, competent journalism is inseparable from morally responsible journalism. At the same time, we should balance Klaidman and Beauchamp's claims by acknowledging that zealousness in reporting and brilliance in writing are not necessarily accompanied by conscientiousness about the full range of moral values, such as respect for privacy and sensitivity to individuals' feelings. As in all areas of life, journalism influences a wide array of moral values, not all of which may be easily compatible. A journalist may be excellent in many respects while simultaneously being open to some moral criticisms.

Finally, there are structural questions about how ethical theories should be applied. Should they be applied to evaluate and justify specific actions, general responsibilities (such as those stated in codes of ethics), or the entire profession as a social institution? Deni Elliott (1986) notes that reference must be made to at least three things: general responsibilities to society shared by all media, specific commitments by news organizations, and individuals' integrity. Perhaps the most detailed answer to this question is worked out by David Luban (1988) with regard to legal ethics. Luban's account, which has implications for journalism, is too complex to fully explain here. Briefly, he suggests that ethical theories can be invoked to justify a social institution or practice, which is then used to justify particular roles within the institution, which in turn are used to justify responsibilities attached to those roles, which, finally, are used to justify particular actions that fall under those responsibilities. For example, ethical theories can be used to justify a free press, which is then used to justify journalists' role of zealously pursuing truth, which in turn establishes the obligation to pursue the truth more aggressively than is permissible in everyday life, which, finally, sometimes justifies particular acts of using deception to uncover vital information. Complicating matters, Luban adds that occasionally direct appeals to ordinary morality are warranted. Attorneys, he says, should be moral activists who are able and willing to subject the legal institution to direct moral assessment. Similarly, it might be argued that journalists should sometimes submit their profession to direct moral scrutiny in the attempt to elevate its moral standards.

Much work remains to be done on the moral foundations of journalistic ethics. To be sure, the importance of ethical theories is itself under dispute. Some writers seek to bypass theoretical disputes in the hope of gaining greater consensus about lower-level principles such as honesty, fairness, and beneficence. They remind us that ultimately what matters is sound practical judgment and genuine moral commitment, not abstract theory. In any case, the study of journalistic ethics benefits from, as it enriches, the burgeoning literature on professional ethics.

References: Christians, Clifford G., John P. Ferre, and P. Mark Fackler. 1993. *Good News*. New York: Oxford University Press.

Daniel, Stephen H. 1992. "Some Conflicting Assumptions of Journalistic Ethics." In Elliot D. Cohen, editor. *Philosophical Issues in Journalism*. New York: Oxford University Press, 50–58.

Elliott, Deni. 1986. "Foundations for News Media Responsibility." In Deni Elliott, editor. *Responsible Journalism*. Beverly Hills, CA: Sage.

Klaidman, Stephen, and Tom L. Beauchamp. 1987. *The Virtuous Journalist*. New York: Oxford University Press.

Lambeth, Edmund B. 1992. *Committed Journalism*. 2d Edition. Bloomington: Indiana University Press.

Luban, David. 1988. *Lawyers and Justice*. Princeton, NJ: Princeton University Press, 128–147.

Martin, Mike W. 1981. "Professional and Ordinary Morality." *Ethics* 91 (July): 631–633.

Merrill, John. 1990. *The Imperative of Freedom*. New York: Freedom House.

Nagel, Thomas. 1978. "Ruthlessness in Public Life." In Stuart Hampshire et al., editors. *Public and Private Morality*. New York: Cambridge University Press, 75–91.

Olen, Jeffrey. 1988. *Ethics in Journalism*. Englewood Cliffs, NJ: Prentice-Hall.

Silvers, Anita. 1985. "How to Avoid Resting Journalistic Ethics on a Mistake." *Journal of Social Philosophy*. Vol. 16: 20–35.

Urmson, J. O. 1978. "Comments by J. O. Urmson." In Allan Casebier and Janet Jenks Casebier, editors. *Social Responsibilities of the Mass Media*. Washington, DC: University Press of America, 65–68.

Conflicts of Interest

Deni Elliott

Conflicts of interest occur when journalists are distracted from doing their jobs by other pursuits in which they have a stake. Interests that create conflicts include those that are financial (e.g., when a reporter stands to lose or gain financially from the handling of a story) and personal (e.g., when a cause or person to whom the reporter is attached stands to lose or gain in some way from the handling of a story). Conflicts of commitment and the appearance of conflicts of interest also need to be discussed under the general notion of conflicts of interest.

A conflict of commitment occurs when journalists are distracted from meeting their journalistic responsibilities because of the moral obligations created by other legitimate roles in the journalist's life. Such roles may include those of parent, life-partner, friend, citizen, or member of a faith community.

The difference between conflicts of interest and conflicts of commitment is that one can avoid conflicts of interest but cannot avoid conflicts of commitment. No journalist lives his or her life totally qua journalist. Successful balancing of loyalties and role responsibilities depends on the journalist being clear about what counts as reasonable expectations for each role and carefully setting boundaries in regard to how one will act when roles conflict.

Conflicts of interest, however, are avoidable. Many news organizations and professional organizations have rules or standards to preclude journalists from becoming involved in stories that might result in financial or personal gain or loss.

Indeed, many news organizations regulate activity that might result in even the appearance of a conflict of interest. Regulating appearance rather than actual conflicts relieves the news organization from the burden of proving that the reporter will actually stand to benefit or lose from involvement with a particular story. As reporters in general could be in conflict if reporting a story that involves their life-partners or one that involves a stock in which they have money invested, many news organizations disallow any reporter from becoming involved with these stories.

Issues and Cases

Freebies and Junkets The most obvious conflict of interest occurs when story sources seek to buy positive coverage. In the early part of the twentieth century, it was common at holiday time for newsrooms and reporters' desks to overflow with presents from local businesses and politicians hoping for a good word (or the withholding of a bad word) in the news columns. By the 1970s, this practice had died out, and journalists perceived themselves as "professionals" who could not and should not be bought. Many news organizations instituted policies that prohibited journalists from accepting anything "of value" from a source. For example, the Society of Professional Journalists Code of Ethics states, "Journalists must be free of obligation to any interest other than the public's right to know the truth. Gifts, favors, free travel, special treatment or privileges can compromise the integrity of journalists and their employers. Nothing of value should be accepted" (Black, Steele, and Barney 1995, 6).

The rule is standard practice in large news organizations when it comes to gifts from individual sources or from local organizations. Yet, many small news organizations accept free tickets for their journalists to attend local events, such as the county fair or the college basketball games. Given the choice between coverage (made possible by the free admission) or noncoverage (due to a nonexistent budget to cover such expenses), news organizations that are struggling financially have determined that it is more important for their audience that they have access.

The importance of the event to the readers can be a helpful tool in determining when it is worth the risk for a news organization to be financially dependent on a source. News organizations, large and small, had an opportunity to test this theory in 1986 when Walt Disney World in Orlando, Florida, celebrated its fifteenth anniversary. Ten thousand journalists were offered an all-expenses-paid trip to attend and cover the celebration. News organizations had the option of paying their reporters' expenses, paying a portion of those expenses, or accepting the free trip.

Among the inducements for news organizations to consider the celebration "legitimate news" was an appearance by former U.S. Chief Justice Warren Burger. U.S. journalist Nicholas Daniloff, who had been detained in the Soviet Union, would also be on hand. Walt Disney World did not disclose how many of those attending did so at the expense of Walt Disney World and Florida tourist agencies, which also contributed to the extravaganza, but the number of small, out-of-town news organizations represented suggests that many in the industry enjoyed the anniversary with no cost to their home organization. News organizations that sent reporters on the basis that the anniversary celebration was a legitimate news story and did pay their reporters' costs condemned those that accepted the financial support. The fact that some news organizations accepted funding from the source made all reporting on the event suspect (Prendergast 1987).

News organizations faced the quandary about accepting support from a news source in a more serious way in late 1990, when the United States sent troops to the Persian Gulf to participate in an exercise dubbed Desert Shield. The positioning of troops in the gulf, with the commencement of military action after the first of the year, was at least as much a public relations success for the U.S. government as it was a success in the battlefield. News organizations had no access to stories relating to the movement of troops into the desert and no access to stories about local men and women participating in the exercise unless that access was granted by the military. In the months between troops first being stationed in Saudi Arabia and the beginning of the actual exchange of fire, the Pentagon offered more than 400 reporters free trips at military expense so that "hometowner" stories could be produced (Nathan 1991, 25). The experience of local men and women on the battleground of a major U.S. military offensive is unquestionably newsworthy, but the military bought and orchestrated the primarily feature stories that resulted from the trips. The resulting stories were supportive of the military; the public approval of the military effort soared.

Conflicts between Economics and Ethics Economically speaking, news organizations exist to create a profit for their stockholders, but the social function of news organizations is to provide citizens with information necessary for self-governance. Financial pressures can get in the way of news organizations meeting their social responsibilities just as financial pressures can get in the way of individual journalists doing their jobs. The number of independently owned news organizations has decreased tremendously, and the trend of media ownership by conglomerates has increased. Influence by owners can be direct. For instance, "when Westinghouse acquired CBS, questions were raised about future coverage of the corporation's interests in electric-power generating equipment used in nuclear power plants. Veteran environmental affairs writer Karl Grossman suggested that CBS coverage of nuclear safety issues was unlikely to occur" (Seib and Fitzpatrick 1997, 25).

In fact, evidence suggests that such economic editing takes place. A report by NBC on bad bolts in commercial airplanes and in missile silos in late 1989 was edited to remove references to the General Electric Company, owner of the network. The incident was labeled an instance of being "overprotective toward a corporate owner" by an executive at an NBC-owned station (Carter 1989, 18).

Most news organizations and professional societies now forbid journalists to moonlight with industries that they cover or to engage in other activities that pay the journalist and might interfere with that reporter's ability to be objective. Journalists in some news organizations are required to complete an annual conflict-of-interest form that discloses to management personal investments or other financial interests. One controversial exception to these policies is the speaking fees paid to well-known and respected journalists. Although such compensation is allowed, it does pose ethical questions. When journalists receive fees (sometimes in the range of several thousands of dollars) to speak to trade or professional associations that consist of members who might well become the subjects of news coverage, their credibility as objective reporters is questionable.

Conflicts between Personal Conviction and Journalistic Responsibility Conflicts between conviction and journalistic responsibility can occur at the corporate as well as the individual level, as do economic conflicts of interest. These conflicts have elements of both conflicts of commitment and conflicts of interest in that public statements of conviction are legitimately part of being a good individual or corporate citizen. Nevertheless, while news organization executives and individual journalists cannot refrain from holding personal convictions on an array of political and community matters, they should refrain from using the news product as a place to broadcast those convictions. They should also be aware that the appearance of conflict between conviction and journalistic role exists when they engage in public endorsements outside of the news columns or programs.

News organizations occasionally decide that they should don their "corporate citizen" hat and endorse a worthwhile community project. In the fall of 1995, the Seattle newspapers (that operate under a joint operating agreement) contributed advertising space for a sales tax initiative. That space was worth $40,000. Opponents of the sales tax initiative objected. "You can't give ads away and make any pretense of being neutral messengers," said one critic (Stein 1995, 22).

Similar conflicts arise when publishers or general managers sit on influential boards. When the publisher of the *Reno Gazette-Journal* accepted a position on the board of a gambling casino, the newsroom was aghast. "You just don't sit on a board when the company is a big player in the city and state and generates news and advertising," one journalist said (Stein 1994, 8). The news organization appears to be a booster, whatever the corporate intent, and the presence of the boss on the board of a newsmaker interferes with the ability of journalists in the organization to report the news. This type of conflict extends to publisher, editor, general manager, and news director involvement in the local boards of United Way and other charities. The message given by such involvement is that these are "good" causes and not newsworthy. Recent scandals in the charities have shown this not to be the case.

Individuals become journalists because they care deeply about the important current issues of the day. It is not surprising that those journalists might wish to participate in social activism as well. Reporters' involvement with social causes, however, are considered to create at least an appearance of a conflict that interferes with the news organization's credibility. Among the recent problems of this sort: "A Tacoma, Washington, education reporter was exiled to the copy desk because of her off-duty involvement in the lesbian-gay civil rights movement; a Santa Rosa, California, reporter was taken off the timber beat after giving an interview to an environmentalist news weekly; and two Fairfield, Iowa, editors were fired after they helped organize an anti-abortion group" (*Columbia Journalism Review* 1991, 6).

News organizations and individual journalists should refrain from involvement in community issues because their job gives them unique access to participate in those issues. No one other than a news organization and its staff can determine which social issues of the day get what kind of public play. That journalistic decision making provides tremendous power to participate in the important events. Extending one's involvement beyond that creates both the appearance and reality of a misuse of power.

Conflict by Association Perhaps the most difficult conflict of commitment and interest occurs when a journalist's life-partner is a news source, subject, or competitor. While news organizations do not seek to control their staffers' personal lives, the employers define the job that a journalist can do based on their personal associations. For example, an assistant managing editor for news of the Newport News (Virginia) *Daily Press* was reassigned to a less "strategic" position after the publisher learned he was living with a woman who is a city editor for the competing Norfolk *Virginian-Pilot* (Radolf 1987, 46). Other news organizations have given the reporter or editor involved with a source, subject, or competitor the choice of resigning or accepting a position that eliminates their ability to influence the news coverage.

The problem with news organizations' response to the problem of conflict by association is that the response denies the ability of journalists to maintain professional confidentiality and is underinclusive.

Other life-partners learn to keep professional secrets from one another, as in the case of married physicians who have an obligation to maintain patient confidentiality even from one another. While it may be impossible for a reporter to do a story on her life-partner in an unbiased way, it does not follow that her mere presence in the newsroom would prevent another journalist from doing the story. The response is underinclusive in that it is not clear which associations create bias and which do not. It is not unusual for reporters and editors to have friends who are sources, subjects, and competitors. It may be as difficult for a reporter to watch a negative story about one's tennis partner come to light as it would be for her to watch her lover become the subject of controversy.

Looking Ahead

As ownership of news organizations moves away from local publishers and into the hands of conglomerates, the economic pressure that journalists and news organizations feel not to bite the hand that feeds them will become more of a problem. As this trend increases, it becomes even more necessary for news organizations to report critically about one another. Critical reporting of competitive media was once considered a conflict of interest that could result in nothing other than claims of bias. Now, critical reporting of the news business is a necessity. News organizations must report on the activities and influences of their own powerful social institution. There is no other industry in society set up to do that job.

References: Black, Jay, Bob Steele, and Ralph Barney. 1995. *Doing Ethics in Journalism: A Handbook with Case Studies.* 2d Edition. Needham Heights, MA: Allyn & Bacon.

Carter, Bill. 1989. "NBC Show Deletes G.E. Mention." *New York Times* (3 December).

Columbia Journalism Review. 1991. "Outside Activities: When Does a Journalist's Personal Opinion Become a Public Issue?" (March/April): 6–7.

Nathan, Debbie. 1991. "Just the Good News Please." *The Progressive* (February): 25–27.

Prendergast, Alan. 1987. "Mickey Mouse Journalism." *Washington Journalism Review* (January/February): 32–35.

Radolf, Andrew. 1987. "Love vs. Career." *Editor & Publisher* (May 2): 46, 143.

Seib, Phillip, and K. Fitzpatrick. 1997. *Journalism Ethics.* Fort Worth, TX: Harcourt Brace.

Stein, M. L. 1994. "Publisher Joins Board of Casino Operator." *Editor & Publisher* (10 September): 8–9.

———. 1995. "Donation of Ad Space Creates Stir in Seattle." *Editor & Publisher* (30 September): 22–23.

Professionalization and Journalistic Education

Elliot D. Cohen

It has been said that the attempt to "professionalize" journalism rests on a mistaken understanding of journalism. Thus, according to Michael Lewis (1993, 24), "the journalist's role is precisely to cut through this sort of obfuscation, not to create more of it. The best journalists are almost the antithesis of professionals. The horror of disrepute, the preternatural respect for authority and the fear of controversy that so benefit the professional are absolute handicaps for a journalist." In a similar vein, John C. Merrill (1974, 142) has charged that "perhaps to far too great a degree journalism education does tend to turn journalism students into robots who can walk 'sure-footedly' into the world of Establishment journalism. It does discourage 'unprofessional' practices and techniques, creativity and individuality, by instilling in all the students the 'proper ways' of journalism."

The idea of a professional as one steeped in the status quo and as such incapable of creativity and individuality, or of fulfilling the role of fourth estate, needs examining. Indeed, those who favor professionalizing journalism typically think doing so will support rather than destroy journalists' ability to serve their public, democratic function. Such is the official view of most schools of journalism, as a cursory survey of their mission statements will reveal. So what does being a professional really imply?

Being a professional has usually been taken to imply possession of a *specialized* fund of knowledge, which the professional is entrusted to apply toward promotion of a certain social good, and for which the professional is (in varying degrees) respected. Professionals also typically have an implied or explicit code of ethics that defines central responsibilities, goals, and aspirations of the profession (Davis and Elliston 1986). Members of a profession are not only expected to regulate their behavior in relation to their code; they are expected to have internalized the code as a measure of what is right or just for any member of the profession. (*See* chapter 6 for specific codes.) Professions also have varying degrees of power to enforce their codes. While some professions, such as the legal profession, have highly organized and effective mechanisms of code enforcement (lawyers must be members in good standing of their state bar associations or they are not permitted to practice in their respective states), other professions, such as the mental health profession, have considerably less enforcement power (Van House and Kottler 1987, 86–87).

Specialized knowledge characterizing a profession is usually acquired through formal training at colleges, universities, or graduate schools. For example, physicians, dentists, and lawyers respectively attend graduate schools of medicine, dentistry, and law, and other professionals such as teachers and accountants (minimally) attain undergraduate degrees in their respective areas. In these schools such professionals are presumed to acquire valuable knowledge that prepares them to become competent practitioners.

If journalism is to resemble these other professions, then the education of journalists will need to include formal, specialized training. As such, the question of what professional courses to include in the journalism curriculum to make journalists competent practitioners will be relevant. If, as authors such as Merrill and Lewis suggest, journalism is really a craft or trade rather than a profession, then it may be learned by way of an apprenticeship or through on-the-job training, without the necessity of attending a professional school of journalism. So, is there any special fund of journalistic knowledge that requires a specialized, formal education?

A look at the credentials of those working in the field suggest that journalism does not necessarily require specialized training taken at either a graduate or undergraduate school of journalism. According to one recent study conducted by Betty Medsger for the *Freedom Forum*, 9 percent of those recently hired for print and broadcast news had journalism master's degrees, while 48 percent held undergraduate journalism degrees, leaving 91 percent without journalism master's degrees and 52 percent without undergraduate journalism degrees (Whitelaw 1996).

Nevertheless, it seems that more people are earning master's degrees in journalism, apparently as a response to a competitive job market. Thus, the enrollment among the nation's 171 journalism and communication master's degree programs increased 25 percent between 1990 and 1994 to over 10,000 (Whitelaw 1996). This increase suggests that, if journalism is not currently a profession insofar as it does not portend specialized training, it may at least be an *emerging* one.

Whether such a trend toward increased professionalization in journalism is a good or bad thing may depend upon whether the knowledge acquired in journalism school proves worthwhile when the student joins the ranks of journalism practitioners. While additional perks of attending journalism school, such as making contacts for prospective employment, may provide extrinsic motivation for attending, the primary purpose of professional education must be sought in the usefulness of what is learned in the practice of journalism.

A common trend in professional training of journalists appears to be toward providing students with a broad liberal education along with technical training. For example, since its founding in 1908, the University of Missouri School of Journalism (1997) has "emphasized in all of its degrees the need for a strong liberal education blended with pragmatic learning experiences." Similarly, the Medill School of Journalism (1997) at Northwestern University "seeks to develop professional writers and editors who are broadly educated in the liberal arts and sciences; who are technically skilled; who understand the historical underpinnings of a free press in America; and who appreciate the social, legal, and ethical issues of the news media in modern-day society." Thus, the Medill core of journalism courses (which includes technical courses such as newswriting, editing, and reporting) comprises 25 percent of the undergraduate curriculum, while nonjournalism courses comprise the remaining 75 percent.

The trend toward a broad liberal education may be justified in terms of the broad nature of journalism itself. Indeed, knowing techniques of reporting, newswriting, and editing may not be sufficient to produce a story. Familiarity or feeling for the subject matter, including its historical, social, ethical, and legal contexts, can make the difference between a mechanical portrayal of an event and an insightful revelation. Since journalists are generalists, their background must similarly suit them for addressing a diverse array of topics. Journalists cannot be expected to be omniscient; nor is it reasonable to expect them to have familiarity with all about which they report. Yet, unless "good journalism" equates to a technically correct record of a bare event severed from all other aspects of reality and devoid of all historical and cultural significance, the richer the journalist's knowledge base, the more enlightening the report is likely to be.

Along with the trend toward liberal journalistic education, the tilt may be toward a theoretical rather than a practical orientation. According to John Wicklein (1994), former reporter and editor for the *New York Times*, the trend in journalism schools is currently toward hiring journalism teachers who have Ph.D.s but who have never worked in a newsroom. Based on a review of 106 *Chronicle of Higher Education* advertisements for tenure-track professors to teach basic newswriting and reporting courses and "dozens of interviews at universities across the country," Wicklein concluded that such a hiring practice has become the rule rather than the exception. Moreover, since these professors tend to be theoreticians, the effect of such a hiring practice is to tilt journalism education toward theory. There is the concern that a theoretical background without instruction by those who have themselves been in the trenches will provide inadequate student preparation.

Perhaps this tendency toward theory and away from practice may to some extent be offset by the common policy of journalism schools requiring internships and other opportunities in which students receive valuable "hands-on" training. For example, at the University of Missouri, a substantial amount of the master's program curriculum is linked to the operation of the daily and Sunday *Missourian* and other media facilities. At Medill's under-graduate School of Journalism, reporting and editing courses are taken on-site at a daily newspaper.

Nevertheless, the role of practical experience as a source of journalistic knowledge may still tend to be discounted in the lectures and texts of jour-nalistic education in favor of abstract theories. Thus, Theodore Glasser (1992, 138) complains that what "ends up in our lectures and texts are not the vividly cultural and historical accounts of journalism that would honor the role of experience in the production of knowledge but rather vague and abstract theories or anecdotes from newsrooms that are disconnected from history and culture."

According to Glasser and Ettema (1989), journalistic knowledge consists largely of knowledge-in-practice, which they dub "common sense" rather than theoretical knowledge. Such common sense is practical in that it sees news as an immediate response to particular needs. For example, the differ-ence between "soft" and "hard" news cashes out in pragmatic terms of know-ing how much control can be exerted over scheduling the news. It is thus a matter of knowing *how* rather than knowing *that*. Furthermore, it is a manner of practice in tune with journalism's customs and traditions, and also with one's own cultural heritage, its principles, and practices. Such knowledge is reflected in proverbs, jokes, anecdotes, and other colloquial expressions—"look before you leap," "a nose for news," "get the story"—rather than in doc-trines, treatises, and theories. It approaches news not as a series of objective facts, but rather as a narrative that can play out with all the vicissitudes, con-flicts and dilemmas of a literary work. This knowledge is the kind acquired and demonstrated in a practitioner's skillful performance. It is not acquired through formal processes ordinarily associated with institutions of higher education. According to Glasser (1992, 138), since those who have not prac-ticed journalism cannot be presumed to possess such knowledge, "it would be almost unthinkable to hire someone to teach a basic reporting course, for example, unless that person has had at least some experience as a reporter."

Insofar as journalistic knowledge-in-practice is animated by cultural norms or values, journalism would appear wedded to a broad liberal educa-tion—grounding in literature, history, and philosophy—in which an appre-ciation for such norms is cultivated. Nevertheless, Glasser sees the attempt to reserve liberal education for courses taken *outside* the journalism major as an unwarranted result of the attempt to professionalize journalism.

The goal of professional education, claims Glasser (1992), is to homoge-nize and standardize knowledge so that all practitioners see things from one common frame of reference. It breeds conformity and runs contrary to the value of diversity, which tolerates differences among journalists. Such knowl-edge is opposed to a liberal education, which aims at diversity. Breaking down the partition between professional training and liberal education can therefore open the door to greater diversity in journalism by allowing stu-dent exposure to more perspectives. This exposure, Glasser thinks, will place journalism education in closer proximity with knowledge-in-practice, which functions within the context of a wide assortment of norms, customs, and traditions. Thus, he states,

> Where better to disabuse students of the orthodoxy of professionalism than in the very classroom where they are expected to abide by the canons of professional conduct? Where better to help our students understand that standards are indeed norms, and norms are not naturally given but historically and culturally contingent, than in a course where standards appear to transcend time and space? And when better to instill among students an appreciation for why journalism is not now and never has been value-free than at the same time they are being taught how to be objective in their newswriting and reporting (Glasser 1992, 137).

While such desegregation of professional and liberal education in journalism appears to be rare, some institutions have embarked upon what Glasser recommends. Brown University's Department of Modern Culture and Media (1997) appears to be a case in point. According to its mission statement, the department

> exists in order to provide a place for the study of the mass media—especially film, photography, print journalism, and television—in relation to modern society itself and to such other cultural products as modern literature, art, and philosophy. In this department, faculty and students attempt to unite aspects of modern culture that are normally separated by university departmental structures (such as fine art, literature, and philosophy). The center also proposes the study of cultural forms (film, video, journalism) that are seldom treated with adequate seriousness in the liberal arts curriculum. . . . In addition . . . we are committed to uniting actual work in the production or creation of media texts with our analytical and theoretical consideration of the arts and media. Specifically, we offer courses in journalistic writing (in cooperation with the English department) and, through our own facilities, courses in film-making and video production. In these courses we are interested in the aesthetic and documentary potential of media. We reject the common distinction between liberal and vocational studies. We are not interested in producing mindless technicians or disdainful aesthetes. Our goal is to help our students become active participants in contemporary American culture, both as thoughtful critics and as creative workers.

Is such a hybrid of study a surrender of professionalism, a move toward giving up the goal of making journalism a profession on a par with the other recognized professions? In a footnote, Glasser (1992, 139) contends that "the lack of a formal systematic core of knowledge neither denies nor contradicts a powerful occupational ethos wedded to the ideal of professionalism." He affirms that the question of which occupations qualify as professions is not really the important issue. Of importance is rather the question of what it means for an occupation to claim to be a profession.

If devotion to the common good is emphasized above all as an earmark of a profession, then journalism does indeed have a legitimate claim to professional status. As clearly reflected in their various codes of ethics, journalists are unified in their commitment to promote general welfare by keeping the public informed about important matters and keeping a watchful eye out for unjust government encroachment of public interests.

Critics of professionalizing journalism fear that professionalization will compromise the independence and autonomy necessary for it to serve its public function. If these critics are correct, then professionalization, at least in the sense that implies a narrow technical education, may prove self-defeating.

It would appear that one benefit of professionalization, for professions other than journalism, has been to increase independence and autonomy rather than diminish it. Insofar as a profession has an institutionalized means of governing itself, it can maintain its independence and autonomy. Without such means, a profession may be subject to external control by government agencies. For example, the American Bar Association is a highly organized association that exists to regulate and enforce standards of practice, admission criteria for practice, and legal education. Consequently, lawyers largely control their own activities rather than having restrictions imposed from outside the profession by government. In this sense, professionalization has served to increase independence and autonomy of the legal profession (Luizzi 1993, 102–103).

Unlike other professions, journalism already has safeguards in place to ensure its autonomy and independence. Protection from government interference with journalists' activities is guaranteed by the First Amendment of the U.S. Constitution, which provides for freedom of the press. The press is free to perform its important public function with little government interference (*see* Freedom of Speech and Press). As such, in seeking to standardize its practice, journalism may have less freedom to gain and more to lose than any other profession.

Journalism is currently in the midst of an identity crisis. On the one hand, going too far along the lines of professionalization may prove self-defeating. On the other, bringing journalism into closer proximity with other more highly respected and well-endowed professions may make further professionalization sound attractive. The future prosperity of this budding "profession" and of the public whom it serves may well depend upon how professionalized it is willing to become in its quest for self-definition.

References: Brown University. 1997. Online information. World Wide Web: http://www.Brown.edu.
Columbia University Graduate School of Journalism. 1997. Online information. World Wide Web: http://www.Columbia.edu.

Davis, Michael, and Frederick A. Elliston, editors. 1986. *Ethics and the Legal Profession*. Buffalo, NY: Prometheus Books.

Glasser, Theodore. 1992. "Professionalism and the Derision of Diversity: The Case of the Education of Journalists." *Journal of Communication* 42 (Spring): 131–140.

Glasser, Theodore, and James S. Ettema. 1989. "Common Sense and the Education of Young Journalists." *Journalism Educator* 44 (Summer): 18–25.

Lewis, Michael. 1993. "Journalism School: Confidential." *New Republic* 208 (19 April): 20–24.

Luizzi, Vincent. 1993. *A Case for Legal Ethics: Legal Ethics as a Source for a Universal Ethic*. Albany: State University of New York Press.

Medill School of Journalism. 1997. Online information. World Wide Web: http://www.nwu.edu.

Merrill, John C. 1974. *The Imperative of Freedom: A Philosophy of Journalistic Autonomy*. New York: Hastings House.

University of Missouri School of Journalism. 1997. Online information. World Wide Web: http://www. Missouri.edu.

Van Hoose, William H., and Jeffrey A. Kottler. 1987. *Ethical and Legal Issues in Counseling and Psychotherapy*. 2d Edition. San Francisco: Jossey-Bass.

Whitelaw, Kevin. 1996. "Is Journalism School Worth It?" *US News & World Report* 120 (18 March): 98–100.

Wicklein, John. 1994. "No Experience Required." *Columbia Journalism Review* (September/October): 45–48.

News Sources and Deception

Deceiving Sources

Sandra L. Borden and Michael Pritchard

The Mirage Bar was a ruse. The *Chicago Sun-Times* set it up with the help of a government watchdog group so that undercover reporters could catch city inspectors accepting bribes. The *Sun-Times* got what it wanted: a compelling series of stories documenting corruption in city government. The series was even nominated for a Pulitzer Prize. The Pulitzer Advisory Board, however, disapproved of the use of deception to get the story, and the award went to someone else (Palmer 1987). Journalists themselves clearly believe that using deceptive reporting methods is a serious matter.

Nevertheless, just a few years later, reporters for the *Lexington* (Kentucky) *Herald-Leader* won a Pulitzer Prize for a series that documented widespread violations of National Collegiate Athletic Association (NCAA) rules in the successful men's basketball program at the University of Kentucky. One difference between this case and the Mirage Bar case is that all sources knew they were speaking on the record and expected to be quoted. What they did not know, however, was that they were secretly being taped. When several former players later denied having made statements attributed to them, the editors responded that they had proof of the statements locked up in a vault (Black, Steele, and Barney 1995).

Both cases involved deception. In the Mirage Bar case, reporters posed as operators of a bar, but the "bar" was set up solely for the purpose of revealing illegal activities. This scheme may have required outright lying, but at the very least it involved deliberate misrepresentation of who the reporters were and what they were doing. In the second case, there was no deception about what reporters were after; the deception concerned only how they went about it (using concealed recorders). Assuming that the normal expectation is that reporters request permission to record when asking for interviews, the players were misled, but there was no outright lying or deliberate misrepresentation. Are these two cases sufficiently different to justify regarding the *Sun-Times'* tactics as objectionable but the *Herald-Leader's* as acceptable? To answer questions like this one, it is necessary to consider the sorts of reasons one might give for or against the use of deceptive tactics in gathering news.

There are several reasons one might offer for using deceptive tactics:

- *Deceptive tactics might make getting the story easier.* Some sources might be more likely to disclose compromising or embarrassing information if they think there is no recorded record or if they think the reporter is their friend.
- *Deceptive tactics might make the story more objective.* Since sources will not be on guard, the story is more likely to be untainted by their efforts to present themselves in a more favorable or less candid light.
- *Deceptive tactics might be the only way to acquire vital information the public needs to know.* Some journalists argue for an even lower standard, the public's basic "right to know" (regardless of whether they actually need to know the information to make important choices).
- *Deceptive tactics might be considered just treatment for sources who have engaged in illegal or unethical behavior.* Arguably, such sources do not deserve any better.
- *Deceptive tactics might be essential for the safety of the reporter.* Someone such as Nashville *Tennessean* reporter Jerry Thompson, who posed as a member of the Ku Klux Klan for a year (Palmer 1987), might be in jeopardy without the protective cloak of a false identity.

Whether these considerations are sufficient to justify deceptive tactics in particular cases depends on how they fare against reasons for not using deceptive tactics. Some reasons are bound up with legal considerations. Others are more straightforwardly ethical. We will address these both in turn.

Some deceptive tactics may be illegal, or at least legally punishable. Most statutes and legal precedents in the area of reporter-source relationships deal with protection of source confidentiality. In *Cohen v. Cowles Media Co.*, 115.Ct. 2513 (1991), the Minnesota Supreme Court established a precedent for legally enforcing promises of confidentiality to sources (Pember 1997). Deception was not an issue in this case since the reporters who made the promise were overruled by their editors, but the message to journalists who would promise confidentiality insincerely is clear: Don't.

Another relevant area of media law concerns surreptitious taping. Taping a news interview without the subject's knowledge is legal for reporters in most states and the District of Columbia. Even in states that outlaw this practice, a subject's consent usually is presumed if the recording device is in plain view and the subject does not object. Secret recording, however, may constitute a legal invasion of privacy even in the most permissive states when it occurs in the subject's home or under circumstances in which the subject has a "legitimate expectation of solitude" (Pember 1997, 243). Of course, the fraud and trespassing lawsuit ABC lost in 1997 to Food Lion puts journalists on notice that there may be legal consequences for deliberately lying to sources for the purpose of going undercover. In this case, the news program *PrimeTime Live* had producers fake references and backgrounds to get jobs at two Food Lion grocery stores in 1992 to document unsanitary food handling and deceptive food packaging reported by a labor union, Food Lion employees, and a government watchdog group. Hidden camera footage suggested that the stores repackaged old meat and sold it as fresh. Despite this revealing footage, the federal jury hearing the case in North Carolina decided ABC had gone too far and awarded Food Lion $5.5 million in punitive damages (*Food Lion, Inc. v. Capital Cities/ABC, Inc. et al.*, 1997). ABC was appealing at the time this essay was being written (Baker 1993; Johnson 1997).

Like the law, the ethical codes of professional associations and individual newsrooms are most specific in the area of confidentiality. Many also deal with ground rules for off-the-record interviews. Most contain general statements urging journalists to be fair and to respect people involved in the news. In 1996, the Society of Professional Journalists added a new "guiding principle" of minimizing harm to its code of ethics. According to this principle, "ethical journalists treat sources, subjects and colleagues as human beings deserving of respect." The code encourages journalists to consider the harm that may come to people involved in the news and to respond with compassion. (*See* chapter 6 for the complete code.)

Some newsroom codes directly address the use of impersonation, entrapment, and criminal methods in reporting. Typically, codes contain a presumption against such methods except in extreme circumstances. Even in such situations, reporters usually are required to consult with at least one editor before proceeding.

A specific set of guidelines for justifying deception in reporting was developed by participants in an ethical decision-making seminar at the Poynter Institute for Media Studies in St. Petersburg, Florida. The checklist (which is discussed in Black, Steele, and Barney 1995) also presumes that deception generally is wrong. Deception is justified only when *all* of the following criteria are met: (1) the information is profoundly important; (2) all other alternatives have been exhausted; (3) the journalists involved are willing to disclose the deception to the public and to provide an account of it; (4) the journalists and their organization commit the necessary resources for fully pursuing the story; (5) the harm prevented by the information outweighs the harm caused by the deception; and (6) the journalists have carefully deliberated about the decision.

The Mirage Bar case with which we began illustrates the complexities involved in applying these criteria. (1) Was the information sought profoundly important? Inspectors were letting health and safety violations slide in return for bribes from bar owners. Two questions are relevant here. First, was the corruption systematic, revealing a flawed system rather than just an isolated incident or two? Second, were health and safety violations (which were allowed to continue without public knowledge) serious public threats?

Assuming the answer to these two questions is affirmative, we still need to ask (2) whether other alternatives were exhausted. The reporters had ample documentation of the corrupt practices. Interviewing real bar owners and others who were "shaken down" could have provided some of the colorful details the reporters were seeking. Perhaps real bar owners would have been willing to try to catch city inspectors red-handed themselves; however, fear of retaliation might have made it hard to secure the cooperation of the bar owners.

Since setting up the fake bar required deception, some justification was called for. In their favor, (3) the journalists were willing to disclose the deception and provide an account of it. Furthermore, (4) the newspaper did commit enough resources to pursue the story fully. It was willing to go to the extreme of operating a fake bar and assigning reporters to work there for hours as bartenders. The paper was evidently willing to go all out, but the question remains whether the resources were put to the best possible use.

So, (5) did the harm prevented by the information outweigh the harm caused by the deception? Law enforcement agencies responded to the illegal activity reported by the paper. Justice was served, and possibly serious threats to public health and safety were remedied. The deception, however, may have harmed the paper's credibility with its readers, especially after it was snubbed by colleagues judging the Pulitzer Prize competition.

What we do not know is (6) whether the journalists carefully deliberated about the decision. Nevertheless, considering that there were other ways to disclose the information (albeit less dramatically) and to alert the proper authorities about whatever health and safety risks existed, the deception in this case does not seem to satisfy the criteria sufficiently to justify the decision.

These criteria reflect more general ethical principles. From an ethical perspective, deception is typically regarded as manipulative and unfair because it fails to respect the right of sources to choose for themselves whether to share or withhold information. Consequently, there is a presumption against deception. One way to remember that the autonomy of sources should be respected is for reporters to imagine a reversal of roles, with reporters themselves being deceived. (This would be an application of the Golden Rule, as well as Immanuel Kant's universalizability test: "Could I will this maxim to be a universal law?")

The deception checklist also calls attention to the possible broader consequences of deception. For example, deception can create distrust between reporters and sources. This distrust will not necessarily be restricted to only those reporters who are known to have used deception. Just as a single deceptive act can raise doubts about the credibility of an individual, reporters who use deceptive tactics can raise doubts about other journalists as well. Such doubts can occur because journalists are commonly viewed together, as members of a profession.

Finally, the criteria urge journalists to consider whether their arguments would stand up to public scrutiny. This test is an application of Sissela Bok's "test of publicity" (Bok 1978). It asks people to consider how the deception they are contemplating would look to an audience of reasonable people. For journalists, whose work is public by nature, this question is more than an academic one. Journalists must be able to give an account for using deception that will be convincing to their readers, listeners, viewers, and peers. If they are unable to provide such an account, their actions may be more deserving of the blame assigned to the *Chicago Sun-Times* for its use of undercover reporters in the Mirage Bar than of the praise given to the *Lexington Herald-Leader* for its surreptitious taping of reluctant sources in the University of Kentucky investigation.

References: Baker, Russ W. 1993. "Truth, Lies, and Videotape: *PrimeTime Live* and the Hidden Camera." *Columbia Journalism Review* (July/August): 25–28.

———. 1995. "Gotcha! Deciding When Sources Are Fair Game." *Journal of Mass Media Ethics*. Vol. 10: 223–235.

Black, Jay, Bob Steele, and Ralph Barney. 1995. *Doing Ethics in Journalism: A Handbook with Case Studies*. 2d Edition. Needham Heights, MA: Allyn & Bacon.

Bok, Sissela. 1978. *Lying: Moral Choice in Public and Private Life*. New York: Vintage.

———. 1982. *Secrets: On the Ethics of Concealment and Revelation*. New York: Pantheon.

Borden, Sandra L. 1993. "Empathic Listening: The Interviewer's Betrayal." *Journal of Mass Media Ethics*. Vol. 8: 219–226.

Braun, P. 1988. "Deception in Journalism." *Journal of Mass Media Ethics*. Vol. 3: 77–83.

Christians, Clifford G., Kim B. Rotzoll, and Mark Fackler. 1991. *Media Ethics: Cases and Moral Reasoning*. 3d Edition. New York: Longman.

Day, Louis A. 1997. *Ethics in Media Communications: Cases and Controversies*. 2d Edition. Belmont, CA: Wadsworth.

Dufresne, Marcel. 1991. "To Sting or Not to Sting?" *Columbia Journalism Review* (May/June): 49–51.

Hodges, Lewis W. 1988. "Undercover, Masquerading, Surreptitious Taping." *Journal of Mass Media Ethics*. Vol 3: 26–36.

Jaksa, James A., and Michael S. Pritchard. 1995. *Communication Ethics: Methods of Analysis*. 2d Edition. Belmont, CA: Wadsworth.

Johnson, Peter. 1997. "Food Lion Awarded Damages," *USA Today* (23 January). Online information. World Wide Web: http://www.usatoday.com.

Klaidman, Stephen, and Tom L. Beauchamp. 1987. *The Virtuous Journalist*. New York: Oxford University Press.

Lambeth, Edmund B. 1992. *Committed Journalism: An Ethic for the Profession*. 2d Edition. Bloomington: Indiana University Press.

Palmer, Nancy Doyle. 1987. "Going After the Truth—In Disguise: The Ethics of Deception." *Washington Journalism Review* (November): 20–22.

Patterson, Philip, and Lee Wilkins. 1994. *Media Ethics: Issues and Cases*. 2d Edition. Madison, WI: Brown & Benchmark.

Pember, D. R. 1997. *Mass Media Law, 1997 Edition*. Madison, WI: Brown & Benchmark.

Seib, Philip, and Kathy Fitzpatrick. 1997. *Journalism Ethics*. Fort Worth, TX: Harcourt Brace.

Undercover Investigations

Steve Weinberg

When journalists discuss ethics, gathering information through undercover techniques is almost always on the agenda. The discussion is usually high-minded, with the conclusion sounding something like this:

> Journalists should avoid undercover or other surreptitious methods of gathering information—except when open methods will fail to provide information vital to the public. If undercover or other surreptitious methods are used, they should be explained to the audience.

The key word in the previous paragraph is *except*, but before discussing the exceptions, definitions are in order. Undercover work involves active deception, passive deception, or a mixture of both. Active deception frequently takes the form of the journalist identifying herself or himself as somebody he or she is not. The misidentification is often accompanied by a hidden camera or hidden audiotape recorder placed according to a well thought-out plan.

Passive deception occurs when a journalist never claims to be somebody else, but allows sources or subjects of investigations to mistakenly assume he or she is something other than a reporter, editor, or producer. Passive deception is often unplanned and carried out ad hoc. A journalist on a sensitive story has a flash of insight that the source mistakenly believes her or him to be a police officer, private detective, government investigator, or whatever. Rather than correct the misconception, the journalist allows it to play out.

The Law

Undercover investigation falls more squarely into the ethical realm than into the legal realm. Active or passive deception might be viewed by a large segment of society as unethical, but it is rarely illegal on its face, except in rare instances when there has been a clear-cut case of trespass or invasion of privacy. Courts regularly find that constitutional principles protect publication/broadcast of stories that touch on the public interest. Those constitutional principles tend to override competing privacy interests.

When subjects of investigations sue journalists for defamation—almost certainly the most common charge made by plaintiffs against investigative journalists—undercover techniques might be prominently mentioned in the complaint, but they are not the foundation of the litigation. Plaintiffs frequently find it satisfying to trumpet journalistic deception, including undercover techniques, in the court of public opinion. Many members of the public, including jurors in defamation cases, automatically dislike and distrust journalists. When those journalists deceive to obtain information, the dislike and distrust grow. That is so even when the reporters' investigations uncover significant wrongdoing. Many members of the public believe that the means simply cannot be justified by the ends.

The Issues

Journalists who fail to factor in public opinion when considering whether to use undercover techniques are shortsighted. A generalized erosion of trust caused by a few journalists using undercover techniques makes information gathering more difficult for all journalists. As a result, journalists need to search their souls: Is the hidden camera or audiotape recorder the only way to capture the information? Is the information that might be captured vital to the investigation, or is it largely glitz? If undercover techniques will be necessary, is the story worth doing at all given the possibility of eroding trust?

Cases

A real-life story that embraces the difficult issues and troubling questions comes from the *Chicago Sun-Times* newsroom. The newsroom received a tip from a government official, who refused to be identified in print or help further, that clinics were falsely telling women they were pregnant then charging them for phony abortions.

Reporters and editors who knew about the tip could have informed health or law enforcement authorities at that point, but did not. The newspaper could have made extensive efforts to obtain evidence from current and former clinic employees in the early stages of the investigation, but that did not happen. Instead, the newspaper practiced deception by sending investigators as phony patients to the clinic. The female patients carried urine samples from males. When the laboratory used by the clinic found those samples to show pregnancy—an obvious impossibility—the newspaper heightened its deception by placing journalists in jobs at the clinic, as receptionists, counselors, and nurses' aides.

During their job interviews, the journalists provided no false information, but they omitted any mention of their journalism connections. For months, the journalists employed at the clinic knew women were being harmed through nonabortion abortions but kept collecting information without informing the victims or government authorities. The collection of evidence included illegally photocopying patients' files.

The printed investigation was convincing and compelling. Could it have been done at all without deception? Yes, through traditional working of paper trails (incorporation papers, lawsuits, tax liens, and the like), supplemented by interviews with current and former employees, current and former patients, lawyers, and regulators. Would the deceptionless version have been as convincing and compelling? Probably not. Was the qualitative difference worth the possible loss of public trust? Hard to say.

Because television journalists are so heavily dependent on pictures to tell the story, they are more likely than print journalists to practice undercover techniques. Many television investigations using hidden cameras fall into the category of consumer journalism—interesting pieces with minimal significance. For example, a television investigative unit decides to look for fraudulent microwave oven repairs. The investigative unit will work with electronics experts to disable an oven by removing a fuse. The disabled oven will then be placed in the kitchen of a television station employee, within range of a hidden camera. Then an investigative unit employee will pose as a consumer seeking repair work. Repair companies might be selected from the telephone directory Yellow Pages, or might be found on complaint lists at the local Better Business Bureau. The "consumer" will leave the repair person alone as the hidden camera tapes every move. Later, the electronics consultant will view the video, helping the journalists distinguish honest repair work from fraudulent work. Some of the secretly filmed footage will be used on the air.

Looking Ahead

As tomorrow's technology becomes even more sophisticated than today's, it is likely journalists will use hidden cameras and audiotape recorders more than ever. As that deception increases, journalists might slip into other forms of deception more easily, including misidentifying themselves to gain access to premises normally off-limits.

Such deception could be a mistake in terms of credibility with the public. Journalists who use undercover techniques should test their judgment by constructing a hypothetical message to readers or viewers that should be able to explain *unequivocally* what significant information the journalists could gather that would be unavailable other ways. Otherwise, undercover techniques should be abandoned.

If the test message offers a satisfactory explanation, journalists should run the next stage of the test. In that stage, journalists should explain how they will justify the undercover techniques on ethical grounds. Is the explanation convincing to everybody in the newsroom? Is it convincing to nonjournalists chosen to evaluate the situation? The answers are rarely unambiguous. Nobody ever said it was easy being an ethical journalist. As the antique joke goes, lawyers incarcerate their mistakes. Physicians kill their mistakes. Journalists, on the other hand, publish or broadcast their mistakes for millions to see.

Recording of Sources and Uses of Such Recordings

Travis Linn

The practice of recording the statements of news sources is as old as the journalistic notepad. The use of pencil and paper or, later, computer or tape recorder to aid memory and to ensure accuracy of quotations is common. Indeed failure to use some recording system, relying entirely on memory, might be considered a lapse of professionalism on the part of a reporter. In this context we think particularly of reporters working for a newspaper.

The growth of broadcasting, bringing with it the use of audiotape and videotape recorders to capture "sound bites," however, has raised questions about the practice of recording news sources. Broadcasting the actual voice (or image and voice) of a news source moves the practice of recording beyond mere note taking, making the "source" not merely the source of information but also a participant in the broadcast report.

Another way of viewing this distinction is to think of the reporter recording a source's comments or behavior for the reporter's own use, perhaps to help the reporter remember a moment, a mood, or the context of a comment, or for the purpose of publication or broadcast. If the record is a written one, the difference is more subtle than if it is a recording. A written account, even one faithfully using quotation marks, is the reporter's characterization of what happened or what was said. An audiotape or videotape recording that is broadcast is, albeit incomplete with regard to context, the transmittal of an event to an audience in a time and place removed from the event itself.

Ethical issues surround the recording in the first place, and the use of the recording in the second place. If the recording is made with the knowledge and consent of the source and there is an understanding that all or part of the recording will be broadcast publicly, no ethical issues arise from the recording itself (although such issues might arise from the way in which the recording is edited), because no deception or breach of confidence is involved. No "rule" of ethical behavior has been broken. Problems arise when the recording is made secretly, or even openly but without the consent of the subject (source) and when the recording, whether secret or not, is used in a manner that is not in accordance with the consent or reasonable expectation of the subject, that is, when deception or breach of promise, expressed or implied, is involved.

The Law

The federal wiretap law (Title III of the Omnibus Crime Control and Safe Streets Act of 1968, as amended by the Electronic Communications Privacy Act of 1986) permits surreptitious recording of conversations when one party consents, "unless such communication is intercepted for the purpose of committing any criminal or tortious act in violation of the Constitution or laws of the United States or of any State." Amendments signed into law in October 1986 expand the prohibitions to unauthorized interception of most forms of electronic communications, including satellite transmissions, cellular phone conversations, and computer data transmissions.

Most states have duplicated the federal law, some expanding on its language to prohibit all recording without the consent of all parties. Some state laws provide additional penalties for divulging or using unlawfully acquired information and for trespassing to acquire it, and in most states the laws allow for civil as well as criminal liability.

Most of the state statutes permit the recording of speeches and conversations that take place where the parties may reasonably expect to be recorded. Most also exempt law enforcement agencies and public utilities that monitor conversations and phone lines in the course of their legitimate duties.

The Issues

Ethical issues in this area, as in so many, have to do with deception and with the concepts of invasion of privacy and of breach of promise. If a recording is made surreptitiously, in a situation in which the source would have a reasonable expectation of privacy, then the very recording of the sound or image might be considered damaging to the source in that the practice fails to respect the human dignity of the source. If the recording is made surreptitiously in a public place, however, an environment in which a person might not reasonably expect any significant degree of privacy, then the recording itself might be considered to be ethical.

Ethical issues more frequently arise from the *use* of recordings that have been made by reporters, either surreptitiously or openly. If an interview is recorded with the understanding that the tape will not be broadcast and then it is broadcast, an obvious ethical problem arises: breach of promise. This was the case in the highly publicized interview between CBS-TV reporter Connie Chung and the mother of House Speaker Newt Gingrich. Chung indicated to Kathleen Gingrich that her response to a question would be "just between us," but then it was broadcast to the world on the "CBS Evening News" of 4 January 1995 and again on "Eye to Eye with Connie Chung" the following evening.

A related problem arises when a recording made for one purpose is used for another, as when video recordings of a scene captured by a security camera are used for news or entertainment purposes. A person who knowingly and willingly enters a space, such as a bank lobby, where there are security cameras, finds her image on a videocassette that is sold to the public for entertainment purposes. This amounts to appropriation of the person's image for commercial purposes without her permission, possibly subjecting her to public ridicule in the bargain.

Surveillance camera tapes often become the stuff of news stories when they reveal the commission of crimes or inappropriate behavior on the part of authorities. The persons depicted in these scenes may complain that, even though they have been recorded in criminal or inappropriate behavior, it is not justified to use the recording to hold them up to public scorn.

Cases

Instances of problems created by journalistic recording, of course, are not hard to find, and many make their way to the courts. A few are mentioned below.

In *Boddie v. American Broadcasting Companies* (881 F.2d 267: 6th Cir. 1989), as part of an ABC expose of judicial corruption in Akron, Ohio, plaintiff Sandra A. Boddie agreed to be interviewed for the program, but she refused to appear on camera. In spite of her refusal, defendants ABC producer Charles C. Thompson and reporter Geraldo Rivera secretly videotaped her interview and broadcast a portion of it. Although the appeals court ruled in favor of ABC, there was a clear ethical violation: Thompson and Rivera broke a promise not to record her and not to broadcast a recording. The ruling was based on the fact that the federal law allows the "interception" of a communication by someone who is a party to the communication, without the knowledge of the other party, "unless such communication is intercepted for the purpose of committing any criminal or tortious act ... or for the purpose of committing any other injurious act (18 U.S.C. 2511(2)(d)). The court ruled that the journalists' action in recording and using the interview was not for a criminal or tortious purpose, and the use of the term "injurious" was unconstitutionally vague.

In a similar case, *Desnick v. American Broadcasting Companies* (44 F.3d 1345: 7th Cir. 1995), ABC's *PrimeTime Live* used "test patients" with hidden cameras inside an eye clinic, even after assuring Dr. James H. Desnick, the owner of the clinic, that no such techniques would be used. The court found that, even though Dr. Desnick might well have refused the network permission to enter his clinic with a camera or to place "test" patients in the clinic, had he known their actual intent, he did grant them permission to enter, and no trespassing occurred. The ruling also noted that no defamation, invasion of privacy, or other tort resulted from the technique the network used to obtain its story, as opposed to the dissemination of the story itself, and added that people of ordinary sophistication should be skeptical of promises made by investigatory journalists. The Desnick clinics specialized in cataract surgery; its patients were primarily elderly persons whose treatment was covered by Medicare.

In both of these cases, the operative question is whether the obvious deception and harm can be justified. The journalists would no doubt argue that the story could not be told without the tape in question and that the story was important to the public's safety and welfare. Both of these claims are subject to question.

In *Huskey v. NBC* (632 F. Supp. 1282, 12 Med. L. Rptr. 2105: N.D. Ill. 1986), a prisoner successfully complained that a network crew filmed him without consent while he was in an "exercise cage." The court ruled that the fact the prisoner could be viewed by a guard did not mean he was in a "public place," such as the dining room, an open visible yard, or the booking area at a jail. He had a reasonable expectation of privacy. An ethical judgment in this case would largely ignore this consideration and focus on the motivation for the filming, the use of the film, and the impact of that use both on the prisoner and on the public.

In *Brooks v. ABC* (737 F. Supp. 431; N.D. Ohio 1990), another Geraldo Rivera case, William Brooks claimed his conversation on a public street had been illegally intercepted (under federal law). The court ruled that the conversation had been intercepted but that, since the conversation had taken place on a public sidewalk, it was not a private conversation and therefore was not illegally intercepted. Despite the technical consideration deemed pivotal by the court, the conversation was in fact taped secretly, when Brooks might be considered to have a reasonable expectation that his conversation was private. The ethical question is whether the secret taping, which obviously violates a "rule" of ethical conduct, can be justified in the light of some greater good.

Looking Ahead

The concept of recording sources is expanded by new technologies. One example might be the appropriation and use of E-mail messages, or excerpts from them, in documents that are published on the Internet without permission of the original writer. Another might be the appropriation of content from an individual's (or institution's) World Wide Web home page without permission for use elsewhere. Certainly a person or organization that places information on a web site may have little or no expectation of privacy, but there is a reasonable expectation of copyright, legally, and of respect for authorship, ethically.

Source Presentation

Kristie Bunton

Selecting the quotations and images that comprise news reports is an integral aspect of journalism. Journalists enjoy considerable freedom in the selection, but ethical questions about truth telling, fairness, and social justice come with that freedom. Should a journalist "clean up" a speaker's poor grammar or offensive language when using a direct quotation? Must a journalist seek out nontraditional sources? When can photographs be staged or digitally altered? Should videotape be edited out of sequence? These are ethical questions about the presentation of sources in news.

The Law

In 1991, the U.S. Supreme Court in *Masson v. New Yorker Magazine* (501 U.S. 496) decided that journalists who alter or fabricate quotations may be guilty of libel. The Court's decision stems from psychoanalyst Jeffrey Masson's complaint against *New Yorker* magazine writer Janet Malcolm. Masson, the former director of the Sigmund Freud Archives, said Malcolm damaged his reputation among his peers by fabricating and attributing to him quotations that made him seem incompetent and unprofessional. For instance, while Malcolm's *New Yorker* article included a quotation in which Masson called himself "an intellectual gigolo," the description appeared nowhere in Malcolm's interview audiotapes and notes, which were examined during the trial. Malcolm also admitted she had reordered Masson's words in direct quotations and condensed interviews conducted over several months into what she presented in her article as a single conversation with Masson.

While the Court said deliberately rearranging quotations so as to damage a person's reputation may be grounds for libel, it acknowledged that journalists who make honest mistakes in using quotations may be protected from libel suits. Still, some journalists worry that the Court's ruling means they can be sued if their quotations are not verbatim reproductions of a source's words.

The Issues

Direct quotations are essential to news reporting. They add spice to news stories by reflecting the speaker's style and tone. They also add credibility, letting readers know the reporter actually conducted interviews.

Few news sources, however, speak in perfectly clear and grammatical sentences. Most speakers' sentences are peppered with "hmm" and "uh," and sometimes speakers say "she ain't" when they mean "she isn't." Because a direct quotation signals to readers that the words inside quotation marks are the speaker's exact words, should interjections and grammatical errors be included in quotations, or should the journalist clean them up?

"Most journalists 'clean up' quotes when they are ungrammatical or difficult to understand, because they believe it is more important to convey the person's thoughts clearly than to confuse the reader," note the authors of *Groping for Ethics in Journalism* (Goodwin and Smith 1994, 232). Nevertheless, many journalists do not clean up the quotations of media-savvy sources who are familiar with the interviewing and reporting process. Columnist Molly Ivins, for example, believes it is not her responsibility to make public officials look good by cleaning up their quotations (Goodwin and Smith 1994, 233).

Another question for journalists is how to treat a speaker's offensive language. If, for instance, a speaker uses "adult" language that might be unsuitable for a "family" newspaper's audience, should that language be quoted? Many news organizations instruct reporters to refrain from using obscenities, vulgarities, or profanities in news stories without a compelling reason for their inclusion. So, as with the case of fixing poor grammar, many journalists contend the speaker's stature determines whether offensive language should be quoted. If the president of the United States uses vulgarity in a public news conference, many journalists would report it as a direct quotation because citizens need to know how their elected leader behaves. If the captain of the high school soccer team uses vulgarity in the locker room, many journalists would not report it because the public does not need to know how a high school athlete behaves after a match.

Given today's easy access to previously published news reports via electronic databases and online services, journalists can be tempted to "recycle" quotations. Recycling quotations from other news accounts is a form of plagiarism, which is, of course, unethical because it is intellectual theft. Plagiarism is also damaging to journalistic credibility, and many news organizations consider plagiarism grounds for dismissal. Nevertheless, in recent years, several well-known journalists and news organizations have found themselves in ethical hot water after using quotations and information that closely resembled the content of other news reports without crediting those reports (see "Plagiarizing in a Copycat Case" and "A Rash of Cases in Fort Worth" in Black, Steele, and Barney 1995).

In addition to raising these truth-telling issues, the quotation process raises fairness and social justice issues. *Who* gets quoted may be as important a question as *how* that person gets quoted. In an increasingly diverse culture, journalists must expand their reporting beyond official sources—often white, middle-class, establishment figures—who are traditionally quoted in news stories. "Diversity is about inclusiveness in choosing sources and about giving voice to the voiceless," note Black, Steele, and Barney (1995, 133), the authors of *Doing Ethics in Journalism*. Ethical journalists seek out the viewpoints of racial and ethnic minorities, women, children, and the poor and quote them in accurate and contextual ways. They refrain from using quotations from a minority person in a token attempt at diversification, and they remain open to the possibility of changing a news story's angle when incorporating new and previously unheard voices (Black, Steele, and Barney 1995, 134).

Just as selecting quotations does, selecting visual images to accompany news stories raises truth-telling issues. Although many people believe a photograph is an objective replication of reality, a photograph is actually an image made by a photographer who makes choices about lighting, angle, and composition. A photograph is as selectively produced as a written news story is, and photojournalists must consider how freely to exercise that selectivity.

One selectivity question for photojournalists is whether to stage or reenact scenes not initially captured. For example, NBC's *Dateline* magazine program attracted worldwide attention after its investigation of faulty pickup truck gasoline tanks included staged video segments that showed a General Motors truck exploding into flames after a collision. Some photojournalists frown on such staged or reenacted images because they believe the images are untruthful, but others believe some staging or reenactment may be acceptable, depending on the circumstances and purpose of the image. The primary ethical problem reported by photojournalists remains "setup" shots, report Philip Patterson and Lee Wilkins (1994, 198), the authors of *Media Ethics: Issues and Cases*.

Ethical problems also persist in the darkroom and in the digital editing of images. Many photojournalists consider it acceptable to "dodge" or "burn" areas of a photograph in the darkroom as long as they are not changing the content and context of the photo, but are instead improving its reproducibility for publication. They draw the line, however, at materially altering the photograph to change its message.

Today's digital-imaging equipment makes it easier to edit images. Because this equipment eliminates the traditional photographic negative, no record of editing decisions is left behind, and readers cannot detect the seamless editing. For example, *National Geographic* used digital editing to scrunch together the great pyramids so they would fit on its cover; the St. Louis *Post-Dispatch* edited a Diet Coke can out of a news photo; *Newsweek* magazine created a cover portrait of actors Tom Cruise and Dustin Hoffman from photos taken in two separate sessions; and *TV Guide* placed talk show host Oprah Winfrey's head over actress Ann-Margret's body for a cover photo. In such instances, digital editing can lead to deception because readers have no way to verify that the images are untrue. In former years, supermarket tabloid readers could detect a "cut-and-paste" job that joined one person's head with another's body. In today's digital age, they cannot. Photojournalists, therefore, must be vigilant in their editing decisions.

Patterson and Wilkins (1994, 202) note that questions about selectivity in editing are most often heated when it comes to television's use of videotape: "Scenes aired out of sequence, answers dubbed behind questions that were not originally asked, and a preponderance of one view dominating the final cut at the expense of another view are some of the most frequently cited instances of selective editing." Even though the authors wonder whether it is logical to encourage news writers to edit and "focus" stories while reprimanding photojournalists for rearranging images to clarify them, they conclude that "as long as readers hold the view that 'seeing is believing,' that view—whether based in reality or not—becomes a promise between the media and their audience that photographers and videographers should be hesitant to break" (Patterson and Wilkins 1994, 203).

Cases

News organizations faced ethical questions about quotations when a recording by the African-American rap group 2 Live Crew was banned by a federal judge in *Luke v. Navarro* (960 F.2d 134) because it contained explicit lyrics. How should news reports explain that the recording contained multiple obscenities and explicit descriptions of violence against women? Would reproducing the lyrics verbatim offend audiences? Would sanitized references fail to adequately illustrate the content? In addition, "the 2 Live Crew controversy was particularly vexing because some social scientists argue that

Crew's use of obscenity, despite its vulgar and misogynist nature, reflects a tradition with its roots in slavery" (Black, Steele, and Barney 1995, 65).

Most news organizations in Florida, where the ban occurred, published descriptions without directly quoting the offensive lyrics. Black, Steele, and Barney (1995, 65), however, argue that the lyrics should have been quoted in the interest of truth telling: "Journalists, while recognizing that some in their audience might find the lyrics offensive, must give heavy emphasis to providing a complete account of this story, including the lyrics, if the public is to understand fully the issue and its ramifications."

Looking Ahead

Because journalism deals with vast amounts of information on a daily basis, the truth-telling questions raised by journalists' presentation of sources in news reports will not disappear. Furthermore, the capabilities offered by new technology, such as electronic databases and digital-image editing systems, may increase the pressure on journalists to make sound ethical decisions about using quotations and images. The continued blurring of the lines between news, advertising, and entertainment, particularly in the area of electronic images, indicates that journalists will have to exercise vigilance to maintain the lines between truth and fiction. A thoughtful commitment to truth telling, fairness, and social justice is required of the ethical journalist.

References: Black, Jay, Bob Steele, and Ralph Barney. 1995. *Doing Ethics in Journalism: A Handbook with Case Studies.* 2d Edition. Needham Heights, MA: Allyn & Bacon.

Christians, Clifford G., Mark Fackler, and Kim B. Rotzoll. 1995. *Media Ethics: Cases and Moral Reasoning.* 4th Edition. White Plains, NY: Longman.

Covington, Bob. 1994. "What TV News Will Do for Ratings: Suit Alleges KSTP Played Loose with Facts in Repair-Firm Story." Minneapolis *Star Tribune* (2 March): 15A.

Goodwin, Gene, and Ron F. Smith. 1994. *Groping for Ethics in Journalism.* 2d Edition. Ames: Iowa State University Press.

Patterson, Philip, and Lee Wilkins. 1994. *Media Ethics: Issues and Cases.* 2d Edition. Dubuque, IA: Brown & Benchmark.

Anonymous Sources

Lee Wilkins

Contemporary journalistic thinking about the role of news sources assumes an active audience. The notion is that readers and viewers may better understand and evaluate journalistic accounts if those accounts identify journalists' information sources. Identification often goes beyond a mere name and address: journalists may provide background so audience members understand why a person or document is cited. The professional standard is that sources should be named and that journalists must have compelling reasons for withholding a source's identity. Furthermore, granting anonymity is a mutual agreement between reporter and source, not a unilateral understanding imposed on one party by the other. Anonymous sources are expected to be the exception rather than the journalistic rule. Professional mores dictate that, should a reporter decide to grant anonymity, she does not have to divulge the source's identity to editors, other supervisors, or, in rare instances, the courts.

The Law

Use of anonymous sources has seldom been the subject of litigation, but two of the best-known court contests illustrate how the law can sometimes erode good ethical reasoning. In *Cohen v. Cowles Media Co.* (Sup. Ct. C8-88-2631 etc., 1992), the U.S. Supreme Court ruled that reporters can be sued for breaking promises to shield a source's identity. The case arose when Dan Cohen, a Republican campaign adviser, offered multiple Minnesota reporters damaging information (for a shoplifting conviction that was later vacated) about a Democratic candidate for lieutenant governor. The reporters agreed to allow Cohen to remain off the record, only to have their agreements over-ruled by editors at two different news organizations. Two other editors allowed Cohen to remain anonymous. When the stories that identified Cohen ran, he was fired. He sued. The Court ruled in Cohen's favor, reasoning that the case was not a First Amendment issue but instead represented the breach of a confidentiality contract. Ultimately, the newspapers paid Cohen $200,000 in damages. Journalists feared many sources would sue based on *Cohen*. In fact, only a few cases have relied on this legal precedent, and not all of those have been decided in favor of the source (Martin 1996).

In *Philip Morris Cos., Inc. v. ABC, Inc.* (Media L. Rep. [BNA] 1434, 1438: Va. Cir. Ct. 1995)—a case that was settled out of court—efforts to uncover an anonymous source's identity took a different twist. In addition to asking journalists to reveal their prized source, "Deep Cough," attorneys for Philip Morris asked the news organization to provide airline, phone, rental car, and hotel records in an effort to track reporters' movements and thereby uncover the source. A judge declined to require ABC to provide the requested information. The case provides some preliminary and very modest assurance of legal protection for journalists who become embroiled in ever more viscous discovery tactics (Calvert 1996).

Finally, some states have enacted shield laws—statutes that provide journalists with full or partial legal protection should they and their anonymous sources wind up in court. These laws have generally been held to be constitutional on First Amendment grounds, but the precise regulations vary from state to state, and not all states have adopted such legislation.

Historic Development

Like many contemporary professional practices, sourcing is not firmly rooted in journalistic history. In the era of the partisan press, story sources were most often the printers who controlled the presses. Further, printers were paid for their efforts by political partisans. Historians suggest that reader understanding of sources in the Revolutionary era parallels contemporary understanding of a signed editorial. Only as the journalistic practice of the interview developed concurrent with the rise of the professional ideal of objectivity did identifying news sources become accepted professional practice (Schudson 1978 and 1995).

The role that sourcing plays with readers and viewers also has been questioned by mass communication research. One of the most widely accepted findings in the field is that audience members tend to disassociate the source from the message, what is known as the "sleeper" effect (Lowery and DeFleur 1988). Studies confirm that most people tend to retain the fact of what is said, while forgetting the context in which they "heard" it. Propagandists, from Goebbels through contemporary political consultants, have intuitively understood this human tendency. Current ethical reasoning, however, asserts the primacy of readers and viewers as morally autonomous actors. Identifying news sources allows audiences to evaluate reports in terms of both content and a source's motives for divulging information.

The Issues

The motives for providing and withholding information are sometimes central to political coverage, and political reporters have added an element of elasticity to the practice of anonymous sourcing.

The phrase *not for attribution* means journalists may quote what is said but agree to veil the source. Thus, the attribution *a high, White House source* may mean anyone from the president himself to cabinet officers to other, well-connected administrative appointees. The phrase *on background* means journalists should consider the information given as an aid in placing facts in context. Background information also may be used as part of a sourcing trail; that is, journalists in possession of background information may use their knowledge to try to get other sources to provide them with the same information on the record.

Journalists continue to debate allowing sources to go "off the record" or "on deep background." A strict interpretation of these synonymous phrases means that the journalist who accepts information may not quote the specific source and, in addition, may not use her knowledge to pry the same information from other sources. This stringent interpretation has meant that editors have instructed reporters to literally leave the room when a source asks for such anonymity. Less stringent interpretations suggest that journalists who accept information off the record may not name or in any way reveal the identity of the source but may use the information itself to leverage similar or related information from other sources.

While such treatment is most common in the political arena, journalists who cover police, the courts, and other areas of public life often develop informal agreements with frequent sources about when and how information may be attributed. Such relationships are necessary but risky. Many journalists have had to decide whether they will "burn a source"—reveal the identity of a source who has been allowed to remain veiled in earlier stories—for a particularly important story. Burning a source means terminating a relationship that worked well for both parties. It is considered a form of promise breaking. Keeping the trust between reporter and source intact is one reason that larger news organizations often will send an investigative reporter to cover a particularly sensitive story that arises on another reporter's beat. Sending an investigative reporter allows the beat reporter's sourcing agreements to remain undisturbed, ensuring a continuing flow of routine information while the investigation continues.

There are significant ethical justifications for using anonymous sources. They are preventing either physical or emotional harm to a source; protecting the privacy of a source, particularly children and crime victims; and encouraging coverage of institutions, such as the U.S. Supreme Court or the military, which might otherwise remain closed to journalistic and hence public scrutiny. It is this final justification that is used most frequently by journalists who cover institutions, such as the Supreme Court or the military, that have historically functioned in secret. Reporters maintain that only when sources are allowed to remain anonymous will they provide newsworthy information that would otherwise place their careers or their physical safety at risk.

Equally respected investigative journalists condemn the practice. They maintain that the well-publicized practice of allowing sources to remain anonymous has infected the profession and that journalists do not work hard enough to get sources on the record. Sources can have their own reasons for seeking anonymity, reasons that put self before public interest. Politicians and government officials "leak" stories to the press for their own purposes, among them misleading political opponents or gauging public opinion without expending political capital (Linsky 1986).

Cases

Certain cases involving anonymous sources have influenced subsequent performance. Four of the best known follow.

Watergate Richard Nixon might have completed his second term in the White House were it not for the anonymous source cultivated by a *Washington Post* reporter in his first year on the job. Bob Woodward's still unknown source, "Deep Throat," set the journalistic standard for use of an anonymous source in an investigation that mattered. "Deep Throat's" knowledge was used to pry information from other sources who did go on the record. Not only did "Deep Throat" help journalists, the courts, and ultimately the political system force to Nixon's resignation, he also helped to make Woodward famous and to spur heightened professional commitment to investigative reporting.

"Jimmy's World" Ten years after Watergate, Woodward was the supervising editor for Janet Cooke, a young reporter at the *Washington Post* who wrote a moving account of an eight-year-old heroin addict living in the District. Jimmy remained anonymous, and the *Post* nominated Cooke's piece for a Pulitzer Prize. She received the coveted award—in a category different from that in which her story was originally entered. When the prize was announced, Jimmy's world unraveled. Cooke revealed her anonymous source existed only as a literary composite of the many children she had met, and she resigned from the *Post*. The incident was a profound embarrassment to the paper, which returned the prize.

A Rape Victim Refuses Anonymity The "Jimmy's World" case prodded journalists to ask whether they had been too willing to allow sources to retain anonymity. The profession, however, continued to allow some kinds of sources—for example, crime victims—to remain veiled. Geneva Overholtzer, editor of the *Des Moines Register*, worked closely with a rape victim who was willing to go on the record with the details of her life and the brutal attack, including her name and photograph. Overholtzer's Pulitzer Prize–winning narrative demonstrated that, even when the issue is as private as rape, sources can be convinced to go on the record in ways that do not assault either the source's dignity or the readers' sensibilities.

The Brock Adams Story Brock Adams, a 20-year Senate veteran, was a liberal Democrat from Washington State. Prior to his 1992 reelection campaign, the *Seattle Times* received a series of off-the-record tips about Adams's sexual victimization of staff members. Journalists could not convince any of 12 women who said they had been victims of Adams's abuse to go on the record. They then crafted a creative agreement with their sources. Eight of them signed an affidavit asserting the events they recounted were true and that, should Adams sue the *Times* for libel, they would reveal their identities in court. The *Times* published the story, declining to identify the women by name but providing significant details of their employment history and work with Adams. Less than 24 hours later, Adams withdrew from the campaign. He never sued. About 200 miles to the south, the Portland *Oregonian* faced a similar set of sourcing challenges when charges of sexual harassment surfaced against longtime Republican Senator Bob Packwood. The *Oregonian* decided to hold the story until after the 1992 election, in large part because it could not get sources on the record. Packwood was reelected; he resigned from the U.S. Senate in disgrace about two years later.

Looking Ahead

While new technology seldom raises new ethical issues per se, the Internet creates additional permutations. Because it substitutes virtual interaction for the face-to-face variety, journalists sourcing their stories via Internet must take additional precautions to authenticate not just information but also sources. In early 1995, *Time* magazine was bamboozled by its exclusive reliance on wired sources for a story about pornography on the Internet. When the magazine later discovered its sources did not possess the claimed academic credentials, it apologized, but not before the story itself became the stuff of congressional debate over the 1995 Communications Decency Act. The constitutionality of that legislation is currently undergoing court review.

References: Calvert, Clay. 1996. "Searching for the Silver Lining: Confidential Sources and the Reporter's Privilege in *Philip Morris Cos., Inc. v. ABC, Inc.*" Unpublished paper presented to the Association for Education in Journalism and Mass Communication, Anaheim, CA, August.

Linsky, M. 1986. *Impact: How the Press Affects Federal Policy Making*. New York: W. W. Norton.

Lowery, S., and M. DeFleur. 1988. *Milestones in Mass Communication Research*. New York: Longman.

Martin, Hugh J. 1996. "*Cohen v. Cowles Media Co.* Revisited: An Assessment of the Case's Impact So Far." Unpublished paper presented to the Association for Education in Journalism and Mass Communication, Anaheim, CA, August.

Schudson, M. 1978. *Discovering the News*. New York: Pantheon.

———. 1995. *The Power of News*. New York: Pantheon.

CONTEMPORARY ETHICAL ISSUES

Chapter 5:
Court Cases

Robert F. Ladenson

Most ethical issues in journalism relate in various ways to circumstances in which activities of journalists present a conflict between values central to the role of the press in democratic society and other morally significant social and individual concerns. Such issues can arise as matters calling for decisions by reporters and editors. Many important ethical issues in journalism, however, merge with broad issues of social and political morality within the scope of the judiciary under the American constitutional system. The following case summaries and discussions of issues thus deal, in effect, with a *public* interpretation of journalism ethics. That is, they deal with this subject from the viewpoints of judicial officers with the responsibility of resolving questions of rights and obligations on behalf of the public. The case summaries and discussions, arranged by topic, all concentrate upon cases decided by the U.S. Supreme Court.

A case citation follows the name of each case, which enables one to locate the published opinion of the Court in connection with the case. For example, the citation for the case of *New York Times v. Sullivan* is 376 U.S. 254 (1964). This means that the case appears in volume 376 of the *United States Reports*, the official reporter series for the U.S. Supreme Court, at page 254, and it was decided in 1964.

Freedom of Speech and Press

Schenk v. United States 249 U.S. 47 (1919)

This case is the first in the history of the Supreme Court in which the Court interpreted the First Amendment guarantee of free speech. The Court rejected a First Amendment challenge to provisions of the Espionage Act of 1917, which authorized the federal government to prosecute anti-World War I activists for preparing to distribute pamphlets opposing military conscription to recent inductees. Justice O. W. Holmes Jr., writing for the majority of the Court, declared in words, later to become famous, that "[t]he most stringent protection of free speech would not protect a man in falsely shouting fire in a theater and causing a panic." Holmes went on to say that speech allowed during peacetime may be silenced when a nation is at war.

Abrams et al. v. United States 250 U.S. 616 (1919)

The Supreme Court upheld the constitutionality, under the First Amendment, of the 1918 amendments of the Espionage Act of 1917, which expanded the range of prohibited speech behavior under the act. In a major shift of position, only a half-year after writing his majority opinion in *Schenk v. United States*, Justice Holmes dissented from the majority opinion of the Court. His dissenting opinion, joined by Justice Louis D. Brandeis, was the first of a series of Holmes and Brandeis dissents in free speech cases, which subsequently became the intellectual cornerstone of the Supreme Court's interpretation of the free speech guarantee of the First Amendment.

Whitney v. California 274 U.S. 357 (1927)

The Supreme Court upheld the constitutionality, under the First Amendment, of a California State statute, entitled the Criminal Syndicalism Act. This act, aimed primarily at prohibiting the spread of radical ideas concerning ownership and control of the means of industrial production, made it illegal to advocate the use of force to bring about "a change in industrial ownership," or to effect "any political change." In a separate opinion, joined by Justice Holmes, Justice Brandeis reluctantly concurred with the majority of the Court for procedural reasons. In doing so, he wrote a statement on the meaning and philosophy of free speech diametrically opposed to the narrow position of the Court majority. Brandeis' words in *Whitney* have become the most frequently quoted statement on free speech in Supreme Court opinions.

Brandenburg v. Ohio 395 U.S. 444 (1969)

In this case, the Supreme Court overruled its decision of 42 years earlier in *Whitney v. California*, declaring unconstitutional, under the First Amendment, an Ohio Criminal Syndicalism Act with language similar to the statute at issue in *Whitney*. In striking down the Ohio statute the Court held that "the constitutional guarantees of free speech and free press do not permit a state to forbid or proscribe advocacy of the use of force or of law violation except where such advocacy is directed to inciting or producing imminent lawless action and is likely to incite such action."

Near v. Minnesota 283 U.S. 697 (1931)

A Minnesota statute made it possible to bring lawsuits for the purpose of perpetually enjoining (i.e., permanently shutting down) any newspaper or periodical judged to be "obscene, lewd, or lascivious" or "malicious, scandalous, or defamatory." The Supreme Court invalidated the statute as unconstitutional under the First Amendment. In this connection, the Court described the statute as a "previous restraint upon speech" and stated that "liberty of the press, historically considered and taken up by the federal constitution, has meant principally, although not exclusively, immunity from previous restraints on speech."

Nebraska Press Association v. Stuart 427 U.S. 539 (1976)

A Nebraska court issued a gag order directed at the press in connection with the trial of a defendant charged with multiple murders. The gag order barred the press from reporting on the testimony and evidence presented at an open preliminary hearing, any confessions or admissions of the accused, or any other "strongly implicative" information. The Supreme Court unanimously declared the gag order an unconstitutional violation of the First Amendment, reaffirming the high constitutional barrier against previous restraints stated in *Near v. Minnesota*.

Discussion

Insofar as one views the basic role of journalism as providing the public with information, commentary, and discussion about subjects of general interest, the topic of journalism ethics presupposes that society accords fundamental status to the right of freedom of the press. It is thus useful to begin a discussion of major ethical issues in journalism by describing, in its broad contours, the right of freedom of the press as the U.S. Supreme Court interprets it.

The First Amendment to the U.S. Constitution says that "Congress shall make no law... abridging freedom of speech or of the press." Does the First Amendment notion of freedom of the press include only printed speech, so that individual persons and media organizations have essentially the same communicational rights under the Constitution? Alternatively, do the words *or of the press* in the First Amendment add anything to the communicational rights of media organizations beyond the constitutional free speech rights that these organizations possess in common with individual persons? The Court has never settled this question, either explicitly or implicitly, and constitutional scholars have different opinions about it. All sides agree, however, on a critical point. The most important rights, by far, at the core of a media organization's right of freedom of the press are its constitutional free speech rights. Thus, to a large extent, understanding the constitutional concept of freedom of the press consists of clearly understanding what freedom of speech means in constitutional terms.

In its earliest First Amendment cases, the Court interpreted the right of free speech in narrow terms, upholding convictions of individuals, under federal laws enacted during World War I that made it a crime to speak out against American involvement in the war. During the more than 75 years since these early decisions, the Court has considered hundreds of other cases, involving a diverse array of issues concerning free speech. In light of accumulated experience and reflection during this period, the Court now views the right of free speech in broad terms, diametrically opposed to the narrow stance the Court originally adopted in its earliest cases.

Under the Court's current interpretive approach, the right of individuals to speak out on issues relating to governmental institutions, policies, or actions is extremely strong, if not absolutely exceptionless. The approach of the Court places a stringently heavy burden upon government to justify regulation of speech concerning public affairs that, in virtually every case, rules out such regulation as constitutionally impermissible. Speech on other subjects, under the Court's current approach, receives protection essentially as strong as that accorded to speech about public affairs, unless the speech at issue falls into an "unprotected category," such as libel and slander, obscenity, or "fighting words." The phrase *unprotected category*, however, can be misleading, because government limitations upon speech in such a category must indeed satisfy significant requirements—most importantly, they must have a reasonable purpose, must be stated in terms that are neither too vague nor too broad, and must not otherwise have a "chilling effect" upon speech.

Controversies about whether or not media organizations have First Amendment free press rights whose content extends beyond the right of free speech, as currently interpreted by the Court, arise in conjunction with a range of diverse issues. These issues include libel and slander, national security concerns, testamentary privilege (i.e., whether reporters have a right not to testify in criminal proceedings about their sources of information for news stories), and informational access rights (i.e., whether media organizations have rights of access to various kinds of information controlled by public officials).

Slander and Libel

New York Times v. Sullivan 376 U.S. 254 (1964)

The Supreme Court held that in lawsuits for defamation (i.e., libel or slander) brought by a public official in regard to statements about his or her conduct in an official capacity, the public official must establish "actual malice" in order to prevail. This ruling means that the public official must prove that the statements at issue were made by the defendant in the case with actual knowledge of their falsity or in reckless disregard of the truth. In justifying this stringent standard the Court stressed that under a less stringent standard public officials could accomplish, through lawsuits for defamation, the same repressive aims they might achieve under sedition statutes making it criminal to libel or slander the government.

Curtis Publishing Company v. Butts and *Associated Press v. Walker* 388 U.S. 130 (1967)

In these two cases, decided jointly, the Supreme Court extended the "actual malice" requirement of *New York Times v. Sullivan* to cover actions for defamation brought by *public figures*, that is, by people in the public eye, whether public officials or not. The Court stressed that public interest in news stories involving nongovernmental public figures generally is no less than in stories relating to public officials, and it also maintained that public figures usually have means available to them to combat ill effects of defamatory speech by virtue of the media attention accorded them.

Rosenbloom v. Metromedia Corporation 403 U.S. 29 (1971)

The Supreme Court applied the *New York Times v. Sullivan* "actual malice" standard in a situation where the plaintiff was neither a public official nor a public figure, but had been prominently involved in a situation that generated substantial media attention. This was, however, a plurality decision—a decision in which the members of the Court could not agree upon the rationale for the decision. Only two members of the Court took the position that, as a general rule, the "actual malice" standard should be understood to cover individuals involved in newsworthy events, even if they are not public officials or public figures.

Gertz v. Welch 418 U.S. 323 (1974)

The Supreme Court stated definitively that the *New York Times v. Sullivan* "actual malice" standard only applies in the cases of lawsuits brought by public officials or public figures. The Court held that extending the "actual malice" standard to cover ordinary individuals, whenever they become involved in a matter of general interest, would unacceptably abridge the right of an individual to protect her or his reputation.

Discussion

The major ethical questions for journalism concerning slander and libel arise from a conflict between the legitimate interest of individuals in protecting their reputations and the range of values, concerns, and interests supporting a broad right of free speech. Decisions of the Supreme Court provide answers to these questions in constitutional terms by adjudicating the conflict predominantly in favor of a broad right of free speech when the aggrieved party is either a public official or public figure.

For many, the words *slander* and *libel* bring to mind the idea of a deeply reprehensible kind of wrong suffered by a person when another individual spreads maliciously motivated harmful untruths about her. It thus often comes as a surprise to people not steeped in the law that the basic legal definitions of slander and libel under common law rules (which still apply to every case except those in which the plaintiff is a public official, public figure, or a private individual suing over a defamation that involves a matter of public concern) do not include the notions of maliciousness, harmfulness, or even untruth. In order for a libel or slander case to be heard in court, one need only allege that someone has communicated words that a reasonable person would regard as defamatory to another individual. One need not allege maliciousness on the individual's part or that the individual's words actually resulted in harm to oneself. A person need not even allege that the individual's words were untrue, although truth is an absolute defense in a lawsuit for slander or libel.

Slander and libel lawsuits are often acrimonious, nasty, long, and expensive. In the landmark case of *New York Times v. Sullivan*, the Supreme Court underscored the severely chilling effect of such lawsuits, when brought by public officials, upon exercise of the right of free speech. For this reason, the Court held in *Sullivan* that a public official's complaint of slander or libel cannot prevail absent a showing of "actual malice," which the Court defined as either knowledge on the part of a defendant that his defamatory words were false or a defendant's reckless disregard for the truth.

Two years after its decision in *Sullivan*, the Court rendered two more decisions, *Curtis Publishing Co. v. Butts* and *Associated Press v. Walker*, in which it extended the "actual malice" standard to include not only public officials but also public figures. These decisions created a period of uncertainty for several years concerning whether the Court would extend the "actual malice" standard beyond public figures to cover individuals involved in newsworthy events. Insofar as the attention of media organizations is precisely what makes events newsworthy, such an interpretation, in effect, would construe the "actual malice" standard as a general rule, applicable in every case involving slander or libel complaints brought against the media. The Court, however, declined to accept this broad interpretation, and in the case of *Gertz v. Welch* explicitly drew the line beyond which the "actual malice" standard no longer applies at public figures.

From the standpoint of constitutional interpretation, the decisions of the Court have thus provided answers, in broad contour, to the key ethical issues for journalism concerning slander and libel. Under these answers, media organizations in the United States enjoy, if not absolute immunity, extremely strong legal protection from lawsuits for slander or libel brought by public officials or public figures.

Privacy

Time, Inc. v. Hill 385 U.S. 374 (1967)

The Supreme Court applied the *New York Times v. Sullivan* "actual malice" standard in a "false light" privacy case. In 1952, James Hill and his family were held hostage in their home for 19 hours by three escaped convicts, but they were released unharmed. Three years later, a play entitled *The Desperate Hours* portrayed a similar incident, only involving much violence. *Life* magazine's story on *The Desperate Hours* involved posing the play's actors in the home the Hills had lived in at the time they were held hostage. (They had since moved out of it.) The Court applied the *Sullivan* "actual malice" standard to overturn a judgment that Hill had recovered against Time, Inc., the publisher of *Life*, under a New York State privacy statute.

Cox Broadcasting Corp. v. Cohn 420 U.S. 469 (1975)

The Supreme Court held that the First Amendment protects a media organization in reporting truthful information about an individual obtained from public records. In this case, a television reporter had learned the name of a 17-year-old gang rape victim during the course of the proceedings against the rapists by examining the indictments. This case is important as much for what it *does not* say as for what it does. The media had sought from the Court a broad holding of an absolute immunity from lawsuits for invasion of privacy when the reported information is true. The Court, while ruling in favor of Cox Broadcasting Corporation, declined to base its ruling upon such a broad principle, stressing instead that the disclosed information had been obtained from public documents.

Discussion

Privacy, in the sense of the word that matters most for journalism ethics, has to do with individual autonomy—specifically with an individual's interest in controlling what, when, and to whom information about oneself is presented. The crucial problem is arriving at a reasonable accommodation between this important interest of individuals and the informational interests of the public entering into the very definition of the journalist's essential role.

As with slander and libel, prevailing law in the United States indicates how the American body politic has approached the problem of reaching such an accommodation. In this regard, most state courts recognize invasion of privacy as a civil law cause of action. Among the kinds of behavior giving rise to a civil lawsuit for invasion of privacy, the following three commonly involve the press as defendants: (1) obtaining information about a person through unreasonably intrusive means; (2) disseminating information about a person that places him in a false light (whether or not doing so amounts to defamation); and (3) publicly disclosing true but "private" information, that is, information of an embarrassing or otherwise objectionable nature.

With respect to cases falling under the first category, courts draw a sharp distinction between whether or not the individual in question is in a public area. If so, then the press may photograph, eavesdrop, or even record the individual's words, so long as doing so is not unreasonable. In contrast, such behavior becomes actionable if the individual is at home, in his office, or otherwise within a domain not open to the public. In situations where the media publicizes information obtained through unreasonably intrusive activity by another party, there is no liability for invasion of privacy arising from reliance upon the other party's unreasonable behavior. Such liability, the courts reason, would place an unreasonable burden upon the media in carrying out its basic role in a democratic society of keeping the public informed.

The reasoning in regard to accommodation of the individual's and the public's interests in connection with the preceding judgments appears sound and straightforward. Issues are less clear cut, however, in connection with the second category of behavior—disseminating information that places an individual in a false light—which can expose the media to lawsuits for invasion of privacy. In the case of *Time, Inc. v. Hill*, the Supreme Court applied the "actual malice" standard, adopted in the defamation case of *New York Times v. Sullivan*, to an invasion of privacy case within this second category. As for the third category, public disclosure of true but "private" information, one cannot summarize the stance of the law concisely in terms of either an authoritative Supreme Court decision or widely adopted legal rules for civil lawsuits. Generally, plaintiffs find it difficult to prevail when alleging disclosure of true but "private" information as a basis for a claim of invasion of privacy. In this regard, courts tend to acknowledge a privilege (i.e., an immunity from legal liability) for reporting of newsworthy events, and they also tend to defer to the judgment of the press concerning the newsworthiness of events. It should be emphasized, however, that the preceding statement expresses a tendency of judicial behavior, not a definite legal rule, applicable to the disclosure of "private" information in connection with civil lawsuits for invasion of privacy.

Right of Access to the News Media

Red Lion Broadcasting Co. v. FCC 395 U.S. 367 (1969)

The Supreme Court unanimously upheld two Federal Communications Commission (FCC) rules applicable to broadcasting that grant rights of reply to individuals or groups singled out for attacks upon their "honesty, character, integrity, or other like personal qualities" in the course of commentary upon matters of public interest. The Court viewed these rules as reasonable exercises of the FCC's congressional authorization to allocate scarce broadcasting frequencies through the licensing process and to promulgate appropriate rules for licensees.

CBS v. Democratic National Committee 412 U.S. 94 (1973)

This case originated with complaints, filed before the Federal Communications Commission (FCC) by the Democratic National Committee and an antiwar group, challenging a CBS policy of refusing all editorial endorsements. The FCC upheld CBS, but the court of appeals reversed, holding that an absolute ban on paid political advertising violates the First Amendment. The Supreme Court disagreed with the circuit court and reinstated the decision of the FCC, upholding CBS.

Miami Herald v. Tornillo 418 U.S. 241 (1974)

The Supreme Court unanimously declared unconstitutional, under the First Amendment, a Florida right of reply statute that required newspapers to grant a political candidate equal space to reply to newspaper criticism and attacks on his or her record.

Discussion

As noted in the discussion above of freedom of the press, the core protections of the First Amendment prohibit governmental actions that forbid or penalize the expression of beliefs and attitudes. Does the idea of the right of free speech also entail rights of access to resources that increase the probability a sizable number of people will receive messages one wants to communicate? In contrast, would statutes creating such rights violate basic principles associated with the idea of the right of free speech?

The *Red Lion* case upheld the constitutional validity of regulations granting a right of reply to individuals or groups subjected to personal attacks communicated by the broadcast media in the course of commentary upon matters of public interest. As *CBS v. Democratic National Committee* and *Miami Herald v. Tornillo* clearly illustrate, however, the Supreme Court does not acknowledge the general idea of a right of access to the news media on the part of individuals or groups under the First Amendment. Nevertheless, the Court's decisions do not consider explicitly the question of whether regulations applicable to broadcasting that create a right of access to media would violate the First Amendment. There are strong reasons to believe the Court would invalidate such regulations on the grounds of being an implicit form of censorship.

In this connection, developments since the Court decided *Red Lion* raise questions about whether the Court would now uphold the constitutional validity of even the rather limited access right at issue in that case. The Court, in *Red Lion*, viewed the FCC's rule requiring broadcasters to allow persons subject to personal attacks a right to respond to be a reasonable exercise of the FCC's congressional authorization to allocate scarce broadcasting frequencies through the licensing process and to promulgate appropriated rules for licensees. It is unclear to what extent the Court would now view new technological developments in broadcasting, such as cable television, which provides a large number of channels, as undercutting this rationale. As a related point, in 1987 the FCC repealed the broad regulatory requirement known as the "Fairness Doctrine," which the personal attack rule partially elaborated. This doctrine essentially required broadcasters to afford reasonable opportunity for presentation of opposing viewpoints on matters of public controversy. In repealing the Fairness Doctrine, the FCC concluded that the doctrine exerted a chilling effect upon the exercise of free speech rights of broadcasters, especially those who air controversial programs.

The topic of an individual's or a group's right of access to the media still poses difficult issues. Advocates of minority positions on important public issues often regard themselves as distinctly shut out of public debate and discussion. In many instances there is good reason to regard these perceptions as correct, which poses troubling questions not only about journalistic fairness but also about the effectiveness of the media in fulfilling its fundamental role in a democratic society—informing the public. Neither media organizations nor anyone else at this time has advanced a clear and plausible idea about how to resolve this problem.

National Security

New York Times v. United States 403 U.S. 413 (1971)

In 1971, the Nixon administration Department of Justice requested the Supreme Court to uphold an injunction issued by a judge in federal court that prohibited the *New York Times* from publishing a set of classified documents about the Vietnam War, known as the Pentagon Papers. The Court overturned the injunction in a 6-to-3 plurality decision. Each of the six justices who declined to support the injunction wrote separate opinions.

Discussion

The basic role of the media in contemporary democratic societies is to inform the public. Public disclosure of information by the media, however, might, in some circumstances, have deleterious effects from the standpoint of national security. Can one state useful guidelines for determining in particular cases whether or not national security concerns outweigh the basic role responsibility of the media to inform the public? Who should have the authority to make these kinds of determinations? Such questions, in turn, give rise to further issues that are complicated, multifaceted, and not easy to resolve.

One can easily imagine scenarios where the disclosure of information by the media would be a grave breach of national security, for example, revealing information about troop movements in wartime. The phrase *national security*, however, has been interpreted in broad and questionable ways, encompassing areas that many would consider important subjects for public debate and discussion. Suppose, for example (as was, in fact, the case), that a newspaper had known about the secret plans for a CIA-backed invasion of Cuba that resulted in the catastrophically unsuccessful Bay of Pigs fiasco in 1961. Would the publishing of a story about the planned invasion (which was not, in fact, the case) have been an unjustifiable breach of national security or a courageous and journalistically responsible action?

Even in cases where a regulation or policy has a reasonable basic purpose from the standpoint of national security, it can be very difficult to avoid framing it in language that invites abuse of power. Consider the Intelligence Identities Protection Act of 1982, which made it a crime to reveal the identities of covert CIA agents. The legislation has a legitimate basic purpose but, nonetheless, raises troubling issues, including the question of whether the law would apply to the investigation by a newspaper, such as the *Washington Post*, of possible CIA involvement in the Watergate break-in or to efforts by a college newspaper to determine if any college employees work covertly for the CIA.

The Supreme Court has never spoken definitively about the complex, difficult issues in regard to balancing the basic role responsibility of the media to inform the public with legitimate national security concerns. The Court's 6–3 decision in the Pentagon Papers case was viewed widely at the time as an immense judicial victory for the media, which it was when compared with the situation that would have resulted had the Court allowed the injunction to stand. Since each of the six justices who declined to support the position of the Nixon administration's Department of Justice, however, wrote a separate opinion to explain his reasoning, it is impossible to view the case as having established any conclusion broader than "the *New York Times* had a right to publish the Pentagon Papers based on the specific facts of the case." The most critical questions about determining the appropriate balance between the basic role of the press to inform the public and legitimate national security concerns are thus equally problematic at this time, from both the standpoint of constitutional case law and that of political morality.

Confidentiality Privilege

Branzburg v. Hayes 408 U.S. 665 (1972)

The Supreme Court held, in a 5-to-4 decision, that newspaper reporters are not entitled, under the First Amendment, to refuse to testify at a grand jury proceeding about information obtained through a promise of confidentiality. Both the majority and the minority acknowledged that a free and independent press is essential to the functioning of democratic government, as envisaged by the Constitution. The critical point of divergence between them concerned the extent to which the freedom and independence of the media necessitates testimonial immunity for reporters from the requirement to disclose confidential information in regard to a criminal proceeding.

Zurcher v. the Stanford Daily 436 U.S. 547 (1978)

This case arose out of a police search of the office of the *Stanford Daily*, the student newspaper at Stanford University, conducted under a valid search warrant. A key issue in the case was whether the First Amendment requires that as a condition of obtaining a search warrant to enter a newsroom, law enforcement authorities first must attempt to obtain the objects sought through the less intrusive means of a *subpoena duces tecum*. This kind of subpoena orders the newspaper to hand over specific items to the police, in contrast to being subjected to a police search conducted on the premises. In a 7-to-2 decision, the Supreme Court declined to hold that the First Amendment requires such a procedure.

Discussion

The closeness of the *Branzburg* decision (5-to-4) suggests there are strong arguments on both sides of the question. The majority stressed the necessarily broad powers of a grand jury in virtue of its role within the criminal justice system, and it dismissed as speculative the concern that requiring reporters to testify would create a diffident atmosphere in newsrooms. The dissenting justices, however, took the latter concern far more seriously, asserting that the case record bore ample evidence that requiring reporters to divulge information obtained in confidence would have precisely this result. In 1980, Congress amended the Federal Privacy Protection Act to provide journalists substantial protection from newsroom searches, applying both to work product materials and to other documents.

Under one interpretation, the ethical significance of First Amendment questions concerning both testimonial immunity for newspaper reporters and immunity from searches of newsrooms relates to the design of basic governmental institutions. In this regard, the critical question can be posed in the following hypothetical terms. If one was to design a governmental system starting from scratch, would one view such immunity as so critical that the Constitution—the blueprint for the system—should specifically include provision for it? This question is not easy to answer insofar as it brings one up against fundamental issues at the core of political philosophy.

Nonetheless, even if a person were uncertain about how to answer this ethically important, but theoretically difficult, question, she could reasonably believe that, as a matter of public policy, newspapers should receive the above kinds of immunities. In this connection, several states have enacted legislation providing testimonial immunity for reporters. Such immunity, however, is limited in all cases in ways intended to reflect an appropriate balance between supporting journalistic freedom and independence, on the one hand, and meeting the requirements of effective law enforcement and criminal justice systems, on the other hand.

Right of Access to Information from Government

Richmond Newspapers v. Virginia 448 U.S. 367 (1979)

The Supreme Court ruled that the media and, more generally, the public cannot be barred from attendance at criminal proceedings. In this case, the Court took the unusual action of overruling one of its own decisions, rendered only a year earlier, in which the Court had interpreted the Sixth Amendment right of a public trial to be exclusively for the benefit of defendants, and thus waivable by them. This earlier decision had prompted a barrage of criticism, not only from the media but from legal scholars as well, which may have been a key factor leading to the Court's decision one year later to overturn it.

Environmental Protection Agency v. Mink 410 U.S. 73 (1973)

The Supreme Court rejected the proposition that the exemption for national defense information in the federal Freedom of Information Act (FOIA) authorizes *in camera* inspection by a court of a contested document bearing a national security classification. In this regard, Mink argued unsuccessfully that the FOIA authorizes a court to separate information on agency disclosure under an FOIA request from information in a document appropriately within the scope of the classification.

Department of Air Force v. Rose 425 U.S. 352 (1976)

This case involved redacted material—material with names deleted—under a Freedom of Information Act (FOIA) request. The Supreme Court held that to justify a redaction an agency must balance the individual's right of privacy against the basic policy of the FOIA of opening agency action to the light of public scrutiny.

U.S. Department of Justice v. Reporters Committee for Freedom of the Press 489 U.S. 749 (1989)

The Supreme Court held that section 7c of the Freedom of Information Act (FOIA), which excludes from the scope of the act records compiled for law enforcement purposes "to the extent that production of such materials could be expected to constitute an unlawful invasion of privacy," applied to FBI rap sheets.

Discussion

Some commentators have argued that the reasoning of the Supreme Court in *Richmond Newspapers* provides the basis for a much more far-reaching conclusion than the one the Court drew, which affirmed the right of the public not to be barred from attendance at criminal proceedings. According to these commentators, insofar as one views such a right as grounded in the idea that criminal proceedings are an activity conducted by public officials on behalf of the public and about which the public has a right to know, this reasoning applies to *every* activity one could view in the same way.

Whether or not the reasoning of the Court in *Richmond Newspapers* implies the idea of a general right of the public regarding access to information from government, the Court has not, at this time, acknowledged such a right in any of its subsequent decisions. Furthermore, were the Court to do so, it could not reasonably view the right as an absolute entitlement, but instead would have to treat it as a kind of rebuttable presumption in favor of providing for public access to information. In this regard, a vast array of legitimate and, in some instances, vital activities conducted by governments require confidentiality, or secrecy, in particular cases. The following two questions thus appear critical for determining the contours of a right of access to information from government in particular situations. First, what is the relationship between various kinds and amounts of information about a particular government activity, on the one hand, and different degrees of democratic accountability with respect to that activity, on the other hand? Second, in what respects, and how seriously, would varying requirements of public access to information adversely affect the conduct of the governmental activity?

A balancing process in which the preceding two questions are posed results in different conclusions for different governmental activities. It would be highly unreasonable, for example, to insist that news reporters have a right to attend the conference meetings of the justices of the Supreme Court when they discuss cases on which they have heard oral argument. This would utterly destroy the conditions necessary for the justices to do their work without enhancing democratic accountability, because all that matters for maintaining such accountability is that the Court explain its reasoning for the public record, which it does through its opinions published in the *United States Reports*. In contrast, the balance does not lean so heavily on one side of the issue in connection with the arguments for and against open meetings laws for lawmakers on the state and local levels. To cite another example, the Freedom of Information Act explicitly lists nine different exceptions intended to strike a reasonable balance between enabling government agencies to carry out their essential functions in an effective way and maintaining an appropriate degree of democratic accountability.

CONTEMPORARY ETHICAL ISSUES

Chapter 6:
Codes of
Journalism Ethics

Elliot D. Cohen

This section includes some major journalistic codes of ethics, including codes specific to newspaper, broadcast, television, and photojournalism. Before proceeding to these codes, what follows is some general background information on professional codes of ethics.

The Nature and Functions of Professional Codes of Ethics

Codes of ethics play several important roles within a profession. First, a professional code of ethics provides a sense of professional identity for practitioners and signalizes the maturity of the profession. In general those practices that have attained social recognition as *professions*, as distinct from jobs or occupations, have organized into associations of practitioners—the American Medical Association, American Bar Association, American

Counseling Association, Society of Professional Journalists, etc. Practitioners belonging to such professional associations share special skills and funds of knowledge required for provision of their special services, and they have typically adopted, and occasionally revise and update, codes of ethics regarding the provision of these services.

The existence of a code of ethics is a healthy sign that those who practice a certain art or science have developed a unified understanding and image of what is expected of them and, indeed, of what they should expect of themselves. Codes of ethics accordingly help to unite individual practitioners in a shared collaborative enterprise.

Second, codes of ethics promote professional autonomy by providing a framework for self-regulation. In the case of journalism, the First Amendment of the U.S. Constitution has granted freedom of the press. With such freedom, however, comes the responsibility to act wisely. A code of ethics thus provides a framework for fulfilling this responsibility.

Third, a code of ethics can provide important guidelines for helping practitioners in making ethical decisions. It is worth noting, however, that codes of ethics are not intended to offer algorithms for ethical decision making. Code statements can sometimes be abstract in character and prescribe positive, aspirational goals (ideals) rather than well-defined (negative) requirements. For example, the Code of Ethics of the Society of Professional Journalists states that "truth is our ultimate goal" and that "objectivity in reporting the news is another goal that serves as the mark of an experienced professional." Truth and objectivity are positive goals to strive for in seeking journalistic excellence. Aspiring to these goals, however, depends much upon journalistic insight, careful reasoning, knowledge, and experience, which no code of ethics alone could provide.

Code rules should also be distinguished from law. Indeed, some less abstract code rules, such as the rule against plagiarism, proscribe conduct that is also illegal. Nevertheless, morally irresponsible journalism need not be, and typically is not, prosecuted. For example, failure to report important information or factual distortion through sensationalizing news constitute fundamental *moral* breaches regardless of whether a news organization can get away with them *legally*. Professional competence in journalism thus demands more than simple conformity to law. It demands respect for a professional code of ethics.

Code rules are not, however, always enforceable. Individual news organizations often fashion their own codes of ethics using a model such as the Code of Ethics of the Society of Professional Journalists. If journalists violate their organizational codes of ethics they may be held accountable for their transgressions and can even be fired; however, insofar as these code rules prescribe ideals, they are unenforceable. For example, it would be senseless to punish journalists for their failure to pursue the practice of photojournalism in a manner "worthy of the very best thought and effort of those who enter into it as a profession" in compliance with Principle 1 of the Code of Ethics of the National Press Photographers Association. Respect for rules expressing ideals must instead be motivated by a journalist's own internalized sense of professionalism.

The codes that follow address such key topics as journalistic responsibility, freedom of the press, honesty, candor, privacy, confidentiality, fairness, impartiality and accuracy. The emphasis and specificity with which each topic is addressed can vary according to the individual code. Viewed in relation to one another, these codes are consistent and mutually supportive. In arriving at an understanding of the ethical standards governing contemporary journalistic practice, it is useful therefore to consider all codes collectively as well as singularly. (All codes are reprinted with permission.)

American Society of Newspaper Editors

Statement of Principles

The American Society of Newspaper Editors (ASNE) last revised its Statement of Principles in 1975, replacing its 1922 Canons of Journalism. Articulated in the Preamble and Article 1 is a clear statement of the press' responsibility to the public. The code makes clear that all other standards of journalistic practice depend upon and are "proportionate to" this primary responsibility.

Statement of Principles

PREAMBLE

The First Amendment, protecting freedom of expression from abridgment by any law, guarantees to the people through their press a constitutional right, and thereby places on newspaper people a particular responsibility. Thus journalism demands of its practitioners not only industry and knowledge but also the pursuit of a standard of integrity proportionate to the journalist's singular obligation. To this end the American Society of Newspaper Editors sets forth this Statement of Principles as a standard encouraging the highest ethical and professional performance.

ARTICLE I—Responsibility.

The primary purpose of gathering and distributing news and opinion is to serve the general welfare by informing the people and enabling them to make judgments on the issues of the time. Newspapermen and women who abuse the power of their professional role for selfish motives or unworthy purposes are faithless to that public trust. The American press was made free not just to inform or just to serve as a forum for debate but also to bring an independent scrutiny to bear on the forces of power in the society, including the conduct of official power at all levels of government.

ARTICLE II—Freedom of the Press.

Freedom of the press belongs to the people. It must be defended against encroachment or assault from any quarter, public or private. Journalists must be constantly alert to see that the public's business is conducted in public. They must be vigilant against all who would exploit the press for selfish purposes.

ARTICLE III—Independence.

Journalists must avoid impropriety and the appearance of impropriety as well as any conflict of interest or the appearance of conflict. They should neither accept anything nor pursue any activity that might compromise or seem to compromise their integrity.

ARTICLE IV—Truth and Accuracy.

Good faith with the reader is the foundation of good journalism. Every effort must be made to assure that the news content is accurate, free from bias and in context, and that all sides are presented fairly. Editorials, analytical articles and commentary should be held to the same standards of accuracy with respect to the facts as news reports. Significant errors of fact, as well as errors of omission, should be corrected promptly and prominently.

ARTICLE V—Impartiality.

To be impartial does not require the press to be unquestioning or to refrain from editorial expression. Sound practice, however, demands a clear distinction for the reader between news reports and opinion. Articles that contain opinion or personal interpretation should be clearly identified.

ARTICLE VI—Fair Play.

Journalists should respect the rights of people involved in the news, observe the common standards of decency and stand accountable to the public for the fairness and accuracy of their news reports. Persons publicly accused should be given the earliest opportunity to respond. Pledges of confidentiality to news sources must be honored at all costs, and therefore should not be given lightly. Unless there is clear and pressing need to maintain confidences, sources of information should be identified.

These principles are intended to preserve, protect and strengthen the bond of trust and respect between American journalists and the American people, a bond that is essential to sustain the grant of freedom entrusted to both by the nation's founders.

Associated Press Managing Editors

Statement of Ethical Principles

The Statement *of Ethical Principles was adopted by the Associated Press Managing Editors (APME) in 1994. Articulated in the section on independence is a detailed statement of types of conflicts of interest that newspaper journalists should avoid. Note that conduct creating even the appearance of a conflict of interest is proscribed. Note also (section on responsibilities) the rule that sources should be disclosed and that any exception to this rule should be explained.*

Statement of Ethical Principles

These principles are a model against which news and editorial staff members can measure their performance. They have been formulated in the belief that newspapers and the people who produce them should adhere to the highest standards of ethical and professional conduct.

The public's right to know about matters of importance is paramount. The newspaper has a special responsibility as surrogate of its readers to be a vigilant watchdog of their legitimate public interests.

No statement of principles can prescribe decisions required in applying ethical principles to newspapers realities. As new technologies evolve, these principles can help guide editors to ensure the credibility of the news and information they provide. Individual newspapers are encouraged to augment these APME guidelines more specifically to their own situations.

Responsibility

The good newspaper is fair, accurate, honest, responsible, independent and decent. Truth is its guiding principle.

It avoids practices that would conflict with the ability to report and present news in a fair, accurate and unbiased manner.

The newspaper should serve as a constructive critic of all segments of society. It should vigorously expose wrongdoing, duplicity, and misuse of power, public or private.

Editorially, it should advocate needed reform and innovation in the public interest.

News sources should be disclosed unless there is a clear reason not to do so. When it is necessary to protect the confidentiality of a source, the reason should be explained.

The newspaper should uphold the right of free speech and freedom of the press and should respect the individual's right to privacy. The newspaper should fight vigorously for public access to news of government through open meetings and records.

Accuracy

The newspaper should guard against inaccuracies, carelessness, bias or distortion through emphasis, omission or technological manipulation.

It should acknowledge substantive errors and correct them promptly and prominently.

Integrity

The newspaper should strive for impartial treatment of issues and dispassionate handling of controversial subjects. It should provide a forum for the exchange of comment and criticism, especially when such comment is opposed to its editorial positions. Editorials and expressions of personal opinion by reporters and editors should be clearly labeled. Advertising should be clearly differentiated from news.

The newspaper should report the news without regard for its own interests, mindful of the need to disclose potential conflicts. It should not give favored news treatment to advertisers or special-interest groups....

Concern for community, business or personal interests should not cause the newspaper to distort or misrepresent the facts.

The newspaper should deal honestly with readers and newsmakers. It should keep its promises.

The newspaper should not plagiarize words or images.

Independence

The newspaper and its staff should be free of obligations to news sources and newsmakers. Even the appearance of obligation or conflict of interest should be avoided.

Newspapers should accept nothing of value from news sources or others outside the profession.... Expenses in connection with news reporting should be paid by the newspaper. Special favor and special treatment for members of the press should be avoided.

Journalists are encouraged to be involved in their communities, to the extent that such activities do not create conflicts of interest. Involvement in politics, demonstrations and social causes that could cause a conflict of interest, or the appearance of such conflict, should be avoided.

Work by staff members for the people of institutions they cover also should be avoided.

Financial investments by staff members or other outside business interests that could create the impression of a conflict of interest should be avoided.

Stories should not be written or edited primarily for the purpose of winning awards and prizes. Self-serving journalism contests and awards that reflect unfavorably on the newspaper or the profession should be avoided.

The Society of Professional Journalists, Sigma Delta Chi

Code of Ethics

The Society of Professional Journalists, Sigma Delta Chi, adopted its first code, borrowed from the American Society of News Editors, in 1926. It wrote its own code in 1973, which was revised in 1987, 1984, and most recently in 1996. In the section under the principle, "Seek Truth and Report It," the Code underscores the importance of providing a balanced, unbiased account of news. It also indicates that, while journalists have a responsibility to present informed analyses, commentaries, and editorial opinions, these must be clearly distinguished and kept separate from news reports.

Code of Ethics

Preamble

Members of the Society of Professional Journalists believe that public enlightenment is the forerunner of justice and the foundation of democracy. The duty of the journalist is to further those ends by seeking truth and providing a fair and comprehensive account of events and issues. Conscientious journalists from all media and specialties strive to serve the public with thoroughness and honesty. Professional integrity is the cornerstone of a journalist's credibility. Members of the Society share a dedication to ethical behavior and adopt this code to declare the Society's principles and standards of practice.

Seek Truth and Report It

Journalists should be honest, fair and courageous in gathering, reporting and interpreting information.

Journalists should:

- Test the accuracy of information from all sources and exercise care to avoid inadvertent error. Deliberate distortion is never permissible.
- Diligently seek out subjects of news stories to give them the opportunity to respond to allegations of wrongdoing.
- Identify sources whenever feasible. The public is entitled to as much information as possible on sources' reliability.
- Always question sources motives before promising anonymity. Clarify conditions attached to any promise made in exchange for information. Keep promises.
- Make certain that headlines, news teases and promotional material, photos, video, audio, graphics, sound bites and quotations do not misrepresent. They should not oversimplify or highlight incidents out of context.

- Never distort the content of news photos or video. Image enhancement for technical clarity is always permissible. Label montages and photo illustrations.
- Avoid misleading re-enactments or staged news events. If re-enactment is necessary to tell a story, label it.
- Avoid undercover or other surreptitious methods of gathering information except when traditional open methods will not yield information vital to the public. Use of such methods should be explained as part of the story.
- Never plagiarize.
- Tell the story of the diversity and magnitude of the human experience boldly, even when it is unpopular to do so.
- Examine their own cultural values and avoid imposing those values on others.
- Avoid stereotyping by race, gender, age, religion, ethnicity, geography, sexual orientation, disability, physical appearance or social status.
- Support the open exchange of views, even views they find repugnant.
- Give voice to the voiceless; official and unofficial sources of information can be equally valid.
- Distinguish between advocacy and news reporting. Analysis and commentary should be labeled and not misrepresent fact or context.
- Distinguish news from advertising and shun hybrids that blur the lines between the two.
- Recognize a special obligation to ensure that the public's business is conducted in the open and that government records are open to inspection.
- Minimize Harm

Ethical journalists treat sources, subjects and colleagues as human beings deserving of respect.
Journalists should:

- Show compassion for those who may be affected adversely by news coverage. Use special sensitivity when dealing with children and inexperienced sources or subjects.
- Be sensitive when seeking or using interviews or photographs of those affected by tragedy or grief.
- Recognize that gathering and reporting information may cause harm or discomfort. Pursuit of the news is not a license for arrogance.
- Recognize that private people have a greater right to control information about themselves than do public officials and others who seek power, influence or attention. Only an overriding public need can justify intrusion into anyone's privacy.
- Show good taste. Avoid pandering to lurid curiosity.
- Be cautious about identifying juvenile suspects or victims of sex crimes.

- Be judicious about naming criminal suspects before the formal filing of charges.
- Balance a criminal suspect's fair trial rights with the public's right to be informed.
- Act Independently

Journalists should be free of obligation to any interest other than the public's right to know.
Journalists should:

- Avoid conflicts of interest, real or perceived.
- Remain free of associations and activities that may compromise integrity or damage credibility.
- Refuse gifts, favors, fees, free travel and special treatment, and shun secondary employment, political involvement, public office and service in community organizations if they compromise journalistic integrity.
- Disclose unavoidable conflicts.
- Be vigilant and courageous about holding those with power accountable.
- Deny favored treatment to advertisers and special interests and resist their pressure to influence news coverage.
- Be wary of sources offering information for favors or money; avoid bidding for news.
- Be Accountable

Journalists are accountable to their readers, listeners, viewers and each other.
Journalists should:

- Clarify and explain news coverage and invite dialogue with the public over journalistic conduct.
- Encourage the public to voice grievances against the news media.
- Admit mistakes and correct them promptly.
- Expose unethical practices of journalists and the news media.
- Abide by the same high standards to which they hold others.

International Federation of Journalists

Declaration of Principles on the Conduct of Journalists

The International Federation of Journalists (IFJ) revised its Declaration of Principles on the Conduct of Journalists *in 1986, replacing its 1954 code. This international journalism code lists several ethical transgressions that also have legal definitions and can carry legal penalties, such as slander, libel, plagiarism, falsification of documents, and malicious misrepresentation.*

Declaration of Principles on the Conduct of Journalists

This international Declaration is proclaimed as a standard of professional conduct for journalists engaged in gathering, transmitting, disseminating and commenting on news and information and in describing events.

1. Respect for truth and for the right of the public to truth is the first duty of the journalist.
2. In pursuance of this duty, the journalist shall at all times defend the principles of freedom in the honest collection and publication of news, and of the right of fair comment and criticism.
3. The journalist shall report only in accordance with facts of which he/she knows the origin. The journalist shall not suppress essential information or falsify documents.
4. The journalist shall use only fair methods to obtain news, photographs and documents.
5. The journalist shall do the utmost to rectify any published information which is found to be harmfully inaccurate.
6. The journalist shall observe professional secrecy regarding the source of information obtained in confidence.
7. The journalist shall be aware of the danger of discrimination being furthered by the media, and shall do the utmost to avoid facilitating such discrimination based on, among other things, race, sex, sexual orientation, language, religion, political or other opinions, and national or social origins.
8. The journalist shall regard as grave professional offences the following:
   — plagiarism
   — malicious misrepresentation
   — calumny, slander, libel, unfounded accusations
   — the acceptance of a bribe in any form in consideration of either publication or suppression.
9. Journalists worthy of that name shall deem in their duty to observe faithfully the principles stated above. Within the general law of each country the journalist shall recognize in professional matters the jurisdiction of colleagues only, to the exclusion of every kind of interference by governments or others.

British National Union of Journalists

United Kingdom Code of Conduct

The British National Union of Journalists (NUJ) adopted its Code of Conduct *in 1994. Of note is the special attention this code gives to the issue of deception. For instance, it enjoins that journalists should as a rule use only "straightforward" means for the acquisition of information and photographs and should employ other means only when they are justified by public interest. It also recognizes as legitimate a journalist's conscientious objection to the use of deceit. Also of note is the special consideration it gives to privacy violations involving intrusions into personal grief and distress.*

Code of Conduct

1. A journalist has a duty to maintain the highest professional and ethical standards.
2. A journalist shall at all times defend the principle of the freedom of the press and other media in relation to the collection of information and the expression of comment and criticism. He/she shall strive to eliminate distortion, news suppression and censorship.
3. A journalist shall strive to ensure that the information he/she disseminates is fair and accurate, avoid the expression of comment and conjecture as established fact and falsification by distortion, selection or misrepresentation.
4. A journalist shall rectify promptly any harmful inaccuracies, ensure that correction and apologies receive due prominence and afford the right of reply to persons criticised when the issue is of sufficient importance.
5. A journalist shall obtain information, photographs and illustrations only by straightforward means. The use of other means can be justified only by overriding considerations of the public interest. The journalist is entitled to exercise a personal conscientious objection to the use of such means.
6. Subject to the justification by overriding considerations of the public interest, a journalist shall do nothing which entails intrusion into private grief and distress.
7. A journalist shall protect confidential sources of information.
8. A journalist shall not accept bribes nor shall he/she allow other inducements to influence the performance of his/her professional duties.
9. A journalist shall not lend himself/herself to the distortion or suppression of the truth because of advertising or other considerations.
10. A journalist shall only mention a person's age, race, colour, creed, illegitimacy, disability, marital status (or lack of it), gender or sexual orientation if this information is strictly relevant. A journalist shall neither originate nor process material which encourages discrimination, ridicule, prejudice or hatred on any of the above-mentioned grounds.

11. A journalist shall not take private advantage of information gained in the course of his/her duties, before the information is public knowledge.

12. A journalist shall not by way of statement, voice or appearance endorse by advertisement any commercial product or service save for the promotion of his/her own work or of the medium by which he/she is employed.

Radio-Television News Directors Association

Code of Ethics

The Radio-Television News Directors Association (RTNDA) adopted its Code of Ethics *in 1987. While the code addresses radio and television journalism, many of its statements are similar to those found in print media and other general codes of ethics. Of note is its emphasis on the avoidance of deception in presenting audio and visual material, including misrepresenting staged or rehearsed material as spontaneous news.*

Code of Ethics

The responsibility of radio and television journalists is to gather and report information of importance and interest to the public accurately, honestly and impartially.

1. The members of the Radio-Television News Directors Association accept these standards and will:
   Strive to present the source or nature of broadcast news material in a way that is balanced, accurate and fair.
   A. They will evaluate information solely on its merits as news, rejecting sensationalism or misleading emphasis in any form.
   B. They will guard against using audio or video material in a way that deceives the audience.
   C. They will not mislead the public by presenting as spontaneous news any material which is staged or rehearsed.
   D. They will identify people by race, creed, nationality or prior status only when it is relevant.
   E. They will clearly label opinion and commentary.
2. They will promptly acknowledge and correct errors.
3. Strive to conduct themselves in a manner that protects them from conflicts of interest, real or perceived.
4. They will decline gifts or favors which would influence or appear to influence their judgments.
5. Respect the dignity, privacy and well-being of people with whom they deal.

6. Recognize the need to protect confidential sources. They will promise confidentiality only with the intention of keeping that promise.
7. Respect everyone's right to a fair trial.
8. Broadcast the private transmissions of other broadcasters only with permission.
9. Actively encourage observance of this Code by all journalists, whether members of the Radio-Television News Directors Association or not.

Radio-Television News Directors Association of Canada

Code of Ethics (Revised 1986)

The Canadian Radio-Television News Directors Association (RTNDA) revised its Code of Ethics in 1986. This code contains more detail than the American RTNDA code (see above). It is more specific about the avoidance of deceit, for instance, in the editing of taped interviews. It discusses the ethical management of news equipment, including a responsibility of broadcast journalists to seek to remove obstructions to the use of electronic news equipment at public proceedings and a responsibility to exercise discretion in the use of broadcast equipment. It also addresses broadcasting undertaken in volatile situations such as hostage situations or other criminal activities.

Code of Ethics

Recognizing the importance to a democracy of an informed public, the members of the RTNDA of Canada believe the broadcasting of factual, accuracy-reported and timely news and public affairs is vital. To that end, RTNDA members pledge to observe the following Code of Ethics:

ARTICLE ONE

The main purpose of broadcast journalism is to inform the public in an accurate, comprehensive and balanced manner about events of importance.

ARTICLE TWO

News and public affairs broadcasts will put events into perspective by presenting relevant background information. Factors such as race, creed, nationality or religion will be reported only when relevant. Comment and editorial opinion will be identified as such. Errors will be quickly acknowledged and publicly corrected.

ARTICLE THREE

Broadcast journalists will not sensationalize news items and will resist pressures, whether from inside or outside the broadcasting industry, to do so. They will in no way distort the news. Broadcast journalists will not edit taped interviews to distort the meaning, intent, or actual words of the interviewee.

ARTICLE FOUR

Broadcast journalists will always display respect for the dignity, privacy and well-being of everyone with whom they deal, and make every effort to ensure that the privacy of public persons is infringed only to the extent necessary to satisfy the public interest and accurately report the news.

ARTICLE FIVE

Broadcast journalists will govern themselves on and off the job in such a way as to avoid conflict of interest, real or apparent.

ARTICLE SIX

Broadcast journalists will seek to remove any impediments or bans on the use of electronic news gathering equipment at public proceedings, believing that such access is in the public interest. They acknowledge the importance of protection of confidential information and sources.

ARTICLE SEVEN

News directors recognize that informed analysis, comment and editorial opinion on public events and issues is both a right and responsibility that should be delegated only to individuals whose experience and judgment qualify them for it.

ARTICLE EIGHT

Broadcast journalists shall conduct themselves politely, keeping broadcast equipment as unobtrusive as possible. Broadcast journalists will try to prevent their presence from distorting the character or importance of events.

ARTICLE NINE

In reporting matters that are or may be before the courts, broadcast journalists will ensure that their reporting does not interfere with the right of an individual to a fair trial.

ARTICLE TEN

Reporting of criminal activities, such as hostage-takings, will be done in a fashion that does not knowingly endanger lives, hamper attempts by authorities to conclude the event, offer comfort and support or provide vital information, to the perpetrator(s). RTNDA members will not contact either victim(s) or perpetrator(s) of a criminal activity during the course of the event, with the purpose of conducting an interview for broadcast.

ARTICLE ELEVEN

The RTNDA will seek to enforce this code through its members and encourage all broadcast journalists, whether RTNDA members or not, to observe its spirit. News directors will try whenever possible and within programming format constraints to publicize the existence of the Code of Ethics, and state that their news department adheres to the code. In any such announcement, it should be mentioned that copies of the code can be obtained by writing the RTNDA or the news director at the station.

National Press Photographers Association

Code of Ethics

This Code of Ethics, *adopted in 1946, is largely aspirational, proposing professional ideals toward which members should "strive." It recognizes the importance of "common sense" and "good judgment" in applying its principles. It provides that photojournalists should strive for photography that "reports truthfully, honestly and objectively."*

Code of Ethics

The National Press Photographers Association, a professional society dedicated to the advancement of photojournalism, acknowledges concern and respect for the public's natural law—right to freedom in searching for the truth and the right to be informed truthfully and completely about public events and the world in which we live.

We believe that no report can be complete if it is not possible to enhance and clarify the meaning of the words. We believe that pictures, whether used to depict news events as they actually happen, illustrate news that has happened or to help explain anything of public interest, are an indispensable means of keeping people accurately informed; that they help all people, young and old, to better understand any subject in the public domain.

Believing the foregoing we recognize and acknowledge that photojournalists should at all times maintain the highest standards of ethical conduct in serving the public interest. To that end the National Press Photographers Association sets forth the following Code of Ethics which is subscribed to by all of its members:

1. The practice of photojournalism, both as a science and art, is worthy of the very best thought and effort of those who enter into it as a profession.
2. Photojournalism affords an opportunity to serve the public that is equaled by few other vocations and all members of the profession should strive by example and influence to maintain high standards of ethical conduct free of mercenary considerations of any kind.

3. It is the individual responsibility of every photojournalist at all times to strive for pictures that report truthfully, honestly and objectively.

4. Business promotion in its many forms is essential, but untrue statements of any nature are not worthy of a professional photojournalist and we severely condemn any such practice.

5. It is our duty to encourage and assist all members of our profession, individually and collectively, so that the quality of photojournalism may constantly be raised to higher standards.

6. It is the duty of every photojournalist to work to preserve all freedom-of-the-press rights recognized by law and to work to protect and expand freedom-of-access to all sources of news and visual information.

7. Our standards of business dealings, ambitions and relations shall have in them a note of sympathy for our common humanity and shall always require us to take into consideration our highest duties as members of society. In every situation in our business life, in every responsibility that comes before us, our chief thought shall be to fulfill that responsibility and discharge that duty so that when each of us is finished we shall have endeavored to lift the level of human ideals and achievements higher than we found it.

8. No Code of Ethics can prejudge every situation, thus common sense and good judgment are required in applying ethical principles.

CONTEMPORARY ETHICAL ISSUES

Chapter 7:
Selected Print
Resources

Bill Pardue

Bibliographies in and of themselves are problematic entities, since they can only represent a small cross section of the published works available on any given topic at a very specific time. Examination of bibliographies from multiple works in any subject will also reveal a vast amount of duplication, as authors try to capture the "essential" works in their field. It is with this in mind that this chapter has been prepared with selected, rather than comprehensive, lists of published books, articles, and journals. The information provided should be adequate for the student or researcher doing basic work in journalistic ethics, and most of the titles themselves have substantial bibliographies, providing a springboard to deeper research on the topic. The articles are listed as a sampling of specialized research primarily from academic journals.

Perhaps more important than being a simple list of reading suggestions, this chapter is fashioned as a guide to doing background research on journalistic ethics, with the aim of assisting the reader to move beyond the works listed here and use the multitude of resources available at any public or academic library. As such, this chapter is intended more as a *pathfinder* than a bibliography.

Books and Basic References

Reference Guides to Journalism Research

The following titles are useful as starting guides for the researcher, not only in journalistic ethics but in all aspects of journalism.

Cates, Jo A. *Journalism: A Guide to the Reference Literature.* 2d Ed. Englewood, CO: Libraries Unlimited, 1997. ISBN 1-56308-374-4.

Cates provides in-depth descriptions to bibliographies and reference titles across the spectrum of journalism research, with helpful insights on how to use each resource. This guide is an excellent introductory resource.

Journalism and Mass Communication Abstracts: Dissertation and Theses in Journalism and Mass Communication. Columbia, SC: Association for Education in Journalism and Mass Communication (Annual). ISSN 1077-694X.

This guide provides long abstracts for theses and dissertations, along with subject indexing. A number of dissertations on ethics are listed each year (17 in 1995, 19 in 1994). To get copies of dissertations and theses, contact your local library (you may have to pay a fee).

Wolseley, Roland E. *The Journalist's Bookshelf.* Indianapolis: R. J. Berg, 1986. ISBN 0-89730-139-0.

This reference work is a wonderful guide to the range of resources in journalism research. A section on ethics is included on pages 134–137. While the work is a bit old, many of the titles listed have a "core" status and remain timely.

Books on Professional Ethics in General

Insofar as it may be helpful to examine the broader field of professional ethics in conjunction with specific works on journalism, the researcher may find the following titles helpful.

Bayles, Michael D. *Professional Ethics.* Belmont, CA: Wadsworth, 1989. ISBN 0-534-09546-1.

This volume is an essential overview of professional ethics, with sections on such broad topics as problems of professions, the structure of professional ethics, and ensuring compliance.

Flores, Albert, ed. *Professional Ideals.* Belmont, CA: Wadsworth, 1988. ISBN 0-534-08688-8

Professional Ideals is yet another collection of essays arranged by broad concepts. This volume, however, includes an essay by noted journalist Penn Kimball entitled "Journalism: Art, Craft or Profession?"

Gorlin, Renee A., ed. *Codes of Professional Responsibility.* 3rd Ed. Washington DC: Bureau of National Affairs, 1994. ISBN 0-87179-849-2.

A massive compendium of codes across all fields, this book includes the American Society of Journalists and Authors Code of Ethics, the American Society of Newspaper Editors Statement of Principles, and the Society of Professional Journalists Code of Ethics. It is good for comparison of codes between professions.

Pellegrino, Edmund D., Robert M. Veatch, and John P. Langan, eds. *Ethics, Trust and the Professions.* Washington DC: Georgetown University Press, 1990. ISBN 0-87840-513-5.

Pellegrino, Veatch, and Langan have put forth one of the most important recent scholarly collections of work on the topic of professional ethics. The intent is to "stimulate discussion between and among disciplines..." (ix).

Windt, Peter D., ed. *Ethical Issues in the Professions.* Englewood Cliffs, NJ: Prentice-Hall, 1989. ISBN 0-13-290081-5.

This book is organized into collections of essays grouped by broad themes, such as "Personal, Professional and Institutional Obligations" and "Regulation of the Professions." It includes a helpful appendix with an "Introduction to Ethical Reasoning" and another with selected codes of ethics, including that of the Society of Professional Journalists.

Books on Journalistic Ethics

Adams, Julian. *Freedom and Ethics in the Press.* New York: Rosen Publishing Group, 1983. ISBN 0-8239-0562-4.

Adams covers a broad range of topics from censorship, libel, and obscenity to privacy and student press issues. The appendix offers a number of professional codes of ethics and guidelines for journalists.

Barbour, William, ed. *Mass Media: Opposing Viewpoints.* San Diego: Greenhaven Press, 1994. Series: Opposing Viewpoints. ISBN 1-56510-107-3.

Barbour covers topics in the general mass media, including a number of journalistic topics, such as liberalism or conservatism in broadcast news and regulatory restrictions on news coverage. Articles are arranged in pairs for and against given proposals (e.g., "Media Campaigns Hinder U.S. Politics" vs. "Media Campaigns Enhance U.S. Politics").

Beam, Randal A. *Journalism Professionalism as an Organizational-Level Concept.* Columbia, SC: Association for Education in Journalism and Mass Communication, 1990. Series: Journalism Monographs.

This book presents the results of a sociological study examining the concept of professionalism in journalism, empirical measures of professionalism, and suggestions for using the concept of professionalism in mass media research.

Belsey, Andrew, and Ruth Chadwick, eds. *Ethical Issues in Journalism and the Media.* New York: Routledge, 1992. Series: Professional Ethics. ISBN 0-415-06926-2.

A collection of essays by a largely academic group of authors, this volume treats journalistic ethics as a subset of the broader field of professional ethics.

Black, Jay, Bob Steele, and Ralph Barney. *Doing Ethics in Journalism: A Handbook with Case Studies.* 2d Edition. Boston: Allyn & Bacon, 1995. ISBN 0-2051-6042-5.

A primer for working journalists on making ethical decisions, this collection is notable for its extensive selection of case studies on accuracy and fairness, conflicts of interest, deception, etc. It features an extensive annotated bibliography.

Cohen, Elliot D., ed. *Philosophical Issues in Journalism.* New York: Oxford University Press, 1992. ISBN 0-19506-898-X.

This volume offers an examination of a broad array of philosophical topics. Among the book's assertions is the idea that the education of the journalist ought to include course work in such philosophical areas as logic, epistemology, and ethics.

Deppa, Joan, et al. *The Media and Disasters: Pan Am 103.* New York: New York University Press, 1994. ISBN 0-8147-1857-4.

Using the 1988 Lockerbie air disaster as a case study, Deppa examines, among other things, the ramifications of the media's ability to cover almost any event "live."

Dodge, Charlie, ed. *Newspaper Ethics Codes and Policies: A Resource Guide for Journalists.* Marina Del Rey, CA: Josephson Institute of Ethics, 1993.

A practical guide assembled for the Associated Press Managing Editors, this work includes their 1975 Code of Ethics and 1993 (proposed) Declaration of Ethics. Organized by "Newsgathering Standards" and "Publishing Standards."

Elliott, Deni, ed. *Responsible Journalism.* Beverly Hills, CA: Sage, 1986. ISBN 08039-2611-1.

Responsible Journalism is a collection of articles discussing the foundations of press responsibility, its relationship to press theory, and the practice of ethical journalism.

Ericson, Richard V., Patricia M. Baranek, and Janet B. L. Chan. *Negotiating Control: A Study of News Sources.* Toronto: University of Toronto Press, 1989. ISBN 0-8020-2659-1.

This scholarly sociological work, focusing on Canadian journalism, is a set of ethnographic studies examining journalists' relationships with their news sources and the role those sources play in determining what the public sees and hears. Topics include the courts, the police, and the legislature.

Fink, Conrad C. *Media Ethics.* Needham Heights, MA: Allyn & Bacon, 1995. ISBN 0-02-337753-4.

By addressing the topic of media ethics, this work covers a broad scope, but it still places its strongest emphasis on journalistic issues. It benefits from the fact that it is fairly recent and can present such cases as the coverage of Bill Clinton's 1992 presidential campaign. Appendixes include a number of professional codes of ethics.

Fuller, Jack. *News Values: Ideas for an Information Age.* Chicago: University of Chicago Press, 1996. ISBN 0-226-26879-9.

Fuller, a Pulitzer Prize winner and the publisher of the *Chicago Tribune*, divides this book into three sections dealing with the issues of truth, expression, and the future in newspaper journalism. It is notable for its extensive use of real-life examples.

Hausman, Carl. *The Decision-Making Process in Journalism.* Chicago: Nelson Hall, 1990. ISBN 0-8304-1203-4.

Hausman discusses decision-making issues relevant to making ethical choices in journalism, for example, "Is it news?," "Is it true?," and "Is it fair?" It includes a section specifically on ethical research and presentation, and it is useful for its extensive use of actual case histories.

————. *Crisis of Conscience: Perspectives on Journalism Ethics.* New York: HarperCollins, 1992. ISBN 0-06-500365-9.

Stating that "the study of journalism has become something of a growth industry," Hausman looks at the logical development of the field. Sections are entitled "The Premise," "Principles," "Principles in Conflict," and "Toward Resolution." The text also provides a "guide for critical self-examination."

Holopainen, Veli, ed. *Case Studies on International Norms and Journalism.* Tampere, Finland: University of Tampere, 1987. Series: University of Tampere Department of Journalism and Mass Communications Publications. Series B. ISBN 951-44-2134-5.

This report is in two parts, the first of which is a summary of the editor's master's thesis on observance of international law in two newspapers. Part 2 consists of case studies of nine media from seven countries and interpretation of the cases in relation to the 1978 Mass Media Declaration of the United Nations Educational, Scientific, and Cultural Organization, an attempt to establish fundamental principles for mass media to work toward peace and international understanding.

Hulteng, John L. *The Messenger's Motives.* Englewood Cliffs, NJ: Prentice-Hall, 1985. ISBN 0-13-577487-X.

Hulteng examines the way in which the media can use reporting practices to influence perception and opinion. Though a little dated, this work is useful for its extensive use of case studies.

Juusela, Pauli. *Journalistic Codes of Ethics in the CSCE Countries.* Tampere, Finland: University of Tampere, 1991. Series: University of Tampere, Department of Journalism and Mass Communications Publications. Series B. ISBN 951-44-2932-X.

This volume is an adapted master's thesis. The author performs a comparative analysis of codes of ethics from countries participating in the Conference on Security and Cooperation in Europe (CSCE). Codes are compared on such common points as truth, acquisition of information, and confidential sources.

Kaplar, Richard T., and Patrick D. Maines. *The Government Factor: Undermining Journalistic Ethics in the Information Age.* Washington, DC: Cato Institute, 1995. ISBN 1-882577-25-6.

The authors examine the intersection of government regulation and ethical decision making in journalism. They find that government interference hinders private morality and blocks the development of a more ethical media.

Klaidman, Stephen, and Tom L. Beauchamp. *The Virtuous Journalist.* New York: Oxford University Press, 1987. ISBN 0-19-504205-0.

Each chapter covers some core theme in journalism ethics, such as reaching for truth, avoiding bias, and avoiding harm. This is a useful primer for basic issues.

Knowlton, Steven R., and Patrick Parsons, eds. *The Journalist's Moral Compass: Basic Principles.* Westport, CT: Praeger, 1995. ISBN 0-2759-5153-7.

An introductory primer to the field of journalistic ethics, this book covers such topics as freedom of the press and the relationship between economic and ethical concerns for the press.

Lambeth, Edmund B. *Committed Journalism: An Ethic for the Profession.* Bloomington: Indiana University Press, 1986. ISBN 0-253-313929.

Lambeth begins with a discussion of research showing that the American public has an abysmally low regard for the press. He goes on to attempt to create a framework for ethical decision making, code creation, etc.

Lee, Martin A., and Norman Solomon. *Unreliable Resources: A Guide to Detecting Bias in News Media.* New York: Lyle Stuart, 1990. ISBN 0-8184-0521-X.

Lee and Solomon examine alleged media bias in both print and broadcast journalism, most often in the form of influence by corporate sponsors. The foreword is written by Edward Asner (television's Lou Grant). The book includes appendixes, listings of media industry facts, alternative media sources, media analysis groups and publications, and journalism organizations.

The Mass Media and the Public Trust: What Is Known and Why It Matters. New York: Gannett Center for Media Studies, 1987.

This book is comprised of transcripts of panel discussions and audience questions from a 1987 conference focusing on the erosion of public trust in journalism and mass media. Participants include professional journalists and academics.

Matelski, Marilyn J. *TV News Ethics.* Boston: Focal Press, 1991. Series: Electronic Media Guides. ISBN 0-240-80089-3.

Matelski discusses the evolution of ethical issues in the television news setting and includes four case studies for consideration. The book includes an essay by Spiro T. Agnew on network censorship and appendixes featuring the

Radio and Television News Directors' Association Code of Broadcast News Ethics and the Society of Professional Journalists/Sigma Delta Chi Code of Ethics.

Merrill, John C. *Legacy of Wisdom: Great Thinkers and Journalism.* Ames: Iowa University Press, 1994. ISBN 0-8183-2041-3.

This book contains brief (5 to 6-page) summaries of a very broad selection of philosophers, from classical to contemporary. Each philosopher's basic tenets are discussed, along with his/her relevance to journalistic ethics.

Merrit, Davis. *Public Journalism and Public Life: Why Telling the News Is Not Enough.* Hillsdale, NJ: Lawrence Erlbaum, 1995. ISBN 0-8058-1982-7.

Merrit discusses journalism's failure to fulfill its obligations "to effective social life" and the need to make substantial changes to improve the relationship between the two. Notable is his inclusion of a chapter on cyberspace and the digital media.

Meyer, Philip. *Ethical Journalism: A Guide for Students, Practitioners and Consumers.* New York: Longman, 1987. ISBN 0-582-28680-8.

Meyer's work is developed from a 1982 survey of newspaper editors, conducted by the American Society of News Editors (ASNE), on the role of editors and publishers in resolving ethical problems. Sections are titled "Major Problems," " Ethics and the Organization," and "Toward a Moral Foundation." He includes four codes of ethics: the ASNE Canons of Journalism; the ASNE Statement of Principles; the ASNE Code of Ethics; and the Society of Professional Journalists/Sigma Delta Chi Code of Ethics.

Nordenstreng, Kaarle, and Hifzi Topuz, eds. *Journalist: Status, Rights and Responsibilities.* Prague: International Organization of Journalists, 1989. ISBN 8-0702-5001-1.

Journalist is an extensive cross section of professional codes of ethics from around the world. Although somewhat dated (it covers the Soviet Union and a split Germany), it is an interesting primer for comparing and contrasting codes.

Olasky, Marvin. *Prodigal Press: The Anti-Christian Bias of the American News Media.* Westchester, IL: Crossway Books, 1988. ISBN 0-89107-476-7.

Olasky contends that American journalism claims to be neutral with regard to religious issues, but in fact it has moved from a position in keeping with a Christian perspective, now embracing the perspective of materialist humanism.

Olen, Jeffrey. *Ethics in Journalism.* Englewood Cliffs, NJ: Prentice-Hall, 1988. Series: Occupational Ethics. ISBN 0-13-290586-8.

This book has a generally solid, textbook-type approach to ethical thought. Case studies are used liberally throughout the text. Included are discussions of moral reasoning in general, ethical codes for journalists, and the relation-ship between the journalist and the public.

Ripley, Casey, Jr., ed. *The Media and the Public.* New York: H. W. Wilson, 1994. Series: The Reference Shelf, vol. 66, no. 5. ISBN 0-8242-0856-0.

This title, as are all others in The Reference Shelf series, is a collection of articles from the mainstream press. Sections include "The Media Business," "Media Evolution and Critique," "Stories and Trends," and "The Future."

Rivers, Caryl. *Slick Spins and Fractured Facts: How Cultural Myths Distort the News.* New York: Columbia University Press, 1996. ISBN 0-231-10152-X.

Rivers examines the role of cultural stereotypes in reporting the news, from coverage of Hillary Clinton's commodity dealings to questions of gender, genetics, race, and violence.

Sabato, Larry J. *Feeding Frenzy: How Attack Journalism Has Transformed American Politics.* New York: The Free Press, 1991. ISBN 0-02-927635-7.

Sabato examines the news media's obsession with investigating the private lives of public figures and concludes that journalism is serving to undermine the American political process. Cases include coverage of Thomas Eagleton, Gary Hart, Dan Quayle, etc.

Taitte, W. Lawson, ed. *The Morality of the Mass Media.* Dallas: University of Texas at Dallas, 1992. Series: Andrew R. Cecil Lectures on Moral Values in a Free Society. ISBN 0-292-71160-3.

This collection of lectures discusses broad themes such as "The News Media and the National Interest" and "Censorship: Historical Background and Justifiable Forms."

Journals

Any researcher on the topic of journalistic ethics will want to keep abreast of writings in a number of different journals and magazines that are either totally devoted to issues of journalistic and/or professional ethics or have regular coverage of the issues with each publication. Simply browsing these titles will help the researcher find out about new controversies, significant publications, and important names in the field. When available, World Wide Web sites are listed.

Core Publications in the Field of Journalistic Ethics

American Journalism Review (AJR). University of Maryland College of Journalism. Bimonthly. ISSN 1067-8654. http://www.newslink.org/gref.html.

AJR covers current events, issues, and trends in journalism and broadcast media. It is an excellent resource for keeping up-to-date on current controversies of ethical importance and a great potential source for case studies.

Columbia Journalism Review (CJR). New York: Columbia University Graduate School of Journalism. Bimonthly. ISSN 0010-194X. http://www.cjr.org/.

Partially supported by the Deer Creek Foundation's Fund for Journalistic Standards and Ethics, the *CJR* offers accessible coverage of current events and trends in journalism in professional and social contexts. It is also considered the oldest journalism publication in the United States.

The Journal of Mass Media Ethics. Mahwah, NJ: Lawrence Erlbaum. Quarterly. ISSN 0890-0523.

This quarterly is certainly one of the premier titles in the field of journalistic ethics and professional ethics in general. Articles are published to "stimulate and contribute to reasoned discussions of mass media ethics and morality among academic and professional groups in the various branches and subdisciplines of communication and ethics." Every issue features scholarly articles, book reviews, and a section on cases and commentaries.

Journalism Quarterly. Minneapolis: Association for Education in Journalism and Mass Communication. Quarterly. ISSN 0196-3031.

With a focus on academic research in journalism and mass communication, this journal regularly features articles on ethical issues.

Nieman Reports. Cambridge, MA: Nieman Foundation at Harvard University (*see* chapter 9). 5 times yearly. ISSN 0028-9817. http://www.nieman.harvard.edu/nieman/nreports.html.

Like the *Columbia Journalism Review*, this journal is another university-based publication covering current issues and trends in journalism. The spring 1994 issue (vol. XLVIII, no. 1) had a special feature, "Ethics on Trial." In addition, most issues include articles directly on or closely related to ethical topics.

Quill. Greencastle, IN: Society of Professional Journalists. ISSN 0033-6475. http://www.spj.org/quill/quill.htm.

One of the most important publications for the newspaper profession in general, *Quill* features a monthly column specifically devoted to ethics, "Ethics and the Media." In addition, the November/December 1994 issue (vol. 82, no. 4) had a special feature on journalistic ethics.

Other Journals Covering Ethics

It may also be helpful to regularly read journals that cover broader topics, such as business or professional ethics in general. Almost all of the following journal titles will carry occasional articles on journalistic ethics in particular, but they are more important in leading the researcher to examine the broader issues (such as theories of professionalism and roles of codes of ethics), which can then be translated to journalism.

Business & Professional Ethics Journal. Troy, NY: Human Dimensions Center, Rensselaer Polytechnic Institute. Quarterly. ISSN 0277-2027.

Business Ethics Quarterly: The Journal of the Society for Business Ethics. Bowling Green, OH: Philosophy Documentation Center, Bowling Green University. Quarterly. ISSN 1052-150X.

International Journal of Applied Philosophy. Fort Pierce, FL: Indian River Community College. Quarterly. ISSN 0739-098X.

Professional Ethics: A Multidisciplinary Journal. Gainesville, FL: University of Florida, Center for Applied Philosophy. Quarterly. ISSN 1027-6579.

Articles

With some notable exceptions, this list does not include articles from the sources listed above, since such an inclusion would have resulted in far too many listings for a given journal. This listing also has a bias toward scholarly articles on the topic, many of which will include footnotes and bibliographies of their own, allowing the researcher to further expand the scope of his or her resources.

It is very important that the researcher be able to locate articles published after this present work is completed. Listings can be located using such commonly available databases as Infotrac's *Expanded Academic Index*, the CARL *Uncover* index, the *Readers' Guide to Periodical Literature*, or Infotrac's *General Magazine Index* for less academic articles. Those seeking more scholarly work might use Wilson's *Humanities Index* or *Social Science Index* or the *Public Affairs Information Service (PAIS)* index.

Those with access to the Internet may wish to examine the Poynter Institute's annual *Bibliography on Media Ethics* or the University of Western Ontario's *Index to Journalism Periodicals* (*see* chapter 8).

Another very useful collection of articles for researchers is the Social Issues Resource Series (SIRS) (Boca Raton, FL: SIRS, Inc.), available in many public and academic libraries. More than an index, SIRS is essentially a "clipping service," pulling complete articles from journals, magazines, and newspapers and organizing reprints by broad categories based on important contemporary issues, such as ethics and communications. Some libraries subscribe to the SIRS collection in electronic format, allowing more extensive keyword searching. Searching for "journalistic ethics" in the 1996 SIRS database resulted in the retrieval of over 30 relevant articles.

Avieson, John. "Chequebook Journalism: A Question of Ethics." *Australian Journalism Review* 14, 1 (1 January 1992): 45–50.

Black, Jay, and Ralph Barney. "Journalism Ethics since Janet Cooke." *Newspaper Research Journal* 13, 4 (Fall 1992): 2–16.

Boeyink, David E. "How Effective Are Codes of Ethics? A Look at Three Newsrooms." *Journalism Quarterly* 71, 4 (Winter 1994): 893–903.

Bunker, Matthew D. "Lifting the Veil: Ethics Bodies, the Citizen-Critic, and the First Amendment." *Journalism Quarterly* 70, 1 (Spring 1993): 98–107.

Christians, Clifford G. "Review Essay: Current Trends in Media Ethics." *European Journal of Communication* 10, 4 (December 1995): 545–558.

Cooper, Thomas W. "Review Essay: Lorraine Code's Epistemic Responsibility, Journalism, and the Charles Stuart Case." *Business & Professional Ethics Journal* 12, 3 (Fall 1993): 83–106.

Cronin, Mary M., and James B. McPherson. "Pronouncements and Denunciations: An Analysis of State Press Association Ethics Codes from the 1920s." *Journalism & Mass Communication Quarterly* 72, 4 (Winter 1995): 890–901.

Dennis, Everette E. "News, Ethics and Split-Personality Journalism." *Television Quarterly* 27, 1 (1994): 29–35.

Elliot, Deni. "Moral Development Theories and the Teaching of Ethics." *The Journalism Educator* 46, 3 (Fall 1991): 18–24.

Encabo, Manuel Nunez. "The Ethics of Journalism and Democracy." *European Journal of Communication* 10, 4 (December 1995): 513–526.

Eveslage, Thomas. "Ethics: No Longer Optional." *Communication: Journalism Education Today* 28, 2 (Winter 1994): 10–12.

"Free Press Threat in Europe." *Editor & Publisher* 126, 45 (6 November 1993): 14, 35.

Glasser, Theodore L. "Communicative Ethics and the Aim of Accountability in Journalism." *Social Responsibility, Business, Journalism, Law* 21 (1995): 31–51.

Goodwin, Ann, and Norma Thiele. "Exercises in Ethics." *Communication: Journalism Education Today* 28, 2 (Winter 1994): 21.

Griffin, Grahame. "Shoot First: The Ethics of Australian Press Photographers." *Australian Studies in Journalism* 4 (1995): 3–28.

Knudtson, Judy. "Literature Shows Recurring Efforts at Finding a Method of Teaching Ethics." *Communication: Journalism Education Today* 28, 2 (Winter 1994): 2–6.

Kruger, Wendy. "How to Teach a Unit on Law, Ethics." *Communication: Journalism Education Today* 28, 4 (Summer 1995): 22–24.

Laitila, Tiina. "Journalism Codes of Ethics in Europe." *European Journal of Communication* 10, 4 (December 1995): 527–544.

Lambeth, Edmund B. "Waiting for a New St. Benedict: Alasdair MacIntyre and the Theory and Practice of Journalism." *Business & Professional Ethics Journal* 9, 1&2 (Spring/Summer 1990): 96–108.

———. "Journalism, Narrative and Community: Implications for Ethics, Practice and Media Criticism." *Professional Ethics* 2, 1 & 2 (Spring 1993): 67–88.

Lambeth, Edmund B., Clifford Christians, and Kyle Cole. "Role of the Media Ethics Course in the Education of Journalists." *Journalism Educator* 49, 3 (Fall 1994): 20–26.

Lichtenberg, Judith. "Truth, Neutrality and Conflict of Interest." *Business & Professional Ethics Journal* 9, 1&2 (Spring/Summer 1990): 65–78.

McCrath, Pam, and Geoff Turner. "The Ethics of Hope: Newspaper Reporting of Chemotherapy." *Australian Studies in Journalism* 4 (1995): 50–71.

Machemer, Peter, and Barbara Boylan. "Ethics and News." *Business & Professional Ethics Journal* 9, 1&2 (Spring/Summer 1990): 53–64.

Mitchell, James C. "The Devil in Disguise: Hybrid News-Commercials and First Amendment Protection for Broadcast Journalists." *Loyola Entertainment Law Journal* 14, 2 (1994): 229–255.

Putnis, Peter. "Television Journalism and Image Ethics." *Australian Journalism Review* 14, 2 (1 July 1992): 1–17.

Serafini, Anthony. "Applying Ethics to Journalism." *International Journal of Applied Philosophy* 3, 4 (Fall 1987): 45–99.

Shepard, Alicia C. "Legislating Ethics." *American Journalism Review* 16, 1 (1 January 1994): 37–41.

Theiele, Norma. "Problems in Ethics." *Communication: Journalism Education Today* 28, 2 (Winter 1994): 22.

Tomlinson, Don E. "Digitexed Television News: The Beginning of the End for Photographic Reality in Photojournalism." *Business & Professional Ethics Journal* 11, 1 (Spring 1992): 51–70.

Turner, Geoff. "Frontline Ethics: The Australian Media's Siege Mentality." *Australian Studies in Journalism* 3 (1994): 25–38.

Westrin, Claes-Goran, and Tore Nilstun. "The Ethics of Data Utilisation: A Comparison between Epidemiology and Journalism." *British Medical Journal* 308, 6927 (19 February 1994): 522–523.

White, H. Allen. "The Salience and Pertinence of Ethics: When Journalists Do and Don't Think for Themselves." *Journalism & Mass Communication Quarterly* 17, 1 (Spring 1996): 17–28.

Yudkin, Marcia. "Epistemological Worries, Philosophy and Freelance Writing." *International Journal of Applied Philosophy* 4, 3 (Spring 1989): 67–79.

CONTEMPORARY ETHICAL ISSUES

Chapter 8:
Selected Nonprint Resources

Bill Pardue

Videotape Resources

In addition to printed materials, there are many videotapes available on topics related to journalistic ethics. For distribution information for specific titles, consult the *Film and Video Finder*, published for the National Information Center for Educational Media by Plexus, Medford, New Jersey (ISBN 0-937548-24-3) at your local public or academic library. (Additional videotape entries contributed by Deni Elliott.)

Buying Time: The Media Role in Health Care
Length: 27 minutes
Date: 1992
Cost: $145
Source: Fanlight Productions
47 Halifax Street
Boston, MA 02130
(617) 524 0980

This documentary provides a thoughtful and disturbing examination of the role of the media in determining the allocation of health care resources. It profiles two very different cases in which patients and their advocates orchestrated media campaigns to solicit contributions.

A Case of Need

Length: 17 minutes
Date: 1989
Cost: $99
Source: Fanlight Productions
47 Halifax Street
Boston, MA 02130
(617) 524 0980

Focuses on the media coverage of a young girl in need of a liver transplant. Interviews with news directors, fund-raising coordinators, and individuals who worked on behalf of the child cover a vast array of issues ranging from the question of fair and equal coverage to competition among news organizations.

Censorship in a Free Society

Length: 30 minutes
Date: 1977
Cost: $49.95
Source: American Humanist Association (AHA)
7 Harwood Drive
Amherst, NY 14226
(716) 839-5080

Part 13 of the AHA's *Ethics in America* series, this videotape examines censorship issues in the context of the Larry Flynt libel trial and its broader implications for free speech.

Communication Is Power: Mass Media and Mass Persuasion

Length: 50 minutes
Date: 1975
Cost: $21.00
Source: Guidance Associates
100 S. Bedford Road
P.O. Box 1000
Mt. Kisko, NY 10549
(800) 431-1242

This videotape focuses broadly on persuasion through all forms of mass media, including newspapers and magazines.

Consuming Images

Length: 58 minutes
Date: 1989
Cost: $89.95
Source. Films for the Humanities
P.O. Box 2053
Princeton, NJ 08543
(800) 257-5126

Host Bill Moyers examines the effect of the media's emphasis on images over words on the public consciousness. This videotape is from the series *Moyers: The Public Mind.*

Different Goals? Different Obstacles? How Scientists and Journalists Think about Mass Media

Length: 60 minutes
Date: 1992
Cost: $30
Source: Sandy Leuck
Purdue University Continuing Education
(800) 359-2968, x90

Doing Ethics in Journalism: Decision-Making in the Newsroom and in the Field

Length: 60 minutes
Date: 1995
Cost· $25
Source: The Poynter Institute
801 Third Street South
St. Petersburg, FL 33701
(813) 821-9494

This video opens with a seminar and then develops into situational decision-making. Discussions center on the use of photos, selection of video coverage, sensationalism, and protection of privacy.

Ethics in Media

Length: 29 minutes
Date: 1992
Cost: $24.95
Source: Ecufilm
810 12th Avenue South
Nashville, TN 37203
(800) 251-4091

Critically examining the manner in which Africa is portrayed in the news and mass media, this videotape is useful for illuminating issues of bias and objectivity.

Illusions of News
Length: 58 minutes
Date: 1989
Cost: $89.95
Source: Films for the Humanities
P.O. Box 2053
Princeton, NJ 08543
(800) 257-5126

As part of the series *Moyers: The Public Mind*, Bill Moyers focuses on the primacy of the image in political reporting and its impact on the American society.

Lines in the Sand
Length: 12 minutes
Date: 1992
Cost: $30
Source: Ed Griffin-Nolan
(315) 471-4953

A video essay examining the Persian Gulf War, the media, and the military. An excellent discussion starter.

Media Ethics: Issues and Cases
Length: 25 minutes
Date: 1995
Cost: Free with purchase of book by same publisher
Source: Brown and Benchmark Publishers
25 Kessel Court
Madison, WI 53711
(608) 273-0040

This videotape, a supplement to the book by the same title, is designed to facilitate discussion in journalism ethics classes. Five vignettes in the book are discussed by the journalists and sources in the situation.

Only the News That Fits
Length: 30 minutes
Date: 1989
Cost: $190
Source: First Run/Icarus Films
153 Waverly Place
New York, NY 10014
(800) 876-1710

This videotape offers an examination of media bias and distortions during the 1987 Nicaragua Peace Plan negotiations.

Politics, Privacy and the Press
Length: 60 minutes
Date: 1989
Cost: $29.95
Source: Annenberg/Corporation for Public Broadcasting Collection
P.O. Box 2345
South Burlington, VT 05407
(800) 532-7637

Part 10 of the *Ethics in America* series (not to be confused with the American Humanities Association's series of the same name), this videotape presents a panel discussion on the issue of press disclosure of details from public individuals' private lives and activities.

Power and Role of the Press
Length: 60 minutes
Date: 1995
Cost: $149
Source: Films for the Humanities
P.O. Box 2053
Princeton, NJ 08543
(800) 257-5126

Australian press examples are used in this documentary questioning the power and the role of journalists today. The program examines the inconsistent and fragmented system of ethics and accountability governing journalism.

Internet/World Wide Web Resources

This Internet section is primarily for sites not officially related to resources already listed elsewhere in this book. If a journal or organization has an affiliated World Wide Web site, the URL is usually listed along with the entry for that resource in chapters 7 and 9. Two significant exceptions are the resources noted below from the Poynter Institute web site, which are useful enough as reference tools to warrant their own separate listings.

It is important to keep in mind that the Internet, besides being a fast-growing entity, is still a questionable tool for many kinds of research. With regard to qualitative issues, it must be remembered that any individual can create a World Wide Web site with little difficulty. It is, therefore, the researcher's responsibility to keep a critical eye on those sites. From a more practical standpoint, it is important to bear in mind that the World Wide Web (and the Internet in general) is a "fluid" medium. A web address that worked at the time this bibliography was written may have moved to a new address, or may no longer exist, by the time the reader finds this volume. It is recommended that the researcher also use such general navigation tools as Yahoo! (http://www.yahoo.com) or AltaVista (http://altavista.digital.com) to verify the current existence of any of the sites recommended below. This process will also lead to discovering new resources that will inevitably be produced in the interim.

EthicNet: Databank for European Codes of Journalism Ethics
Department of Journalism and Mass Communications
University of Tampere (Finland)
URL: http://www.uta.fi/ethicnet/

An extremely important source for international codes of ethics as of late 1996, this site promises to become a strong general resource on journalistic ethics for students, scholars, and practitioners.

Ethics Bibliography
David Shedden
Poynter Institute for Media Studies
URL: http://www.reporter.org/poynter/biblio/bib_me.htm

This annually updated service of the Poynter Institute Library has references to both print and online resources. Users can link up to the general Poynter Institute site for broader coverage of professional issues in journalism and the media.

Ethics on the World Wide Web
School of Communications
California State University–Fullerton
URL: http://www5.fullerton.edu/les/ethics_list.html

This extensive web clearinghouse of ethics links includes lists of links for media ethics, professional codes, associations, and research centers. It is a valuable "one-stop" source for ethics on the World Wide Web.

Ethics Resources on the Internet
Association for Practical and Professional Ethics
URL: http://ezinfo.ucs.indiana.edu/~appe/links.html

This resource is an extensive listing of links to web sites of organizations covering all areas of professional ethics (not only journalism). It is useful for locating research centers and doing comparisons between general topics, journalistic ethics, and ethics in other professional fields.

Index of Journalism Ethics Cases
School of Journalism
University of Indiana
URL: http://www.journalism.indiana.edu/Ethics

This resource is a searchable database of journalistic ethics case studies excerpted from the school's publication *FineLine*.

Index to Journalism Periodicals
Graduate School of Journalism
University of Western Ontario
URL: http://www.uwo.ca/journ/rc.html#ijp

This site is a useful resource for identifying print articles focused on journalism. With a database of over 24,000 citations, a quick search on the word *ethics* revealed several hundred hits. It is especially helpful if other proprietary indexes are unavailable.

Journalism Web Sites
David Shedden
Poynter Institute for Media Studies
URL: http://www.poynter.org/poynter/jsites.html

This useful reference tool is a subsection of the Poynter Institute site. Links are broken into the broad categories of Libraries, News Research, Newspapers and Television, Organizations, Publications, and Schools and Institutes.

CONTEMPORARY ETHICAL ISSUES

Chapter 9:
Organizations

Bill Pardue

Certainly, there is no shortage of organizations that the ambitious researcher can contact for background on professional responses to journalistic ethics. The *Encyclopedia of Associations* (published by Gale Research, 1996) lists well over 100 organizations, both in the United States and internationally, that either have the descriptor *journalism* or have the word *journalists* in their name. Many of these organizations have their own codes of ethics, statements of principles, etc., and many offer a broad range of publications (either free or at cost) to the public. The following list is intended primarily to guide the reader to a broad but short sampling of these organizations and centers. When available, World Wide Web site addresses have been included.

Accuracy in Media (AIM)
4455 Connecticut Ave., NW
Suite 330
Washington, DC 20008
(202) 364-4401
URL: http://www.aim.org/aim.html

Accuracy in Media (AIM) is a politically conservative group with the self-described purpose of acting "as an independent watchdog and critic" against alleged liberal bias in journalism and mass media. It produces extensive print and broadcast material.

American Society of Magazine Editors (ASME)
919 3rd Ave.
New York, NY 10022
(212) 872-3700

Affiliated with Magazine Publishers of America, the American Society of Magazine Editors is the primary organization for practicing magazine editors. It also sponsors an annual internship program for college juniors, presents the National Magazine Award, and holds an annual conference.

American Society of Newspaper Editors (ASNE)
P.O. Box 4090
Reston, VA 22090-1700
(703) 648-1144
URL: http://www.asne.org/

A major organization with numerous publications, the American Society of Newspaper Editors (ASNE) also features a committee on ethics and values. It produces numerous publications and holds an annual conference.

Associated Press Managing Editors (APME)
50 Rockefeller Plaza
New York, NY 10020
(212) 621-1552
URL: http://apme.com

Associated Press Managing Editors (APME) specifically addresses the workings of the Associated Press and its affiliated news and editorial staff. It also presents the Freedom of Information Award to a newspaper or journalist for upholding the principles of freedom of information or broadening free access to information.

Association for Education in Journalism and Mass Communication (AEJMC)
University of South Carolina
1621 College St.

Columbia, SC 29208
(803) 777-2005
URL: http://www.aejmc.sc.edu/online/home.html

The Association for Education in Journalism and Mass Communication is also affiliated with the Carol Burnett Fund for Responsible Journalism (Journalism Dept., 2550 Campus R., Crawford 208, University of Hawaii, Honolulu, HI 96822). It promotes excellence in journalism and mass communication education via its extensive scholarly publications and annual meetings.

Association of British Editors (ABE)
c/o Westminster Press, Ltd.
8-16 Great New St.
London EC4P 4ER, England
01480-492133

The Association of British Editors is a professional society that addresses professional editorial issues, including ethical conduct. It publishes the quarterly journal *The British Editor* and holds an annual convention in London.

Canadian Association of Journalists (CAJ)
Carleton University
St. Patrick's Bldg.
Ottawa, Ontario, Canada K1S 5B6
(613) 788-7424
URL: http://www.eagle.ca/caj/

The Canadian Association of Journalists is the premier Canadian organization for professional journalists. It organizes conferences, presents several awards, and publishes *Media* magazine.

Center for Mass Communications Research and Policy
Department of Mass Communications
University of Denver
Denver, CO 80210
(303) 753-2166

The Center for Mass Communications Research and Policy focuses on theoretical research, especially on the effects of mass media on individuals, groups, and society as a whole.

Fairness and Accuracy in Reporting (FAIR)
130 W. 25th St.
New York, NY 10001
(212) 633-6700
URL: http://www.igc.org/fair/

A "national media watch group" with a decidedly liberal slant, Fairness and Accuracy in Reporting produces a wide array of resources, both print and broadcast, which seek to combat alleged conservative bias and misinformation in mass media.

Gay and Lesbian Press Association (GLPA)
P.O. Box 8185
Universal City, CA 91608
(818) 902-1476

The Gay and Lesbian Press Association examines ethical issues both in the professional conduct of its members and in the gay/lesbian media in general. It also addresses the coverage of gay/lesbian issues in the general mass media. It publishes the quarterly newsletter *The Media Reporter* and holds biennial conferences.

International Organization of Journalists (IOJ)
Celetna 2
Prague CS-110 01, Czech Republic
2-2365916

Claiming 265,000 members, the International Organization of Journalists addresses all areas of the journalistic profession. It includes a committee on professional ethics and hosts a conference every five years. It also publishes the monthly magazine *Democratic Journalist*.

International Press Institute, American Committee (IPI)
c/o Gene Giancarlo
819 N. Kiowa St.
Allentown, PA 18103
(610) 432-6700

The International Press Institute, American Committee, addresses professional issues among those who are involved in establishing news policy in the mass media. It also conducts research on news activities, publishes numerous reports, and holds an annual conference.

Investigative Reporters and Editors (IRE)
University of Missouri
26A Walter Williams Hall
Columbia, MO 65211
(314) 882-2042
URL: http://www.ire.org

A fairly large organization (over 4,000 members), Investigative Reporters and Editors focuses on practical and professional issues for practitioners of investigative and in-depth journalism. It produces a number of periodicals and sponsors several conventions and workshops each year.

Mass Communications Research Center
School of Journalism and Mass Communication
University of Wisconsin
Vilas Communication Hall
Madison, WI 53706
(608) 262-3642

The Mass Communications Research Center conducts research on such topics as the effect of television news upon viewers and the roles of media organizations.

National Association of Hispanic Journalists (NAHJ)
National Press Bldg.
529 14th St., NW
Suite 1193
Washington, DC 20045
(202) 662-7145
URL: http://www.nahj.org/

The National Association of Hispanic Journalists addresses topics for practicing Hispanic journalists and covers Hispanic issues in the general mass media. It publishes the monthly *NAHJ Newsletter* and sponsors an annual convention.

Nieman Foundation
Harvard University
Walter Lippmann House
1 Francis Ave.
Cambridge, MA 02138
(617) 495-2237
URL: http://www.nieman.harvard.edu/nieman.html

The Nieman Foundation provides research opportunities to practicing journalists and publishes the quarterly journal *Nieman Reports*.

Poynter Institute for Mass Media Studies
801 Third St. South
St. Petersburg, FL 33701
(813) 821-9494
URL: http://www.reporter.org/poynter/home/index.htm

The Poynter Institute for Mass Media Studies is a nonprofit, educational journalism school. It produces publications, bibliographies, and special events. Its web site also offers a number of useful reference tools (*see* chapter 8).

Radio-Television News Directors Association (RTNDA)
1717 K St., NW
Suite 615
Washington, DC 20006
(202) 659-6510
URL: http://www.rtnda.org/rtnda/

The Radio-Television News Directors Association closely examines legal and regulatory issues that affect the practice of broadcast journalism and seeks to improve the ethical standards of conduct in the profession.

Society of American Business Editors and Writers (SABEW)
University of Missouri
P.O. Box 838
Columbia, MO 65205
(314) 882-7862

The Society of American Business Editors and Writers covers special issues of interest to the business journalism community. It publishes the bimonthly magazine *The Business Journalist* and holds an annual convention. It is affiliated with the Society of Professional Journalists (SPJ).

Society of Professional Journalists (SPJ)
P.O. Box 77
16 S. Jackson St.
Greencastle, IN 46135-0077
(317) 653-3333
URL: http://spj.org

The nation's largest journalism association (with over 13,000 members), the Society of Professional Journalists addresses issues in nearly all aspects of journalism practice and publishes the very important magazine *Quill*. The SPJ Code of Ethics is considered among the most significant in the field. The society also sponsors a major annual convention.

CONTEMPORARY ETHICAL ISSUES

Glossary

Anonymous Source: A news source that the news organization has agreed not to disclose.

Applied Ethics: The branch of philosophical ethics that attempts to clarify or resolve practical moral problems, for example, abortion, gays in the military, and capital punishment.

Background: A basis for supplying information negotiated between source and reporter. Information given on background may be used by the reporter to develop additional material for the story but may not be published or attributed.

Balanced News Report: A primary goal of mainstream journalism. A balanced news report is said to accurately and fairly represent all sides of the event or issue.

Broadcast Journalism: A form of journalism including news reports appearing on radio and television news programs.

Burn a Source: Disclose a source's identity after a reporter has promised not to do so.

Confidential Source: An anonymous source.

Conflicts of Commitment: A conflict among legitimate roles (parent, life-partner, member of faith community, etc.) that is unavoidable. Decisions on how to balance one's commitments include decisions about how to parcel out one's time as well as how to coordinate roles in an integrated fashion.

Conflicts of Interest: A situation in which a journalist's professional choice could result in financial or other personal gain. Journalism codes of ethics typically admonish journalists to avoid such situations inasmuch as they compromise journalistic objectivity or create the appearance of such.

Culturalism: A biased outlook in which one cultural group is viewed as superior or inferior to another.

Deception: The intentional leading of others to a false conclusion. Acts of deception may be acts of commission (false statements) or acts of omission (failing to disclose information that one is reasonably expected to disclose).

Descriptive Ethics: The branch of ethics that attempts to report or describe the moral outlooks of diverse cultural groups or subgroups.

Devices of News Slanting: The techniques whereby some facts, opinions, or points of view are played up or played down at the expense of others. *See also* hiding; highlighting.

Digital Film Technology: The technology that permits translation of film into computer code for purposes of manipulating or changing the image.

Docudrama: A fictionalized true story. Docudramas raise ethical concerns because of the blurring of fact.

Editor: A journalist whose job involves preparing reports for publication or broadcast. The editor also often assigns stories.

Ethical Theory: The branch of philosophical ethics that defines and justifies abstract normative standards, principles, or ideals for identifying and distinguishing between morality and immorality.

Ethics: The study of morality. Can be divided into the descriptive, or anthropological, study of morality (descriptive ethics) and the philosophical study of morality (philosophical ethics).

Fairness Doctrine: The Federal Communications Commission (FCC) broadcasting regulation requiring that important, controversial issues be aired and that reasonable opportunity be afforded for the airing of contrasting viewpoints. Repealed by the FCC in 1987.

False Light: A legal term signifying the portrayal of someone before the public in such a way as to create a false impression.

Federal Communications Act (1996): The federal legislation (S652) that aims at stimulating competition in the communications industry through deregulation. The act also bans "indecent" materials from being disseminated online.

Federal Communications Commission (FCC): The U.S. governmental agency regulating wire, radio, and television communications.

Freedom of Information Act (FOIA): The federal legislation enacted in 1966 providing a qualified right of public access to government documents and records. *See also* Privacy Act.

Freelance Journalist: A journalist who is self-employed and paid by the story or project.

Harm Principle: The ethical principle that prohibits harming persons unless there is some overriding reason for doing so. *See also* publicity test.

Headline: The copy in bold type that appears above a news story and that summarizes the major story content.

Hiding: In journalism, a device of news slanting whereby some facts in a news report are played down as, for example, by placing them at the back of a newspaper article or at the end of a news program where they are less likely to be noticed or inspected by the audience.

Highlighting: In journalism, a device of news slanting whereby some facts in a news report are played up through such means as devoting extra time to them, placing them up front, headlining them, and using colorful language in their presentation.

Inside Information: Information that becomes available to journalists through their professional roles that can be used to their personal benefit. It is immoral and sometimes illegal to use such information before it is available to the public.

Internet: The system of interconnected computer networks throughout the world, including facilities for electronic exchange of messages (E-mail), bulletin boards, and other online information resources.

Investigative Journalist: A journalist specializing in the examination of documents, computer tapes, and other complex material in the development of in-depth reports.

Journalism: Mass communication that discovers and reports information to citizens, telling them what they can expect from society and what society can expect from them. In the United States, the reported information includes that which is necessary for self-governance.

Journalism Ethics: The branch of professional ethics addressing moral problems arising in the context of the practice of journalism.

Lead: The first paragraph of a news story.

Libel: A legal term referring to defamation of another through print, writing, signs, or pictures. *Compare* slander.

Lifting Out of Context: Presenting misleading or inaccurate accounts of an event by omitting relevant data in reporting or photographically depicting the event.

Mass Media: The collection of information outlets targeted to segments of the population or to the public at large. Mass media includes print media (newspapers, periodicals, books), broadcast media (radio, television), and cybermedia.

Multiperspectivism: A news philosophy that attempts to resolve the problem of news bias by presenting news events from as many different human perspectives as possible.

New Journalism: Journalism that is written from the subjective experience of a reporter.

News: A timely published report of an event fulfilling a public need to know.

News Beat: A particular area that a journalist covers, most usually an area in which the journalist has particular education or expertise, such as business, science, or ethics.

News Bias: A term often used to imply an objectionable (for instance, unfair, dishonest, or unbalanced) slanting of the news.

News Leak: The disclosure of information that the news source has implicitly or explicitly promised to keep secret.

News Source: The point from which a journalist develops information. A source may be a person, a document, or an event.

News Staging: Re-creating or dramatizing a news event.

Newshole: The amount of physically available space to be filled by news items.

Newsroom Diversity: The practice of hiring journalists who come from a variety of distinct racial, ethnic, religious, sexual, and socioeconomic backgrounds.

Newsworthy: A value term applying to reports of events deemed worthy of publication.

Not for Attribution: A term referring to permission to quote a source only if the source's identity is not disclosed.

Nut Graph: A paragraph early in a news story that sums up the point or content of the story.

Objective Reporting: A primary ideal of journalism implying a truthful and unbiased account of the news.

Off the Record: A condition negotiated between reporter and news source in which the reporter promises not to disclose particular information. The secret information can include the source's identity or the information supplied.

Ombudsman: An independent source who hears and investigates complaints against news organizations or other institutions, reports findings, and helps to reach a settlement.

Op-Ed Pages: The opinion/editorial pages of a newspaper, which provide a public forum and an opportunity for the publication of well-reasoned arguments relating to the issues of the day. As the news columns are expected to contain well-balanced stories, op-ed columns are expected to contain thoughtful opinion.

Pack Journalism: The phenomenon of journalists from competing news organizations attempting to be the first to access the identical information.

Philosophical Ethics: The branch of ethics that rigorously examines, defends, or justifies moral judgments, rules, principles, or ideals.

Photojournalism: The practice of taking, cropping, and presenting news photographs.

Plagiarism: The appropriation of another person's work (words, ideas, etc.) as one's own without giving due credit.

Print Journalism: Printed news media such as newspapers and news-magazines. *Compare* broadcast journalism.

Privacy Act: The federal legislation enacted in 1974 providing individuals in most cases a right of access to federal agency records about themselves and regulating the collection, recording, and use of personal information. *See also* Freedom of Information Act.

Privacy Tort: The harm/injury arising from violation of a person's privacy, such as the media's disclosure of private facts, placement of another in a false light, intrusion into solitude, and appropriation of a name or likeness for commercial purposes. *See also* tort.

Professional Ethics: The branch of applied ethics that addresses moral problems arising in the context of professional practice.

Publicity Test: A justification test for determining if the harm principle is being violated. Harm caused in the performance of professional duties is often justifiable if the journalist is willing to publicly defend the action.

Publisher: The person who makes the final business decisions in a news organization and who oversees the entire operation of the news organization, including the editorial and fiscal sides.

Pulitzer Prize: The most coveted set of journalistic awards for reporting by U.S. news organizations and their journalists.

Reporter: The journalist who gathers the news and writes the initial news story.

Sensationalism: A problem of overemphasizing elements of a story that panders to public curiosity over need to know.

Situation Ethics: The theory of ethics according to which moral judgments must be justified in relation to the context or situation. For example, journalists' use of deception may be justified in some contexts while not in others.

Slander: A legal term referring to verbal defamation of another. *Compare* libel.

Stereotype: A rigid, oversimplified characterization of a group of people without regard to individual differences among group members.

Tabloid Journalism: Print or broadcast journalism that is sensationalized. *See* sensationalism.

Tort: In law, a private or civil injury, arising independently of contract, resulting from a breach of legal duty.

Trial Balloon: An attempt by a source to gauge public opinion on an idea or proposed public policy prior to enactment.

Undercover: A term implying the use of deception in investigative work.

Utilitarianism: An ethical theory according to which the morality of an action or type of action is determined in relation to its ability to maximize happiness.

Videographer: The journalist who collects information for news programs using a videotape recorder.

Whistleblowing: The publicizing of (allegedly) dangerous, illegal, or unethical activities of an organization such as a business or government agency.

Index

organizational bias, 62–64
Newspaper Research Journal, 36
Nieman Foundation, 27, 181
Nixon, Richard. *See* Watergate.
Not for attribution, 119
NPR. *See* National Public Radio

Objectivity, 2, 43, 44, 45, 48, 54–58,
    65–67, 115, 119, 140
Obligation. *See* Social responsibility.
Off the record, 119
Olen, Jeffrey, 89
Ombudsman, 31, 33, 36
Online news service, 51
Opinion, 4, 72
Organization of News Ombudsmen, 27
Overholtzer, Geneva, 121
Ownership. *See* Economics.

Packwood, Bob, 121
Partisanship, 54–58, 81, 118–119
Patterson, Philip, 47, 116
PBS. *See* Public Broadcasting System.
Pentagon Papers, 132–133
Perot, Ross, 60
Perspective, 43–45, 57, 58–62, 85
Philip Morris Cos., Inc. v. ABC, Inc., 118
Philosophical ethics, 2
The Photographers' Guide to Privacy, 70
Photography, 51, 72, 115–116
Photojournalism, 61, 116, 139
Plagiarism, 115
Plato, 44, 55
Pluralism, 89
Politics, 81–86, 119–122
Polls, 59, 82–83
Post-modernists, 56–58
Power, 8, 45, 67, 73
Poynter Institute, 21, 24, 25, 26, 27, 31,
    32, 34, 38, 39, 104, 174, 175, 181
Poynter, Nelson, 21, 38
Pratt, Cornelius, 38
Press council. *See* News council.
Press-Enterprise v. Superior Court, 76
Press responsibility. *See* Social
    responsibility.
Principles, 15–16, 87–88, 141–153
Pritchard, Michael, 24, 102
Privacy, 3, 32, 39, 47, 69–70, 72, 74,
    77–81, 86, 104, 107, 111–113, 120,
    129–130, 141–153
Profession, journalism as a, 2, 16, 92,
    96–102, 139–141

Professional ethics, 2, 86–90
Promise, 5, 111–113, 116, 120
Public Broadcasting System (PBS), 4
Public figure, 74, 80, 127–129
Public forum, 18
Public interest, 17, 18, 77–78, 101
Public journalism, 32, 37
Public officials, 114, 127–129
Public opinion, 107–109
Pulitzer, Joseph, 16, 39
Pulitzer Prize, 5, 22, 31, 32, 34, 56,
    102, 105, 121

Race, 32, 46, 59, 71
Racial stereotypes. *See* race.
Racism. *See* race.
Radio-Television News Directors
    Association, 68, 150–151, 182
Radio-Television News Directors
    Association of Canada, 151–153
Rape. *See* Sex crimes.
Reasonable person (as a standard), 78
*Red Lion Broadcasting Co., v. Federal
    Communication Commission*, 75,
    131–132
Relativism, 89
Reporters Committee for Freedom of
    the Press, 70
Representation, 37, 43, 65–66, 72
Resource allocation. *See* Economics.
Responsibility. *See* social responsibility.
Rich, Carole, 45
Richmond Newspapers v. Virginia, 76,
    135–137
Rivera, Geraldo, 112
Role. *See* Social responsibility.
Rosenbloom v. Metromedia Corporation,
    127
Rotzoll, Kim, 32, 70
Rowe, Anita, 66

*Sable Communications of California v.
    Federal Communications
    Commission*, 74
Schad v. Borough of Mount Ephron, 74
Schenk v. United States, 124
Schools. *See* Education.
Self-governance, 5, 7
Self-interest, 4
Self-regulation, 24
    as voluntary compliance, 17
Sensationalism, 16, 19, 39, 49–50, 60
Seto, Benjamin, 68

About the Contributors

SANDRA L. BORDEN (Ph.D., Indiana University) is assistant professor of communication at Western Michigan University. Specializing in media ethics, she has published articles in the *Journal of Mass Media Ethics* and in *Communication Monographs* regarding ethical issues involved in reporter-source relationships and on the choice processes used by journalists in making ethical decisions. Borden serves on the executive board of the Center for the Study of Ethics in Society.

KRISTIE BUNTON is an assistant professor of journalism and mass communication at the University of St. Thomas, where she teaches the senior seminar in media ethics. Her doctoral degree in mass communication ethics and law is from Indiana University, and she completed master's and bachelor's degrees at the University of Missouri School of Journalism.

CLIFFORD G. CHRISTIANS is research professor of communications and director, Institute of Communications Research at the University of Illinois. He is coauthor of *Media Ethics: Cases and Moral Reasoning* (Longman, 1995), now in its fourth edition, and *Good News: Social Ethics and the Press* (Oxford University Press, 1993). His most recent publication is *Communication Ethics and Universal Values* (Sage, 1997), coauthored with Michael Traber.

ELLIOT D. COHEN (Ph.D., Brown University) is professor of philosophy at Indian River Community College and editor in chief and founder (1981) of the *International Journal of Applied Philosophy*. His books include *AIDS: Crisis in Professional Ethics*, with Michael Davis (Temple University Press, 1994) and *Philosophical Issues in Journalism* (Oxford University Press, 1993). He is cofounder of the American Society for Philosophy, Counseling, and Psychotherapy (ASPCP), the North American chapter for philosophical counseling. As the society's ethics committee chair, he drafted its *Principles of Ethical Practice* (1995). A version of his proposed "contagious, fatal diseases" rule (addressing notification of sex partners of HIV-seropositive clients) was adopted by the American Counseling Association in its revised Code of Ethics (1995). Professor Cohen is also inventor and U.S. patent holder of computerized belief scanning technology that detects logical fallacies in articles produced on word processors.

DENI ELLIOTT is the university professor of ethics and director, Practical Ethics Center at the University of Montana. She is also a professor in the Department of Philosophy and adjunct professor in the School of Journalism there. Elliott is book review editor for the *Journal of Mass Media Ethics* and serves on the editorial board of *Professional Ethics Journal*. She is coauthor or editor of four books and coproducer of three documentaries in areas of applied ethics. She has also authored several dozen articles and book chapters in the field for lay, trade, and academic audiences.

MARTIN GUNDERSON (Ph.D., J.D.) is an associate professor of philosophy at Macalester College, St. Paul, Minnesota. His areas of specialization are bioethics and philosophy of law. He has written various articles on informed consent and physician-assisted death as well as on other topics in bioethics and philosophy of law. He is also a coauthor of *Aids: Testing and Privacy*.

ROBERT F. LADENSON is professor of philosophy at the Illinois Institute of Technology (IIT) and faculty associate in IIT's Center for the Study of Ethics in the Professions. Professor Ladenson's areas of specialization are the philosophy of free speech, ethics in the professions, moral and political philosophy, and employment relations. He is the author of *A Philosophy of Free Expression* (Rowman and Littlefield, 1983).

PAUL MARTIN LESTER is an associate professor in the Department of Communications at California State University, Fullerton. He invites you to visit his web site at: http://www5.fullerton.edu/les/homeboy.html for more information.

TRAVIS LINN is professor of journalism at the University of Nevada, Reno, where he teaches broadcast journalism, media technologies, and media ethics. A former dean of the school, Linn was previously Southwest bureau manager for CBS News and news director of WFAA-TV in Dallas.

MARTY LINSKY returned to the faculty of Harvard's John F. Kennedy School of Government in 1995, after being chief secretary to Massachusetts Governor William Weld. He teaches and writes about the press, leadership, politics, and public management. A graduate of Williams College and Harvard Law School, he has been a journalist, a lawyer, and a politician, as well as a member and assistant minority leader of the Massachusetts House of Representatives.

MIKE W. MARTIN (Ph.D., University of California, Irvine) is professor of philosophy at Chapman University in Orange, California, where he is also the chair of the Department of Philosophy. His books include *Love's Virtues* (University Press of Kansas, 1996); *Virtuous Giving: Philanthropy, Voluntary Service, and Caring* (Indiana University Press, 1994); *Self-Deception and Morality* (University Press of Kansas, 1996); and *Ethics in Engineering*, 3d edition, with Roland Schinzinger (McGraw-Hill, 1995). Currently, he is working on a book exploring the role of personal ideals in professional ethics.

BILL PARDUE is an electronic resources specialist at the Arlington Heights (Illinois) Memorial Library and holds an M.A. in philosophy from Pennsylvania State University. He is coauthor of "A Bibliography on AIDS and Professional Ethics" (with Dr. Sohair W. Elbaz) in *AIDS: Crisis in Professional Ethics* (Temple University Press, 1994). He was formerly the librarian/information researcher at the Illinois Institute of Technology's Center for the Study of Ethics in the Professions.

MICHAEL PRITCHARD is professor of philosophy and director, Center for the Study of Ethics in Society at Western Michigan University, where he has taught since 1968. Professor Pritchard has published many books and articles in various areas of ethics and political philosophy as well as philosophy for children. Among his books are *Communication Ethics: Methods of Analysis*, with James Jaksa (Wadsworth, 1994, 2d edition); *Engineering Ethics: Concepts and Cases*, with C. E. Harris and Michael Rabins (Wadsworth, 1995); *Reasonable Children: Moral Education and Moral Learning* (University Press of Kansas, 1996); and *On Becoming Responsible* (University Press of Kansas, 1991). His edited books include *Responsible Communication: Ethical Issues in Business, Industry, and the Professions*, with James Jaksa (Hampton Press, 1996).

CAROLE RICH is the author of *Writing and Reporting News: A Coaching Method*, 2d edition (Wadsworth, 1997). She was an editor at the *Hartford Courant* in Connecticut and the *Sun-Sentinel* in Fort Lauderdale and a reporter at the former *Philadelphia Bulletin*. She teaches journalism at the University of Kansas.

STEVE WEINBERG is an associate professor of journalism at the University of Missouri. He is the author of books and articles on investigative journalism and biography. His books include *Armand Hammer: The Untold Story* (Little, Brown, 1989); *Trade Secrets of Washington Journalists* (Acropolis Books, 1981); and *Telling the Untold Story: How Investigative Reporters Are Changing the Craft of Biography* (University of Missouri Press, 1992). Weinberg is also editor of the *IRE (Investigative Reporters and Editors) Journal*.

LEE WILKINS has focused much of her research and writing on the media's impact on the American political system. Her work examines the ethical dimensions of environmental journalism and of coverage of political leaders. She is a professor at the University of Missouri School of Journalism.

KEITH WOODS is a faculty associate in the ethics program at the Poynter Institute for Media Studies. He teaches ethics, writing, and reporting on race, and he writes occasionally on issues of ethics and race relations. Woods spent his 16-year journalism career at the *Times-Picayune* in New Orleans as an award-winning sportswriter, news reporter, and columnist. As city editor, he helped lead the newspaper's massive series on race relations that earned national acclaim and a National Headliner award. He left the newspaper's editorial board to join Poynter in 1994.